CAMBRIDGE MUSICAL TEXTS AND MONOGRAPHS

*General editors: Howard Mayer Brown, Peter le Huray, John Stevens*

# THE EARLY HISTORY OF THE VIOL

# THE EARLY HISTORY OF
# THE VIOL

IAN WOODFIELD

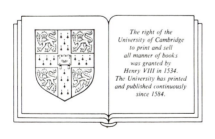

The right of the
University of Cambridge
to print and sell
all manner of books
was granted by
Henry VIII in 1534.
The University has printed
and published continuously
since 1584.

CAMBRIDGE UNIVERSITY PRESS

*Cambridge*

*London    New York    New Rochelle*

*Melbourne    Sydney*

Published by the Press Syndicate of the University of Cambridge
The Pitt Building, Trumpington Street, Cambridge CB2 IRP
32 East 57th Street, New York, NY 10022, USA
296 Beaconsfield Parade, Middle Park, Melbourne 3206, Australia

First published 1984

Printed in Great Britain at
the University Press, Cambridge

Library of Congress catalogue card number: 83–18876

*British Library Cataloguing in Publication Data*
Woodfield, Ian
The early history of the viol –
(Cambridge musical texts and monographs)
1. Viol – History
I. Title
787′.42′08   ML760
ISBN 0 521 24292 4

*To Thérèse*

# Contents

# Illustrations

## FIGURES

# Acknowledgements

My first debt of gratitude is to Howard Mayer Brown who suggested the early history of the viol as a possible topic for my thesis while I was a research student at King's College, London in 1973. Since then, he has continued to offer advice and encouragement which I now acknowledge with much pleasure. Many other individuals have contributed helpful suggestions or replied to requests for information, among whom are Pierluigi Petrobelli, John Stevens, Sibyl Marcuse, Trevor Dadson, Ian Harwood and Martin Edmunds. I should like to acknowledge, too, the assistance of Mrs Rosemary Dooley and the staff at Cambridge University Press.

Of all the published works that I consulted in the preparation of this study, by far the most useful was Professor Post's monumental fourteen-volume *History of Spanish Painting* (Cambridge, Mass., 1930–1966). Without this exceptionally erudite investigation into the obscure corners of late-medieval and early-renaissance Spanish painting, the task of compiling material for the early chapters of this study would have been very difficult.

The following institutions have kindly supplied me with photographs and granted permission for their reproduction: Ampliaciones y Reproducciones Mas, Barcelona; Museu Nacional de Arte Antigua, Lisbon; Fratelli Alinari, Florence; Biblioteca Riccardiana, Florence; Soprintendenza per i Beni Artistici e Storici di Napoli; Museo Civico Medievale, Bologna; Soprintendenza per i Beni Artistici e Storici di Modena e Reggio Emilia; Soprintendenza per i Beni Artistici e Storici di Milano; Monumenti, Musei e Gallerie Pontificie, Vatican; Kunsthistorisches Museum, Vienna; Städelsches Kunstinstitut, Frankfurt; Germanisches Nationalmuseum, Nuremberg; Musée du Louvre, Paris; Musée d'Unterlinden, Colmar; Bibliothèque Nationale, Paris; Institut Royal du Patrimoine Artistique, Brussels; Gemeentemuseum, The Hague; The Hermitage, Leningrad; The British Library; The National Gallery, London; The National Portrait Gallery, London; The Ashmolean Museum, Oxford; The Fitzwilliam Museum, Cambridge; Birmingham City Museum and Art Gallery; The Metropolitan Museum of Art, New York; The Hispanic Society of America, New York. I should also like to thank the Worshipful Company of Goldsmiths for permission to reproduce extracts from their records.

xi

I have received financial assistance from the research funds of King's College, London and The Queen's University of Belfast. These contributions I record with gratitude.

Finally, I should like to thank most warmly Mrs Eileen Dunwoody for typing the manuscript of this book quickly and efficiently, and my wife for her many helpful suggestions and her constant support and encouragement.

Ian Woodfield

*The Queen's University of Belfast*
1 July 1983

# Abbreviations

| | |
|---|---|
| Acta | Acta Musicologica |
| AIM | American Institute of Musicology |
| AM | Anuario Musical |
| AMw | Archiv für Musikwissenschaft |
| AnM | Analecta Musicologica |
| AnnM | Annales Musicologiques |
| Ch | Chelys: Journal of the Viola da Gamba Society |
| CHM | Collectanea Historiae Musicae |
| EM | Early Music |
| EMH | Early Music History |
| GSJ | Galpin Society Journal |
| JAMIS | Journal of the American Musical Instrument Society |
| JAMS | Journal of the American Musicological Society |
| JLSA | Journal of the Lute Society of America |
| JVdGSA | Journal of the Viola da Gamba Society of America |
| LSJ | Lute Society Journal |
| MB | Musica Britannica |
| ML | Music and Letters |
| MRM | Monuments of Renaissance Music |
| Note | Note d'Archivio per la Storia Musicale |
| PRMA | Proceedings of the Royal Musical Association |
| RdeM | Revue de Musicologie |
| RIdIM | Répertoire International d'Iconographie Musicale |
| RIM | Rivista Italiana di Musicologia |
| RMI | Rivista Musicale Italiana |

# Introduction

Speculation about the origins of the viol is almost as old as the instrument it-self. Ganassi, author of the first comprehensive viol tutor,[1] claimed that he had often wondered whether the viol or the lute was the more ancient instru-ment. Having discussed this question with various people, he became con-vinced of the greater antiquity of the viol after recalling that he had once noticed, among some Roman relics, a marble relief of the figure of Orpheus playing a 'viola d'arco'.[2] The belief that bowed instruments like the viol and the *lira da braccio* could be traced back to the golden age of the Greek and Roman civilisations was not uncommon in the 16th century, and Ganassi, like many of his contemporaries, was prepared to back up this assertion with wholly spuri-ous evidence, archaeological 'fakes' to use Winternitz's term for objects such as this figure of Orpheus.[3] An even more absurd attempt to establish the an-cient pedigree of the viol was later made by Rousseau in his *Traité de la Viole*.[4] In his comments on the origins of the viol, Rousseau claims that if Adam had wished to construct a musical instrument, it would have been a viol! ('On peut juger que si Adam avoit voulu faire un Instrument, il auroit fait une Viole.') Theories such as these, prevalent during the lifetime of the viol, eventually fell into disrepute when it was realised that the art of bowing was a comparatively recent phenomenon. As Bachmann[5] put it, 'toward 1800 it became generally accepted that bowing was unknown to the Mediterranean peoples of classical antiquity'.

By the early years of the 19th century, the viol was no longer in common use, and so interest in the instrument became increasingly theoretical rather than practical. Scholars now began to study the viol in terms of its supposed contri-bution to the development of the violin. In accordance with the evolutionary spirit of the age, a number of genealogical tables were constructed with the aim of tracing the ancestry of the violin back to its 'primitive' origins.[6] The position of the viol in such genealogies was usually that of 'parent' or direct ancestor to the violin. Schlesinger, for example, argued that the violin was 'directly descended in body as well as in name from the Kithara of the Greeks through the guitar'.[7] The application of the bow to the guitar had produced the 'guitar–fiddle' which in 15th-century Italy had given way to the viol, the

I

'immediate precursor' of the violin. This approach was regarded with scepticism by many subsequent writers. E. S. J. van der Straeten[8] rejected it completely: 'it must be clearly understood that the viols were not the parents of the violin family, but they were cousins who came into existence about the same time, both being descendants of the guitar–fiddle'. The viol was thus freed from the stigma of its earlier station as a mere forerunner of the violin. (This long-held and rather facile belief that the viol somehow 'gave rise' to the violin does at least highlight the dangers of the uncritical use of terms such as 'parent', 'ancestor', 'precursor', 'cousin', 'descendant' and 'offspring'. Though it is impossible to avoid this kind of terminology completely, it should always be borne in mind that words like 'parent' imply a direct relationship that may not have existed.)

With the revival of viol playing in the early years of the present century, scholars began to investigate the origins of the instrument with renewed interest. At this period the consensus of opinion seemed to be that the viol could be traced back in Europe at least as early as the 12th century. This theory was based to a considerable extent on iconographic evidence, much of which had come to light as a result of previous research into the origins of the violin. In the 12th century a large bowed string instrument, remarkably like a viol with its waisted outline and its downwards playing position, was frequently depicted. Even the bowing techniques of its players were those traditionally associated with the viol. Faced with so much pictorial evidence of this viol-like instrument, early modern historians of the viol understandably assumed that it was the direct ancestor of the renaissance viol and accordingly began to evolve theories linking the two instruments. Almost without exception, these attempts foundered on the lack of evidence of a continuous line of development during the 14th and 15th centuries. Galpin,[9] for example, having stated that the viol was 'the result of adapting the bow to the guitar-shaped instruments of antiquity', and having cited a number of examples of the instrument in 12th- and 13th-century art, then jumped 150 years or so to the latter part of the 15th century when the Italians 'altered the flowing outline of the viol by the addition of corners'. Bessaraboff[10] also attempted to connect the two instruments, but was honest enough to admit that he had uncovered hardly any evidence from the 14th century. Like Galpin, he moved on hastily to the end of the 15th century when 'the viols began to assume their final form and proportions'. Hayes,[11] too, author of the most extended monograph on the subject, opted for this theory, arguing that like other bowed instruments the viol was developing along its characteristic path from the 12th century onwards.

Attempts such as these to trace early forms of the viol back to the 12th century are now regarded with disfavour. Contemporary scholarship prefers the view that the viol was a product of the late 15th century. As Munrow[12] put it, 'there are two long-standing misconceptions about early bowed instruments, which have still not entirely vanished. One is that the viol is a medieval as well as a renaissance instrument.' The changed climate of opinion is partly due to the publication of new research on medieval bowed instruments which has suggested that the supposed ancestor of the viol had more or less disappeared by the early 14th century. In Remnant's words, 'the medieval viol' – a useful term for the instrument – was 'losing favour to the fiddle during the early 14th century'.[13] A direct connection between this instrument and the later viol seemed more and more unlikely. Baines[14] exemplifies the more cautious approach now prevalent. While noting the appearance of 'fiddles held downwards' in 12th-century pictures, he argues that the history of the viol is best begun in the second half of the 15th century.

Another reason for the growing reluctance of present-day writers to accept the medieval ancestry of the viol is a well-founded mistrust of much of the philological evidence presented by earlier authorities.[15] It is now generally realised that terms such as 'viola' (It.), 'vielle' (Fr.) and 'vihuela' (Sp.) were generic ones, applied not only to the viol but to other waisted string instruments such as the medieval fiddle, the *lira da braccio* and (in the absence of the modifying phrase 'de arco') the *vihuela*. As Munrow[16] points out, generic terms such as 'vielle' are frequently translated too specifically as 'viol' with the result that there is 'confusion about the period to which the viol belongs'. Marcuse,[17] to take a recent example, writing of the 'gamba-to-be' in the second quarter of the 15th century, refers to two blind musicians hired by Philip the Good who are described in some accounts as 'joueurs de vielle', a phrase she translates as 'viol players'. The term 'vielle', however, could equally well have denoted a medieval fiddle, and so its use cannot be regarded as proving the existence of viols at the mid 15th-century Burgundian court. Only in the 16th century did a more specific terminology for waisted string instruments begin to emerge.

While there is now a certain measure of agreement about the date of the viol's first appearance, opinion is still divided about the place of its origin, Spain and Italy being the two most popular candidates for the honour. A significant contribution to the debate was made by Dart,[18] who proposed the case for the Spanish origins of the instrument. The viol, he argued, was in essence a bowed guitar, the result of a cross-fertilisation between the 15th-century Spanish plucked instrument known as the *vihuela de mano* and the medieval fiddle. Not everyone accepted this thesis. One reviewer[19] accused Dart of making sweeping generalisations and cast doubt on the idea of the viol as a bowed guitar. Notwithstanding reservations such as these, Dart's theory greatly influenced subsequent scholarship. Speculation about the Spanish provenance of the viol is now commonplace, though scholarly caution leads many authorities to prefer a 'non-proven' verdict. Boyden,[20] for example, while alluding to the possibility that 'the viols originated in 15th-century Spain as a bowed species ('vihuela de arco') of the Spanish guitar ('vihuela de mano')', concludes that 'this cannot be the whole story'.

It has long been assumed that Italian instrument makers played a significant part in the evolution of the characteristic body shape of the viol; both

Schlesinger[21] and Galpin[22] accredit Italy with the invention of instruments with 'corners' to their waists. Recent supporters of this theory, however, have tended to concentrate on the evidence of theorists. In his article on 16th-century ensemble viol music, Morrow[23] states that the viol 'came to Germany from Italy about the end of the 15th century', its transalpine provenance being confirmed by the term 'welsche Geige' (Italian fiddle) sometimes applied to the instrument in German sources. Agricola, for example, in *Musica instrumentalis deudsch* (Wittenberg, 1545) terms the viol family 'grossen welschen Geigen'. Marcuse[24] cites the opinion of Vincenzo Galilei, expressed in his *Dialogo della musica antica, et della moderna* (Florence, 1581), that the *viola da gamba* and *viola da braccio* families were of Italian origin, possibly Neapolitan ('La Viola da Gamba, & da braccio, tengo per fermo che ne siano stati autori gli Italiani, & forse quelli del regno di Napoli'). But the case for the Italian origins of the viol has yet to be argued convincingly.

In view of the large amount of general research on the organological antecedents and the place of origin of the viol, there have been surprisingly few attempts to fathom the specific reasons for the appearance of the instrument. Sachs,[25] ever ready to advance an hypothesis, considered that the *viola da gamba* became a distinct type in the 15th century 'when musical evolution made large fiddles necessary'. (Why large fiddles should have become necessary in the 15th century is not stated.) The appearance of large fiddles, Sachs also claimed, meant that the players had to stretch further to stop the strings in the correct places. The strings were therefore tuned to smaller intervals (i.e. fourths and a major third) for the convenience of players, while the number of strings was increased to six to maintain the overall range. This none-too-convincing idea was supported by Hortense Panum.[26] Baines[27] recently put forward the more plausible theory that the viol was developed to meet the need – he does not, however, elaborate upon what precisely this 'need' was – for a bowed instrument 'corresponding in compass, string length and tuning to plucked instruments', in effect an extension of Dart's view of the viol as a bowed guitar.

To sum up the current state of research, it would be fair to say that broad agreement has been reached on two points: first, that the viol as we know it originated in the late 15th century; and secondly, that it was profoundly influenced by plucked instruments of that period. On the other hand, very little progress has been made in charting precisely how the viol rose to importance. Boyden's comment of 1965 thus remains valid: 'to date there is no satisfactory account of the origins and early history of the viols'.[28]

The present study begins with a brief discussion of the 12th-century instrument still known as the 'medieval viol' and long regarded (though wrongly) as an early form of the viol itself. Concerning the rise of the viol in the late 15th century, the central topic of this work, an attempt will be made to answer the following questions: (i) Which medieval instrumental traditions contributed to the evolution of the viol? (ii) Where were the first viols made and played? (iii) What were the physical characteristics of the early viol and how quickly did the 'classic' instrument begin to emerge? (iv) What kinds of music did the first viol players perform? (v) Why did the viol spread from its place of origin so rapidly and become successful throughout Europe? The rest of the book will be devoted to an account of the growth of viol playing in Europe during the 16th century. Among the most important topics to be discussed here will be: the development of the instrument itself, both its internal construction and its external physical characteristics; tunings; playing techniques as advocated by contemporary theorists; the repertory of music, solo and consort, played by violists. The final chapter is devoted to the history of the viol in 16th-century England. The relatively late date of its appearance here – the viol was essentially a southern instrument for the first half-century of its life – means that the emphasis will be on a slightly later period, the mid to late 16th century. The study will conclude with an extended discussion of the music played by viols in Tudor England, a topic of interest to players of the English consort repertory.

In writing of the viol during its first great period of popularity, the mid 16th century, I have been able to draw upon a wealth of information: several major treatises were published at that period which deal thoroughly with the instrument, its playing techniques, tunings and music; documentary evidence of the viol in renaissance society is plentiful; and from the mid 16th century onwards a number of viols have survived in their original condition. But for the earliest years of the viol's existence, the crucial period of about 1480 to 1520 when the newly-emerging instrument was beginning to spread across Europe, firm evidence of this kind is lacking. No treatise on the viol was published during its formative years; only after the instrument had achieved a measure of popularity was it commercially viable to do so. Nor have the vagaries of chance been kind to the instrument itself; no viols are known to have survived from this early period.[29] I have thus been compelled to fall back on the evidence of contemporary works of art, paintings, miniatures and sculptures, in order to answer a whole range of questions about the early viol's physical structure and also the manner of its spread throughout Europe. Some remarks about the use of iconographic evidence as a research tool in this study are therefore necessary.[30]

The primary use of musical iconography in this book is in helping to determine the structure of instruments that have failed to survive the ravages of time. Since, as is only to be expected, some artists reflect reality more closely than others, single works of art (which may result as much from the artist's imagination as from his powers of observation) are of doubtful value as evidence. It has therefore been my aim to collect a substantial number of examples, before using the evidence of works of art to establish the physical characteristics of any given instrumental type. In a report on his work on music-making angels in *trecento* art, Brown[31] notes that, even though it was not necessarily their intention to do so, artists depicted quite small structural details of instrumental types 'with surprising and comforting consistency'. It has been my experience, too, that once a particular viol-type has been isolated – the late 15th-century Valencian *vihuela de arco* and the early 16th-century German *gross Geigen* are two good examples – artists in the area do seem to depict the type with reassuring consistency. If a substantial number of depictions of a single instrumental type can be located, iconography has a further use: that of helping to distinguish between 'normal' and 'variable' features. The early Valencian *vihuela de arco* again illustrates this point well. The type is an easily recognisable one with many commonly recurring features. Yet Valencian makers could not be held guilty of slavish adherence to the local custom; the position, number and size of sound-holes, for example, varies from instrument to instrument (see Chapter 4).

The value of iconographic evidence in this kind of research can be tested objectively, once it becomes possible to compare paintings with surviving instruments. The results of such comparisons have, on the whole, been encouraging. It is very reassuring to find in a mid 16th-century Venetian painting an instrument closely resembling extant examples of the Venetian viol maker's craft (see Chapter 7).

More problematic is the use of iconographic evidence in tracing the development of playing positions or bowing techniques. Certain categories of musician depicted in paintings of the period – the hovering angel; the gracefully reclining muse; the grotesque marginal figure – are obviously of little use. Angel musicians, however, cannot always be dismissed out of hand, especially if a large number of examples follow a consistent pattern. Almost all 15th-century Aragonese depictions of angels playing the *rabāb* illustrate the downwards playing position (*a gamba* – that is, on or between the legs – if the angel is seated) and the underhand bow grip. It is therefore reasonable to assume that the artists were copying what they observed in real life, a supposition confirmed by non-angelic Aragonese *rabāb* players who adopt an identical posture and playing technique (see Chapter 2).

Most controversial of all is the use of iconographic evidence in the study of performance practice. 'If the student of organology needs to exercise caution in using pictorial evidence, anyone wishing to learn how music was actually performed during earlier times must be even more prudent in his use of works of art as evidence, for the questions he can answer using pictorial material depend entirely on the notion that artists depict contemporary reality. The extent to which an individual art work reflects true and common practice must be assessed before its testimony can be accepted as literal fact.'[32] This is a very necessary caution, and it is probably best, as in the present study, to use the testimony of paintings in this field only when it can be corroborated from other sources. On the other hand, it would be foolish to neglect entirely the detailed visual information about performing customs that is often only available in works of art; at the very least, it can be useful in confirming aspects of performance practice that are, perhaps, rather ambiguously described in contemporary literature. To take an example, there are a number of descriptions of mid 16th-century *intermedio* performances which imply that a consort of viols consisting largely, if not exclusively, of bass instruments ('bassi di violoni') was used. The fact that two mid 16th-century Italian paintings depict a consort of four viols, one tenor and three basses, is important confirmation of this practice. The players themselves are undeniably denizens of the celestial realm, but in this instance their identity does not detract from the value of the evidence (see Chapter 11).

Apart from the study of musical iconography, there is only one other potentially valuable source of information about the early years of the viol's development – references in archival documents and literary sources. Unfortunately the problems of string instrument terminology at this period are almost insuperable. Boyden[33] has aptly categorised this field as 'a treacherous quicksand ready and eager to engulf those who mistake it for *terra firma*'. Furthermore, it is during precisely the earliest years of the viol's history, when references to the instrument would be most valuable, that the problems are at their most intractable. As the viol emerged, it became customary to refer to it, not with a newly coined set of terms, but with the old, well-tried generic terms for string instruments: *vihuela* (Sp.); *Geige* (Ger.); *viola* (It.). Many different ways of qualifying these all-embracing terms were tried out, but the more distinctive terminology that eventually emerged for the viol family was for many years inconsistently used. (A glance at the index to the present study under 'viol, terminology of' will give a good idea of the lack of consistency.) Nor is the problem confined to the viol family. The period in question witnessed a momentous revolution in the development of all Western bowed string instruments; old medieval types such as the fiddle and the rebec were declining, and new instruments, the *lira da braccio*, the viol and the violin families, were replacing them. Ambiguity of terminology was therefore endemic, the unmodified generic terms being used for the old and new instruments alike. It is usually impossible to do more than make an informed guess about the specific meaning of generic terms such as 'viola' during the crucial period. To take one well-known example, Castiglione[34] refers to the practice of 'singing to the viola' ('il cantare alla viola'); in this context 'viola' could signify any of the following: lute; *vihuela de mano*; *lira da braccio*; viol. It could even be interpreted in a general sense: 'singing to a string instrument'. In view of this degree of uncertainty, I have tried to avoid using references to string instruments during the period of maximum ambiguity (the late 15th century to the early 16th century) except when the generic terms are modified in a helpful way (e.g. 'viole grande da archetto') or (rarely) when there is independent confirmation of the likelihood of the instruments in question being viols.

As the situation becomes clearer in the 16th century, one can use unmodified references more freely. Four 'viole' performing in 1495 may or may not have been viols; four 'viole' (or more likely 'violoni') performing in 1535 would very probably (though not certainly) have been viols.

Finally, a word should be said about the problems of classification. All too often, the history of musical instruments has been written as though all instruments fit into a rigid classification scheme of instrumental types. Research for this study has convinced me that this approach is of limited value for the early viol. Two examples will suffice. In examining the late 15th-century *vihuela* (Chapter 3), we shall encounter the concept of a dual-purpose instrument, a *vihuela* that could equally be plucked or bowed – in other words, a single instrumental type that transcends the bowed/plucked division of many conventional classification schemes. Later in the study (Chapter 7), there will be examples of hybrid instruments, for instance, viols that are so profoundly influenced by the violin that it makes little sense to classify them in either of the major string families. Instruments are depicted in 16th-century art that have the body of the violin (and hence probably its acoustical properties) but the frets and six strings of the viol (and hence probably its tuning and playing techniques). These problems in classifying the early viol are in part caused by the length of time that the instrument took to find a widely acceptable physical form. Whereas the violin seems to have found its 'ideal' form very quickly, for the viol it was a protracted struggle, and it was only at the end of the 16th century, with the instruments of John Rose (the son) and his English contemporaries, that any one form became sufficiently dominant to merit the description 'ideal' or 'classic'. To write of 'the renaissance viol' as a single type is therefore highly misleading. It implies a uniformity that never existed. It would almost be more realistic (though this could verge on an opposite fallacy) to regard the early viol as something of an abstract concept, a large bowed string instrument with frets, held downwards and bowed underhand, whose precise physical form remained flexible enough to be determined by local custom or even individual preference. Any stricter definition would soon exclude the violin-shaped French viol, which was tuned in fourths throughout. Whether in discussing the viol's physical structure, its tunings or its playing techniques, it is an insistence on the significance of local variation that runs like an *idée fixe* through this survey of the early viol.

# I

## The medieval viol

As noted in the introduction, the term 'medieval viol' is now used to refer to a large, waisted fiddle, popular in 12th- and 13th-century Europe, which was played with the instrument held downwards and the bow supported above the palm. The idea of an unbroken line of development between the medieval viol and its renaissance counterpart has, as I have shown, been questioned, and the two instruments are now thought to belong to two quite distinct traditions, separated by at least a century and a half. The medieval viol is nonetheless relevant to the central topic of this book, for, together with the *rabāb*, it was one of the first European bowed instruments to adopt the downwards playing position and underhand bowing techniques that were, many centuries later, to become distinctive characteristics of the viol family.

The earliest representation of a bowed string instrument in European art so far discovered is in a Mozarabic manuscript in the Biblioteca Nacional, Madrid dating from *c*920–930.[1] Four standing musicians play large, bottle-shaped instruments which are held downwards and bowed with large, almost semicircular bows. Bachmann aptly comments that the artist 'seems to have gone out of his way to draw attention to the process of bowing, as if representing something new and special in this musical scene'. Other early depictions of bowed instruments in European art also illustrate the downwards playing position. A manuscript written in a Benedictine abbey near Burgos in Spain in about 1100 (British Library, Add. ms. 11695, fol. 86) shows a dancing minstrel using, somewhat awkwardly, the downwards position.[2]

During subsequent centuries, as bowed instruments became widespread in Europe, two distinct methods of playing them evolved: the *a braccio* method with the instrument held against the upper arm or shoulder and bowed 'overhand', that is, with the bow held under the palm; the *a gamba* method with the instrument held downwards, supported on the knees or between the calves, and bowed 'underhand', that is, with the bow supported above the palm. This latter method of playing string instruments has always been associated with the Orient; to this day, a wide range of bowed instruments are played *a gamba* in North Africa, the Middle East, Central Asia and the Far East.[3] In many of these countries musicians may still be observed seated upright on the ground, their legs crossed, their instruments held vertically downwards resting either on the ground (as in the case of spike fiddles) or on the loose folds of their clothes. The introduction into Europe of this characteristically oriental playing position may have been the result of the influence of Moorish culture in Spain. By the 12th and 13th centuries, however, it had spread throughout Europe, even to those northern countries (such as England) furthest removed from the immediate sphere of Islamic influence. Bachmann reproduces an excellent selection of illustrations, including a number of northern examples, such as a miniature of King David with his musicians from an early 12th-century English psalter in St. Alban's Abbey (Albani Psalter, fol. 447).[4] A later English example from the early 13th century (British Library, Arundel ms. 157, fol. 71ᵛ) shows a player of a medieval viol seated on a bench with his feet neatly crossed (Plate 2).

By the 12th century the *a gamba* playing position had come to be associated very closely with one group of instruments in particular, the waisted fiddles. Remnant terms these instruments 'medieval viols',[5] but they could equally well be described as 'medieval fiddles played downwards'. It is possible to dis-

1    King David and his musicians: detail of a minstrel playing a medieval viol
(mid 12th-century German Bible: British Library, Harleian ms. 2804, fol. 3ᵛ)

2   Initial 'E' with musicians: detail of a minstrel playing a medieval viol
(early 13th-century English: British Library, Arundel ms. 157, fol. 71ᵛ)

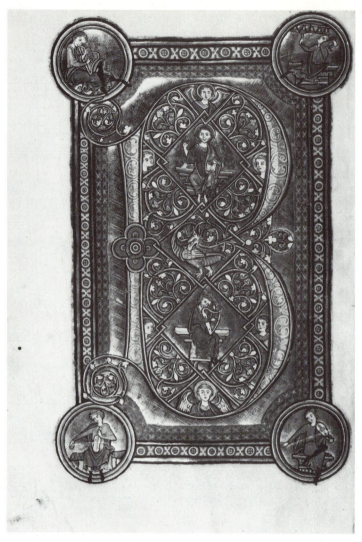

3    Initial 'B' with roundels depicting musicians
(mid 13th-century English psalter: British Library, Add. ms. 44874 , fol. 7ᵛ)

tinguish three main types: fiddles with gently incurving, guitar-shaped waists; 'figure-of-eight' fiddles with bodies formed from two circular resonators such as gourds; fiddles with a small central 'bump' separating the two main sections of the belly (Figure 1). Other types of medieval fiddle with circular, square, rectangular or oval bodies (i.e. non-waisted fiddles) were normally played *a braccio*. This was a distinction frequently observed by miniaturists of the 12th and 13th centuries; a waisted fiddle held *a gamba* and a non-waisted fiddle held *a braccio* are often to be seen in a single illustration, as in a mid 13th-century English psalter (British Library, Add. ms. 44874, fol. 7ᵛ). Usually, as in this

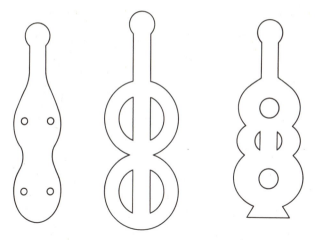

Figure 1    Typical outlines of the medieval viol

case, the artist took care to match the appropriate bowing action to each playing position (Plate 3). Bachmann is once again an excellent source for illustrations of miniatures which depict the two playing positions side by side. To pick
one more example at random, an early 13th-century French miniature
(Koninklijke Bibliotheek, The Hague, ms. 76 E 11) shows a figure-of-eight
fiddle played *a gamba* and bowed underhand, and a club-shaped fiddle played
*a braccio* and bowed overhand.[6].

During the early 14th century the medieval viol, for reasons that are still not
fully understood, suffered a substantial decline in popularity and eventually
disappeared altogether. One theory that has been advanced to account for the
instrument's decline is that its playing position may have proved inconvenient
for the minstrels who might otherwise have played it. In the view of Remnant,
'mediaeval minstrels often walked around as they played, for instance in processions or dances, and for this the mediaeval viol was unsuitable'.[7] Bachmann
cites a remarkable passage from *Fadet Joglar* (1210) concerning the skills that a
minstrel might be expected to possess in addition to his musical abilities;
these included story-telling, rhyming, trials of skill, throwing and catching
little apples on knives, imitating birdsong, doing card-tricks and jumping
through hoops.[8] For this type of all-round entertainer, the argument runs, the
*a gamba* posture may have been too constricting, whereas the *a braccio* playing
position would certainly have allowed much more mobility, thereby freeing
minstrels to take part in processions and dances while playing. The difficulties
that might have been encountered by a musician playing the medieval viol
(especially one of the larger variety) in a standing position are well illustrated
in a miniature of King David dating from the 12th century (British Library,
Harleian ms. 2804, fol. 3ᵛ). One of the musicians supports an unusually large

medieval viol on the calf of his right leg while standing on his left, an obviously unrealistic posture (Plate 1). This explanation, however, has one serious drawback; it conveniently ignores the fact that the downwards playing position with all its supposed inconveniences had been used by fiddle players for over four centuries before its demise. If it was so inconvenient, why was it not abandoned much sooner?

Whatever the reasons for its decline – and it may, of course, have been nothing more significant than a change of fashion – there can be no doubt that the medieval viol was defunct by the end of the 14th century. There are, it is true, occasional depictions of fiddles held downwards in 14th- and 15th-century art, for example, two early 15th-century Sienese miniatures (British Library, Add. ms. 30014, fol. 124[v] and fol. 145).[9] In many cases, however, these turn out to be fiddles held downwards for the purposes of tuning. A clear example of this is to be seen in the central panel of a triptych by Giovanni di Benvenuto (1479) in the National Gallery, London.[10] Despite its undeniably viol-like appearance and playing techniques, the medieval viol was thus not the immediate ancestor of the renaissance instrument, which did not appear until the end of the 15th century. To quote Munrow again, the concept of the viol as a medieval as well as a renaissance instrument is a 'long-standing misconception'.[11]

# 2

---

# The Moorish *rabāb* in Aragon

After the decline of the medieval viol in the early 14th century, players of most western bowed instruments opted for the *a braccio* playing position, the one best suited to their needs. The older *a gamba* posture, however, did not die out completely in Europe. In certain areas of the Kingdom of Aragon it not only survived but flourished throughout the 14th and 15th centuries as a result of its continued use by players of the Moorish *rabāb*, a provincial tradition that proved an important factor in the eventual emergence of the renaissance viol. As the only bowed instrument in western Europe still regularly played *a gamba* by the late 15th century, the *rabāb* of the Aragonese must be considered the chief bowed precursor of the viol.

In the Islamic world the term *rabāb* covered a wide variety of string instruments. The type of *rabāb* so popular in medieval Aragon was a North African, Moroccan instrument, shaped rather like a small segment of a circle, long and thin with straight sides and a rounded lower end.[1] Early depictions of this instrument in European art, such as the frescos in the Capella Palatina at Palermo, show it being played in the downwards position.[2] The *rabāb* was almost certainly introduced to southern Europe from North Africa through areas under Moorish domination. Indeed, the subsequent fortunes of the instrument were largely determined by the proximity of Moorish culture. In northern countries furthest from the sphere of Islamic influence the *rabāb* underwent modifications in shape and size and eventually lost its association with the downwards playing position. But in those areas of Europe to the South where Moorish influence remained powerful, notably in the Kingdom of Aragon, the *rabāb* changed very little and was still almost universally played in the downwards position. Not until the mid 15th century was the *rabāb* significantly affected by north European instrument-making practices. At this period, as we shall see, some remarkable instruments were constructed combining the traditional *rabāb*-shaped body with sickle-shaped pegboxes and carved heads of the type associated with early 16th-century Italian viols (Plate 16). Instruments of this type could, of course, be termed 'rebecs' – their all-wooden construction and generally Western features are those of the instrumental type usually associated with the term 'rebec' – but for convenience I have chosen to retain the Arabic term 'rabāb' for all instruments of the genre in the 15th-century Kingdom of Aragon, even though, strictly speaking, the term 'rabāb' is only really apt for instruments constructed in the oriental fashion with parchment bellies.

Early references to the Moorish rabāb in Spanish sources retain the r–b stem of the Arabic term. Variants such as rabé, rabeu and rabel are found. The r-b stem is also frequently found in early northern sources. Jerome of Moravia (c1280) writes of the 'rubeba', and among the instruments mentioned in part two of the Roman de la Rose (c1275) are 'rubebes'.[3] Variants of the form rubeba remained in use throughout the 14th century in both France and England. Machaut's list of instruments in Remède de Fortune[4] included a 'rubebe', and Jean Lefèvre[5] writes of 'la rebebe a corde terne' in La Vieille. In The Miller's Tale[6] Chaucer refers to a 'smal rubible', while John Lydgate in Reson and Sensuallyte (c1408) uses the plural 'rubibis'.[7] By the 16th century, however, r-b-b forms of the word were giving way in both England and France to the r–b–c group still in use today. Remnant[8] cites the various forms found in John Palsgrave's Lesclarcissement de la Langue Francoyse (1530): 'Rebecke' (Eng.); 'robecq', 'rebecq', 'rebeq', 'rebecquet', 'rebec' (Fr.). In Spain the form rabel was firmly established by the 16th century when it occurs frequently in the pastoral literature of Cervantes, Jorge de Montemayor and others. The Spanish form also occurs on occasion in northern sources. According to Martin le Franc's poem Le Champion des Dames (c1442), two blind musicians from Spain put Dufay and Binchois to shame with the music of 'leur rebelle'.[9] The main forms of the word current by the end of the 16th century are given by Minsheu in The Guide into Tongues (London, 1617): 'Rebecke' (Eng.); 'Rebec' (Fr.); 'Rebeccino' (It.); 'Rabel' (Sp.).

The main stronghold of the Moorish rabāb in Europe was the Kingdom of Aragon, which extended over a wide area of the western Mediterranean (see Figure 2a): the provinces of Catalonia, Aragon, Valencia, on the Spanish mainland; the small Catalan-speaking province of Roussillon to the north of the Pyrenees; the Balearic Islands, Majorca, Menorca and Ibiza; Sicily; and (by the mid 15th century) Naples. (For the purposes of this study the 'Kingdom of Aragon' refers to the whole of this area, the 'province of Aragon' to the much smaller area around the city of Zaragoza. The term 'Aragonese', unfortunately, can refer to the population of either area, and so its meaning will need to be clarified each time by the context.) The beginnings of the expansion of the Kingdom of Aragon can be traced back to the second half of the 12th century when, having successfully concluded a dynastic alliance with the Count of Barcelona, the Aragonese committed themselves fully to the reconquista, the holy crusade to recapture the lands occupied by the Moors in southern Spain. After a prolonged conflict James I of Aragon eventually took Valencia from the Moors in 1238. This was followed by the fall of the Balearic Islands, which had always enjoyed close cultural links with Valencia. After the *reconquista* and the official reconversion of their lands to the Christian faith, large numbers of Moors remained in their Aragonese homelands, living for much of the time in remarkable harmony with their Christian neighbours. Poulton[10] has summed up the changing attitudes of the two communities thus: 'There was no consistent, unalterable policy, with the Christian forces drawn up on one side and the Moors on the other. There were periods of hostility, and periods of peaceful co-existence; both sides suffered attack and betrayal from their co-religionists, while greed and political gains played as strong a part as religion in the various aspects of the struggle.' Systematic repression of the Aragonese Moors was not undertaken until the late 15th century, with the setting up of the Inquisition.

By the 15th century the largest and most concentrated community of Moors in Christian Spain – Granada did not finally capitulate until 1492 – inhabited the provinces of lower Aragon and Valencia from the Ebro valley to the coastal plains.[11] It has been estimated that up to thirty per cent of the Valencian population were Moors. Many of these conversions, though, were purely nominal, the Moorish Christians being Islamic in all but name. There is a good deal of evidence of the continuing vitality of Moorish culture in the enclaves of Valencia and Aragon. The well-known late 14th-century reliquary chest from the monastery at Piedra, now kept in the Real Academia de Historia at Madrid, is a striking example of the combination of the Gothic and Moorish styles.[12] Numerous paintings from the region depict artefacts such as musical instruments patterned with intricate black and white geometric motifs in the style perfected by Moorish artists. Musicians, too, remained faithful to the instruments of their own culture; the *rabāb* in particular was widely played here throughout the 14th and 15th centuries.

In the province of Catalonia many artists depicted the *rabāb* around the end of the 14th and the beginning of the 15th centuries, but there are comparatively few Catalan examples from later periods: this possibly reflects the more cosmopolitan nature of Barcelona and the greater distance of Catalonia from the really concentrated centres of Moorish population to the South. The frequency of the instrument's appearance in Catalan paintings may also be related to the rise and decline of an important indigenous school of painting in Catalonia – the flowering of medieval Catalan art in the works of Jaime Serra and Luis Borassá coincides exactly with the appearance of the *rabāb*. By the mid 15th century, however, the most important centres of the *rabāb* were undoubtedly the provinces of Aragon and Valencia. The city of Zaragoza in the province of Aragon seems to have been particularly significant at this period to judge by the large number of examples from towns and villages in the vicinity such as Daroca, Morata de Jiloca, Villarroya, Lanaja and Albalate (see Figure 2b). The rather isolated inland situation of this area and the rugged nature of its terrain may have helped to protect the instrument with its long-established traditions of performance from contact with changing cus-

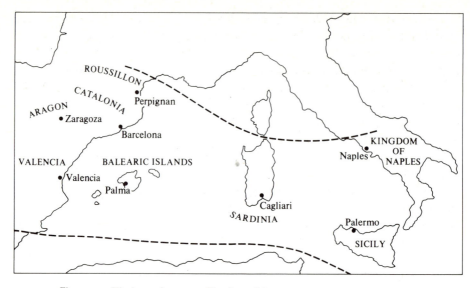

Figure 2a    The late 15th-century Kingdom of Aragon

Figure 2b    Towns and villages in the province of Aragon in which local artists
depicted the *rabāb* during the 15th century

toms elsewhere. The evidence is once again chiefly provided by an indigenous
school of painting headed by an unknown but prolific artist, active around
Zaragoza, known as the Lanaja Master, upon whose works, wrote Professor
Post, 'the Aragonese stamp is most profoundly impressed'. Post further considered that the works of this school 'emanate as truly from the very marrow of
the Aragonese aesthetic temperament as the production of the Serras and of
Borassá issues from the heart of Catalonia'.[13] It is surely not in the least surprising that local traditions of music-making were reflected most faithfully by
indigenous painters with their awareness of local customs. The survival of the
*rabāb* further south in the city and province of Valencia is particularly note-
worthy, since it was in this area that players of the newly emerging renaissance
viol first adapted for their own use the techniques of the Moorish *rabāb* players,
the downwards playing position being ideally suited to the rather tall viols so
popular at that period (see Chapter 4).

There is some evidence that the *rabāb* survived elsewhere in southern
Europe in a few isolated localities. In Castilian painting, for example, there is
one charming example in the work of a mid 15th-century artist known as the
Nicolás Francés Master, a panel of the Madonna and Child seated in a fenced
garden with music-making angels in attendance.[14] A much later example
(*c*1535) is Juan Correa de Vivar's *Adoración de los Padres* in the Prado in which
one of the trio of serenading angels plays a *rabāb*.[15] These fairly isolated cases,
however, do not add up to a strong Castilian tradition. There are also quite a
few examples of the instrument in Italian art. The late 14th-century Pistoiese
artist Cristiani on several occasions depicted a pair of angel musicians playing
*rabābs* of the traditional two-string variety. Even in the 15th century the *rabāb*
still makes an occasional appearance in Italian art, perhaps reflecting Aragonese involvement in Naples.[16] The relative scarcity of Italian pictorial
evidence by the mid 15th century, though, does tend to suggest that the tradition was declining outside the Moorish areas of Aragon and Valencia.

Archival and literary references from the 14th century confirm that the *rabāb*
was considered a Moorish instrument; there are a number of references to the
'rabé morisco' and the 'rabeu morish'. Other sources record players of the *rabāb*
with Moorish names, and in one case it was specifically noted that the musician was a Moor. Lamaña[17] cites two instances: '1313 Sarracelio de Xátiva,
Jutglar de rabeu morisch; 1337 Halezigua, moro, juglar, tocador de rabeu'.
Among the many instruments mentioned in the *Libro de Buen Amor* (*c*1330) by
Juan Ruiz, Archpriest of Hita, is the Moorish *rabāb* ('el rabé morisco'),[18] and
the great 14th-century historian of the Arab world, Ibn Khaldūn, referred to
an instrument shaped like 'the segment of a circle', surely the Moorish *rabāb*.[19]

The instrument seen in 14th-century Spanish illustrations of the *rabāb*
resembles very closely indeed the traditional Moroccan instrument still
played today. The best-known examples come from the *Cantigas de Santa
María*, which date from the early part of the century. One of the miniatures

depicts a pair of musicians bowing tiny *rabābs*, both of which are fretted. A much clearer and more detailed example may be seen on the back of a late 14th-century reliquary chest found in Perpignan (Plate 4). The characteristic features of the moorish *rabāb* in the late 14th century are illustrated in Figure 3. They may be summarised as follows: a long, thin, straight-sided body with

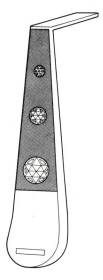

Figure  3    A *rabāb* depicted in a late 14th-century Majorcan painting

a curved lower end; reverse pegbox; two strings; a distinct division between the two halves of the belly, the lower section made from parchment, the upper from wood; ornamental roses on the upper half.

The 15th century was a period of transition for the *rabāb* in the Kingdom of Aragon; some features of the traditional instrument illustrated in Figure 3 defied the changing fortunes of fashion, other aspects were modified to conform to northern European practices. This whole process is a fascinating one to observe, as the rising influence of the Western 'rebec' slowly transformed the Moroccan *rabāb*. In one important respect, however, there was no alteration; the straight-sided instrument remained popular throughout the century. Various similes have been used to describe this basic outline; Khaldūn's 'shaped like the segment of a circle' is clearly appropriate; more recent epithets such as 'club-shaped' or 'boat-shaped' are also apt, especially the latter, since in Islamic legend the *rabāb* sometimes appears as a boat. A European visitor to Morocco recalled hearing the *rabāb* described as the 'boat of Fatma' and reported the traditional belief that the Prophet's daughter sailed down the Red Sea on a *rabāb*.[20] Pear-shaped instruments with the characteristic bulge in the lower half of the belly do not appear in Aragonese paintings of this period. The length of the *rabāb* varied considerably; in certain areas of southern Aragon and Valencia there seems to have been a vogue for tall *rabābs* of at least 18″, about the length of the modern Moroccan instrument, an instrument of which type appears in a panel of the Madonna and Child in the Ermita de San Roque at Jérica (Plate 7); further north, around Zaragoza, a slightly shorter version was preferred (Plate 11).

The belly of the Moorish *rabāb* was divided into two sections, the lower of which was made from animal skin. The soundholes were therefore placed in the upper wooden section. By the mid 15th century this essentially oriental method of construction was beginning to fall into disfavour; Aragonese and Valencian *rabābs* of the 1470s and 1480s were often constructed with completely wooden bellies. As soon as the wooden belly became fashionable, the position of the soundholes was altered. There had usually been two or three roses in the wooden segment of the belly, the lower quite large and often ornamented with a geometric pattern in the Moorish style, the upper, by contrast, quite tiny, sometimes no larger than a recorder hole (Plate 18). With the advent of the completely wooden belly, these upper holes were superseded by a single large rose in the lower half of the belly (Plate 13). The mid 15th century also saw a significant change in the construction of the pegbox. Hitherto, the *rabāb* had usually been made with a simple reverse pegbox, the angle of the pegbox to the neck being quite acute (Plate 6). During the 15th century, however, sickle-shaped pegboxes often surmounted by a carved animal head became increasingly popular (Plate 16). The lion's head was favoured, although a few makers preferred a more original theme; a devilish canine mask glares out over the pegbox of one *rabāb* (Plate 13).

The number of strings was extremely variable; the traditional two-string *rabāb* predominates in the early period (Plates 4 and 6), but later, instruments appeared with three, four, five or even six strings (Plates 11 and 13). There was no need for the two-string *rabāb* to be fitted with an arched bridge, since whatever its shape either string could be sounded individually. In most cases the strings passed over a thin, flat piece of wood placed on the parchment belly and were fixed directly to the lowest part of the back by means of a button inserted into the wood. The flat-topped bridge was usually retained even after the number of strings had increased, so that, except for the outer strings, no single string could be sounded individually. Arched bridges were still comparatively rare even in the late 15th century. Tailpieces were not used, although the idea was undoubtedly known to string instrument makers of the area, as is shown by a most interesting string-playing duo depicted by one late 15th-century Aragonese artist (Plate 13); the fiddle has a tailpiece, but not the *rabāb*, the strings of which are attached directly to a 'bridge' or stringholder as it might more accurately be termed. This latter method of string fastening became quite common in the late 15th century.

Two-string *rabābs* were probably tuned with their strings a fifth apart. In his late 13th-century *Tractatus de Musica* Jerome of Moravia described an instru-

4    Madonna and Child with angel musicians: detail of an angel musician playing a *rabāb* (late 14th-century reliquary chest, Roussillon school: private collection, Perpignan)

5   Madonna and Child with angel musicians: detail of angel musicians playing a *rabāb*, a lute and a recorder
(*c*1417-1419, Catalan school: Museo de Bellas Artes, Barcelona)

6   Madonna and Child with angel musicians: detail of an angel musician playing a *rabāb* (*c*1412, Catalan school: private collection)

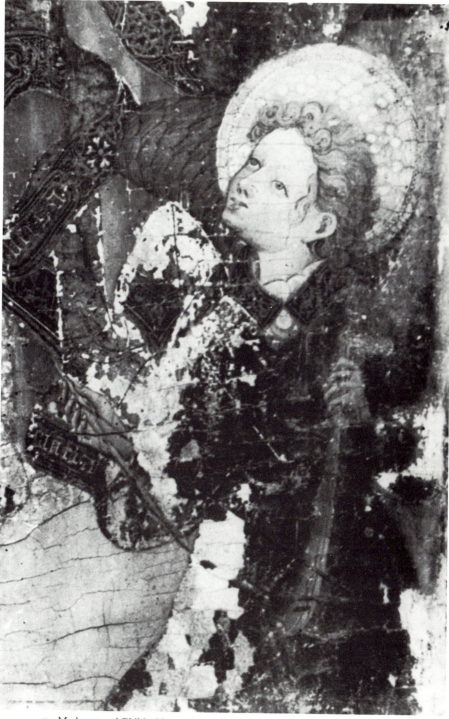

7  Madonna and Child with angel musicians: detail of an angel musician playing a *rabāb*
(late 14th/early 15th century, Valencian school: Ermita de San Roque, Jérica)

8   Madonna and Child with angel musicians
(early/mid 15th century, Aragonese school: Museo Provincial, Zaragoza)

9   Angel musician playing a *rabāb*: detail of Plate 8
(early/mid 15th century, Aragonese school: Museo Provincial, Zaragoza)

ment called the 'rubeba' (probably the *rabāb*) tuned *c–g*.[21] The nominally low pitch of Jerome's 'rubeba' would certainly have suited some of the very tall *rabābs* popular in the province of Valencia, as it does the contemporary Moroccan instrument, the tone of which has been compared to that of a 'deep viola'.[22] To judge by the variety of sizes depicted in medieval paintings, though, the actual pitch must have varied considerably from instrument to instrument. Jerome gives the range of the 'rubeba' as a major ninth *c–d'*, above which 'the rubeba may ascend no more' ('et non plus rubeba potest ascendere').

The traditional downwards playing position adopted by Moorish *rabāb* players remained popular throughout the 15th century, if the evidence of paintings from the Kingdom of Aragon – and there is no other – is to be trusted. However, it is worth repeating and indeed amplifying a point made in the introduction concerning the use of iconographic evidence in the discussion of playing techniques. Celestial beings, it hardly needs to be said, are able to per-

10   Madonna and Child with angel musicians
(early/mid 15th century, Aragonese school: Städelsches Kunstinstitut, Frankfurt)

II   Angel musician playing a *rabāb*: detail of Plate 10
(early/mid 15th century, Aragonese school: Städelsches Kunstinstitut, Frankfurt)

form, at the whim of the artist, in postures which mere mortal players would find impossible to emulate. In some Catalan paintings, for example, the Virgin Mary and the Holy Child are attended by angels hovering in the air. The beautiful Cervera Madonna is worshipped in this way by an orchestra of tiny, fluttering musicians (Plate 5), the artist being prevented from depicting the true *a gamba* posture with the instrument resting on the knees or in the lap of a seated player. In this case the *rabāb* is held vertically downwards without visible means of support, a playing position that terrestrial musicians may not have been required to assume. Not all angel musicians, though, were intended to represent ethereal heavenly beings remote from the human race, a point made vividly by Professor Post when describing the physical manifestations of the Aragonese character (i.e. of the inhabitants of the province of Aragon) in paintings of angels: 'the Aragonese temperament', he wrote, 'has partially emptied the music-making child–angels of the spiritual *élan* and artificial

12    Retable of St Thomas: a panel depicting a servant rebuking St Thomas for refusing to eat
with the heathen
(mid/late 15th century, Aragonese school: Museo, Daroca)

beauty of their Catalan and Valencian brothers, but it has compensated by
rendering them more humane and winsome'.[23] Certainly some 'Aragonese'
angels of the mid 15th century seem to be performing their musical duties with
rather less *élan* than might be expected on such a joyous occasion! A few look
positively doleful (Plate 18). Yet the greater 'humanity' of Aragonese angels is
reflected in their more 'down-to-earth' postures; they are inclined to disport
themselves around the Madonna's throne, standing or sitting on part of its
structure, or even leaning rather casually against it (Plate 8). Aragonese artists
of the 1430s and 1440s delighted in constructing magnificent Gothic thrones
upon which to seat their Madonnas, and they were particularly adept at positioning tiny angel musicians on the numerous turrets and platforms of these

13   Madonna and Child with angel musicians: detail of angel musicians playing a fiddle and a *rabāb*
(late 15th century, Aragonese school: private collection, Barcelona)

intricate structures (Plate 8): instrumentalists sometimes appear airily situated on lofty pillars; others stand on the seat of the throne itself; one relaxed player reclines languidly against an arch with his *rabāb* resting on a ledge (Plate 11). That the *a gamba* posture normally required a seated player is borne out by the few examples of non-angelic *rabāb* players in Aragonese art. In the museum of the Daroca Colegiata there is a late 15th-century retable of St Thomas, one of the panels of which displays a most unusual scene of music-making (Plate 12). During his travels in India, St Thomas was reputedly struck across the face by a servant for refusing to eat with the heathen. In the artist's version of this dramatic incident a small meal is in progress, the music being provided by a single young lady, seated and playing a *rabāb*. Whether standing or seated, most *rabāb* players are depicted gripping their instrument in the manner advocated by Jerome of Moravia (Plate 6), just below the reverse peg-box between the thumb and index finger ('inter pollicem et indicem iuxta capud').[24]

The bows used by *rabāb* players at this period were made from fairly thick pieces of wood and were arched quite strongly. In size they varied considerably;

some were tiny, almost semicircular in shape (Plate II), others appear to have been huge, ungainly implements, often as long as the instruments themselves (Plate 7). The method of bowing traditionally associated with the downwards playing position was the underhand or reverse method with the bow held above the palm. This was almost invariably the grip adopted by angelic musicians in paintings. On the back of the Perpignan reliquary is a charming *rabāb* player (Plate 4) who appears to be using the third and fourth fingers to increase the pressure on the hair of the bow, a technique that was described almost three centuries later by Christopher Simpson in *The Division Violist*.[25]

Information about the musical repertory and performance practices of players of the *rabāb* in the late 15th-century Kingdom of Aragon is scarce. There are however, a few comments in Tinctoris's *De inventione et usu musicae* (c1487)[26] about another instrument in use at this period in Spain, the gittern. These remarks at least provide a background to the instrumental practices of the area. Tinctoris refers to a small tortoise-shaped instrument 'invented by the Catalans, which some call the *guiterra* and others the *ghiterne*' ('a Catalanis inventum: quod ab aliis ghiterra: ab aliis ghiterna vocatur').[27] Concerning the use of this instrument Tinctoris wrote: 'The *ghiterra* is used most rarely, because of the thinness of its sound. When I heard it in Catalonia, it was being used much more often by women, to accompany their love songs, than by men.' ('Ghiterre autem usus: propter tenuem ejus sonum: rarissimus est. Ad eamque multo sepius Catalanas mulieres carmina quaedam amatoria audivi concinere: quam viros.') Tinctoris's uncomplimentary description of the tone of the gittern as 'thin' certainly has a parallel in medieval reaction to the Moorish *rabāb*. To quote from Bachmann,[28] even cultivated Muslim musicians and theorists were at first 'unimpressed by the bowed instrument's thin, unattractive tone, and regarded it as a most imperfect instrument, to be included in their writings only for the sake of completeness'. Al-Farabi wrote that 'owing to its construction, the sound of the *rabāb* is not as strong as that of certain other instruments; from this point of view, the *rabāb* is inferior to most others'. In Spain reference was made to the screeching *rabāb* ('el rabé gritador') in the *Libro de Buen Amor* (c1330). Tinctoris's observation that the gittern was usually played by women to accompany love songs is also worthy of comment. The practice may well relate back to the long-established tradition of the female musical slave, so highly prized by the Moorish rulers of Spain. Fabulous prices were sometimes paid for outstanding performers, and accounts of the effects of their musical talents are almost legendary in tone. One report stated that it was customary in Cordoba during the time of Al-Mansur for a girl's education to include learning to play the lute, *rabāb* and other instruments 'in order to be a solace to her husband'.[29]

A possible source of information about the use of the *rabāb* in 16th-century Spain is the pastoral literature of Cervantes, Jorge de Montemayor, Gaspar Gil

Polo and others, in which the instrument occupies a significant place. References to the 'rabel' abound in Montemayor's *Diana* (*c*1559) and Gil Polo's continuation *Diana Enamorada* (1564), both of which works were translated into English by Bartholomew Yong and published in 1598.[30] Montemayor was himself a musician, and his works mention many instruments of the day, as do those of Gil Polo. Groups of courtly instruments appeared in important set pieces in the pastoral, but two instruments, the *zampoña* and the *rabel*, were much more frequently and closely associated in the mind of the playwrights with the daily life of their principal characters, the shepherds. The chief function of both instruments was to accompany the songs of the shepherds which formed such a significant part of the genre. Despite the evidently symbolic position of the *rabel* as a pastoral emblem, some specific, practical details of the shepherd's performance practice may derive from contemporary usage.

At the very start of *Diana* we are informed that Syrenus was never without his *rabel*: 'sometimes picking up his *rabel* which he always carried very neatly in a pouch' ('tomando a vezes su rabel que muy polido en un çurrón siempre traya').[31] The performance of a song would frequently commence with the shepherd tuning his instrument. Indeed, the strong impression is given that tuning was part of the performance itself; the tuning session would then merge into a short instrumental prelude before the voice entered: 'and picking up a *rabel* that he had by him, he began to tune it, to do that which the Shepherdess requested . . . and having played on it a little, with a voice more heavenly than human, he began to sing this song' ('Y tomando un rabel que cerca de sí tenía le començó a templar para hazer lo que la pastora le mandava . . . y aviendo tañido un poco con una voz más angélica, que de hombre humano, dió principio a esta canción').[32] Presumably, having tuned the instrument and played a prelude, the musician would then use the *rabel* as a background drone, with perhaps the occasional instrumental interlude to rest the voice. On some occasions the tuning had a practical purpose when several shepherds were performing together: 'Now, good Shepherd, said Syrenus, take up your *rabel*, and I will take up my *zampoña* . . . then the two Shepherds, tuning their instruments with much grace and sweetness, began to sing' (' – Aora, pastor – dixo Sireno – , toma tu rabel e yo tomaré mi çampoña . . . y templando los dos pastores sus instrumentos con mucha gracia y suavidad, començaron a cantar').[33] The seated posture of the performers is sometimes mentioned. In a pastoral episode of *Don Quixote* a young musician called Antonio is asked by a goatherd to sing a love song, upon which the lad 'sat down on the trunk of a fallen oak and then tuned his *rabel*' ('se sento en el tronco de una desmochada encina, y templando su rabel').[34] There are a few references to the *rabel* combining with other instruments such as the harp, and also to groups of *rabels*; Cervantes speaks of the 'triste y agradable música de varios rabeles'.[35] Not only shepherds sang to the sound of the *rabel*; in the third book of *Diana Enamorada* a sea fable is recounted of a rough journey to Valencia (perhaps the most important centre of the Moorish *rabāb* in Spain by the 16th century), during which 'one of the sailors, taking out of a chest a *rabel* with which he was accustomed to amuse himself during long and dangerous voyages, began to play and sung thus' ('uno de los marineros sacando de una arca un rabel, con que solía en el pesadumbre de los prolixos y peligrosos viajes deleitarse, se puso a tañer y canto ansí').[36] Like other instrumentalists, players of the *rabel* sometimes took their name from their instrument; in one of Juan del Encina's eclogues, a musician called Juan Rabé makes an appearance.[37] There are many more references to the *rabel* in 16th-century Spanish literature than have been cited here, most of them in the context of song accompaniment. Though it would be unwise to place much reliance on this evidence in matters of detail, yet the position of the *rabel* in the Spanish pastoral does show that it was widely perceived as an instrument of vocal accompaniment.

A potential source of information about the medieval *rabāb* may be its modern descendant which is still played today in Morocco. The degree of similarity between the modern *rabāb* and its Moorish ancestor is sometimes quite astonishing. Compare, for example, the instrument depicted in a late 14th-century Majorcan painting (Plate 14) with the modern *rabāb* presented to the South Kensington Museum by His Highness the Viceroy of Egypt, illustrated in Engel's catalogue (Plate 15).[38] The modern instrument might almost have been copied from the medieval painting; even its size, given as 19", seems to be roughly that of the average medieval instrument. In his note on this instrument Engel correctly identifies the *rabāb* as a favourite instrument of the Moors in Spain and then imparts the fascinating piece of information that in his day (1870) the *rabāb* was still occasionally found 'among the country people of Spain, who call it *rabel* or *arrabel*', a remarkable testimony to the tenacity of the tradition in Spain. A variant form with slight waists to the lower half of the belly is illustrated in Munrow;[39] this instrument's parchment belly is very clear, as is the button inserted into the lower part of the back to which the two strings are tied, a feature not visible in medieval paintings which almost invariably give a front view. Although the *rabāb* played today in North Africa is closely related in its physical appearance and construction to the instrument popular in the medieval Kingdom of Aragon, it would be very rash to conclude from this that its musical traditions survived equally unchanged through the centuries. Nonetheless, the musical rôle of the modern *rabāb* in traditional music is, at least in general terms, consistent with the little we know about the medieval instrument. In common with many other bowed instruments of North Africa and the Middle East, the *rabāb* is used to provide a drone accompaniment to the human voice. According to Sachs,[40] the quadrilateral Egyptian *rabāb* with one string 'accompanies the endless recitations of public narrators', while the instrument with two strings 'accompanies songs'. The Moroccan *rabāb* is described by a pre-war European traveller thus: 'Its tone is like a deep viola and its compass an octave and four notes. The lower

14    Madonna and Child with angel musicians: detail of angel musicians playing a flute and a
*rabāb*
(late 14th/early 15th century, Majorcan school: Santa María del Puig, Pollensa)

15    *Rabāb*
(illustrated in C. Engel: *A Descriptive Catalogue of the Musical Instruments in the South Kensington
Museum*, London, 1870, 9)

16    Madonna and Child with angel musicians: detail of an angel musician playing a *rabāb*
(*c*1500, Rodrigo Osona, Valencian school: Iglesia de Nuestra Señora, Ibiza)

string is often played as a drone for the accompaniment of vocal singing.'[41] As an example of *rabāb* drone accompaniment, Farmer[42] cites a short transcription of a piece for three *rababs*, two of which are playing single-note drones.

All this rather speculative and fragmentary evidence concerning the possible musical usage of the medieval Aragonese *rabāb* may be summed up as follows:

  i   Tinctoris referred to the Catalan tradition of women playing the gittern to accompany their love songs.

  ii  In 16th-century Spanish pastoral literature the 'rabel' is frequently played by shepherds to accompany songs, the vocal performance being preceded by a brief tuning session acting as, or merging with, an instrumental prelude.

  iii  The modern Moroccan *rabāb* shares a traditional function of bowed string instruments of the area, that of playing drone accompaniments.

  iv  The medieval *rabāb* was constructed like the modern instrument and would therefore have been well equipped for a similar rôle as a drone accompanist.

Perhaps the only safe conclusion to be drawn from this is a negative one: that the *rabāb* in its traditional form was not used in performances of polyphonic art-music. Yet the appearance of transitional instruments with wooden bellies may indicate a desire to equip the *rabāb* for playing in part-music, in effect changing it into the type of 'rebec' for which Gerle[43] arranged some consort pieces in the early 16th century.

The *rabāb* with its traditional playing techniques survived in the Kingdom of Aragon long after it had disappeared elsewhere in Europe, the continuing vitality of Moorish culture protecting such survivals from the Islamic past. Outside Aragon, the 'rebec', as it came to be known, was usually played in the *a braccio* position and bowed overhand, techniques of string playing that remained dominant throughout the 14th and 15th centuries. The Moorish musicians of the Kingdom of Aragon can thus claim the important distinction of having maintained in Europe the ancient, oriental method of string playing from which the viol was to copy its own playing techniques. In a very real sense, therefore, the viol was as much a product of medieval Islamic civilisation, represented by the Moorish enclave in Valencia, as that of Christian Europe. That is not to say that its Moorish origins were not very speedily forgotten. Indeed, Ganassi,[44] author of the first important viol tutor, specifically rejected the use of any 'Moorish gesture' ('atto di moresca') in playing the viol, a considerable irony, since posture and playing method were the most significant contributions of the Moors to the development of the viol.

# 3

---

## The *vihuela de mano*

The survival of the downwards playing position was by no means the sole contribution made by late-medieval musicians from the Kingdom of Aragon to the evolution of the viol. Aragonese instrument makers of the mid 15th century were also responsible for the development of the large, waisted, plucked instrument known as the *vihuela de mano*, from which the construction and body shape of the earliest viols were derived. Dart was the first to appreciate the true significance of the *vihuela* in understanding the origins of the viol. In an oft-quoted passage,[1] he argued that the viol was in essence a bowed *vihuela*, the result of a union between the plucked *vihuela de mano* and the bowed medieval fiddle. Somewhat surprisingly perhaps, his theory was not examined very thoroughly by subsequent historians of the *vihuela*, and most recent accounts have concentrated on the instrument in the 16th century and the marvellous repertory of music provided for it by Spanish composers.[2] Indeed, the last decades of the 15th century when the *vihuela* exerted a profound influence on the viol, have often been glossed over, sometimes with the erroneous excuse that the instrument was 'illustrated comparatively rarely'.[3]

One of the problems of discussing the growth of the *vihuela* in the latter part of the 15th century is knowing how to distinguish between early examples of the true renaissance *vihuela* and depictions of medieval fiddles being plucked. This difficulty is well illustrated by a miniature in a mid 15th-century Italian manuscript[4] which shows a man standing before a table apparently plucking an accompaniment to his own singing (Plate 17). Should his instrument be regarded as an early form of the plucked *vihuela*, or should it be classified merely as a plucked medieval fiddle? It certainly resembles the latter instrument with its gently waisted form, five strings and circular pegbox.[5] It could be argued, of course, that the renaissance *vihuela* first evolved as a species of plucked fiddle which, having lost its association with bowing, developed characteristics more specifically suited to its rôle as a plucked instrument, yet there is very little evidence to back up such an hypothesis, convenient though it is.

Whatever its origins, we have the authority of Tinctoris that the *vihuela* was 'invented' by the Spanish. In his treatise *De inventione et usu musicae* (c1487)[6] he described various instruments descended from the lute, among which was an instrument 'invented by the Spanish, which both they and the Italians call the *viola*, but the French the *demi-luth*' ('hispanorum invento . . . quod ipsi ac Itali violam Gallici vero dimidum leutum vocant'). Tinctoris continued: 'this viola differs from the lute in that the lute is much larger and tortoise-shaped, while the viola is flat, and in most cases curved inwards on each side' ('que quidem viola in hoc a leuto differt: quod leutum multo majus ac testitudinem est: ista vero plana: ac – ut plurimam – ex utroque latere incurvata'). The date of the invention of the *vihuela* by the Spanish is not known for certain, but the mid 15th century seems the most likely period, since there is certainly no trace of any waisted plucked instrument in Spanish painting of the late 14th and early 15th centuries. The celestial orchestras so frequently depicted by artists from the Kingdom of Aragon include myriads of angels plucking lutes, harps and gitterns and bowing fiddles, but of a waisted plucked instrument there is no sign (Plates 8 and 10). Thus, there is no obvious precedent for the early renaissance *vihuelas* which Aragonese artists of the 1460s and 1470s began to include in their works. Indeed, as Poulton[7] has pointed out, the whole phenomenon of the *vihuela* in Spain is a puzzling one, given the immense popularity of the lute in that country and the similar, not to say identical, musical capabilities of the two instruments.

The plucked *vihuela* makes one of its earliest appearances in an anonymous mid 15th-century painting of the Virgin and Child from the province of Aragon, now in a private collection in Barcelona (Plate 18). Few details are visible, but a useful comparison may be made with a nearby lute; both instruments are played with a plectrum, both are strung with courses. The small size of the *vihuela* compared with that of the lute is of particular interest in view of Tinctoris's comment that the lute was 'much larger' than the *vihuela*.[8] In Spanish paintings of the period the *vihuela* is, if anything, usually the larger of the two, as is the case in another version of the Madonna and Child, originally to be found in the village of Maluenda near Zaragoza in the province of Aragon, but now in the Museo Maricel, Sitges (Plate 19). The *vihuela* depicted by this artist is a large instrument with extremely sharp, clean-cut corners to its waists. As in the previous example, its head and pegbox are obscured from view. In some ways these two early examples of the *vihuela* are not very alike; one is a large instrument with huge waists, the other is quite small with comparatively insignificant waists, yet together they do confirm that a waisted, plectrum-plucked instrument was beginning to be played in this region of eastern Spain.

By the 1480s the plucked *vihuela* had established itself firmly in the Kingdom of Aragon and was, therefore, included more and more in scenes of angelic music-making. There was, moreover, a growing consensus about its general shape; the typical late 15th-century *vihuela* had a reverse lute-like pegbox, a long thin neck and waists with corners (Figure 4), all of which features are well

17    Musician plucking a medieval fiddle (?)
(mid 15th century: Biblioteca Riccardiana, Florence, ms. 492, *Aeneid* 745-7, fol. 75)

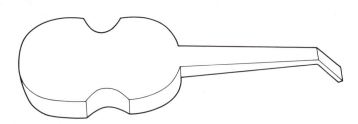

Figure  4    A *vihuela de mano* depicted in a late 15th-century painting from the province of Aragon

18   Madonna and Child with angel musicians
(mid 15th century, Aragonese school: private collection)

illustrated in a Valencian retable by the Perea Master dating from the 1470s
and kept, prior to its destruction in the Spanish Civil War, in the Colegiata at
Játiva (Plate 20). The belly of this *vihuela* is decorated with small geometric
motifs of the type commonly found on Spanish instruments of the period. A
slightly later example by a painter working in the province of Aragon appears
in the parish church of the village of Tamarite de Litera (Plate 21). The length
of this instrument's neck is worth noting.[9].

19   Madonna and Child with angel musicians (mid 15th century, Aragonese school: Museo Maricel, Sitges)

The use of 'corners' to define more exactly the shape of the waists of the early *vihuela* was a development of considerable importance, the origins of which can be traced back to the 1430s and 1440s when some instrument makers working in the province of Aragon began to experiment with the gently incurving waists of the medieval fiddle by incorporating definite angles to mark the point at which the waists join the sides.[10] Fiddles of this type, combining traditional features such as the flat, circular pegbox with the new outline, appear in two retables of the period, one in the Museo Provincial, Zaragoza (Plate 27), the other in the parish church at Villarroya del Campo (Plate 28). During the second half of the 15th century the new shape gained fairly

20 Madonna and Child with angel musicians: detail of angel musicians playing shawms and
a *vihuela de mano*
(mid/late 15th century, Valencian school: Colegiata, Játiva)

general acceptance throughout the Kingdom of Aragon, perhaps because it
allowed fiddlers to use a rather freer bowing action – there would be less
chance of the hair of the bow striking the side of the instrument, provided that
the strings were bowed opposite the waists. A fairly typical late 15th-century
fiddle of this type is played by one of a trio of angels in a Valencian retable in
a private collection (Plate 29). The older style of circular pegbox retained on
this instrument was now often replaced by the reverse, lute-like pegbox as
depicted in a late 15th-century panel of the Madonna and Child in another

21   The Holy Family with angel musicians: detail of angel musicians playing shawms and a *vihuela de mano*
(early 16th century, Aragonese school: Iglesia Parroquial, Tamarite de Litera)

private collection (Plate 13). In their outward physical appearance fiddles of this kind differ very little from the early viol, especially when they are as large as the instrument in a late 15th-century Catalan Madonna and Child in the Museo Diocesano of Gerona Cathedral, the huge body of which looks far too bulky to be played with comfort against the upper part of the arm (Plate 31). The invention and development of corners was a notable achievement for the Aragonese school of instrument making, for it signalled the start of the long period of transition between the gently incurving shape of the medieval fiddle and the rather more sectional outlines of the renaissance viol and violin families.[11] Moreover, the fact that fiddles with corners appeared at about the same time as cornered *vihuelas* lends support to the idea that the two instruments may have been quite closely related at that stage.

The next period in the history of the *vihuela* is somewhat complicated, and so it may be helpful to the reader to summarise the main trends before attempting a detailed discussion: (i) By the mid 1480s the plucked *vihuela* with its long neck and waists with well marked corners was firmly established in the Kingdom of Aragon. (ii) In and around the city of Valencia two distinct off-

22 Retable of the Visitation: detail of a panel illustrating the
celebration of the Mass
(mid 15th century, Aragonese school: Hispanic Society of America,
New York)

23 St Anne, the Virgin and St
Michael: detail of a musician playing a *vihuela de mano*
(mid/late 15th century, Aragonese
school: Metropolitan Museum of
Art, New York)

24 St Vincent with angel musicians: detail of miniature figure playing a *vihuela de mano*
(early 16th century, Catalan school: Museo Diocesano, Lerida)

25    Madonna and Child with angel musicians: detail of an angel musician playing a *vihuela de mano*; see also Plate 16
(*c*1500, Rodrigo Osona, Valencian school: Iglesia de Nuestra Señora, Ibiza)

26   Madonna and Child with angel musicians: detail of an angel musician playing a *vihuela de mano*
(*c*1500, Sardinian school: Castelsardo)

27    Angel musician playing a fiddle: detail of Plate 8
(early/mid 15th century, Aragonese school: Museo Provincial, Zaragoza)

28    Madonna and Child with angel musicians: detail of an angel musician playing a fiddle
(early/mid 15th century, Aragonese school: Iglesia Parroquial, Villarroya del Campo)

29    Retable of St Nicholas: detail of angel musicians playing a fiddle, a harp and a lute
(late 15th century, Valencian school: private collection, Barcelona)

shoots of this instrument began to emerge: the bowed *vihuela de arco* or viol,
structurally identical to its ancestor, but borrowing its playing techniques
from local Moorish players of the *rabāb*; and the plucked *vihuela de mano* which
reverted to the guitar shape and abandoned the use of corners.

The development of a bowed version of the *vihuela* resulted, quite simply,
from the application of an old playing technique to a new instrument. The
playing technique and the instrument are shown side by side in many paintings of the second half of the 15th century. To take but one example, in a panel
from the province of Aragon in the Museo Maricel at Sitges one of the angel
musicians is bowing a Moorish *rabāb* in the traditional downwards position,
while a nearby colleague is plucking a new *vihuela* (Plate 19). In effect, such
paintings illustrate the two principal ancestors of the bowed *vihuela* immediately prior to their profitable union. The change was therefore almost
wholly one of playing technique, the earliest bowed *vihuelas* being structurally
indistinguishable from their plucked ancestors. The first Valencian musicians
to play the new *vihuela de arco* presumably copied the playing techniques of
their *rabāb*-playing colleagues because the downwards playing posture would
have been ideally suited to the rather tall instruments so popular at that time.

The relationship between the bowed and the plucked *vihuela* is clearly
reflected in the terminology which the Spaniards applied to the two instru-

30   Madonna and Child with angel musicians: detail of an angel musician playing a fiddle; see also Plate 26
(c1500, Sardinian school: Castelsardo)

31    Madonna and Child with angel musicians
(late 15th century, Catalan school: Museo Diocesano, Gerona)

ments. Whereas in Italian usage the various types of string instruments were commonly differentiated by size (*viola / violone*), playing position (*viola da braccio / viola da gamba*) or some physical feature such as the presence or absence of frets (*viola tastarda / viola senza tasti*), the Spaniards often defined a string instrument by its playing technique, a method peculiarly appropriate to the various types of *vihuela*. In fact, the generic term *vihuela* could be modified in three ways: *vihuela de péndola* (a *vihuela* plucked with a plectrum); *vihuela de mano* (a *vihuela* plucked with the fingers); *vihuela de arco* (a *vihuela* played with a bow) – one basic instrumental type with three playing methods. Two of these types appear side by side in a privately-owned Valencian painting of the early 16th century. The *vihuela de arco* (Plate 37) is strung exactly like the plucked instrument with the strings tied round a stringholder fixed to the belly; the *vihuela de mano*, however, has one important distinguishing feature, its gently incurving, guitar-shaped waists (Plate 36). Instruments of this type first began to appear in and around the city of Valencia at the very end of the 15th century, replacing the older cornered *vihuelas* previously popular throughout the Kingdom of Aragon. The change in body design reflected the growing divergence between the two instruments as each developed its own distinct identity. There was probably no reason to maintain the deep waists with corners once the instrument was used exclusively for plucking. To put it another way, the early cornered *vihuelas* of the 1480s and 1490s were probably dual-purpose instruments to be bowed or plucked at will, whereas by the turn of the century two separate offshoots had emerged, each with a specific shape, each with an individual playing technique. The transitional period is perfectly illustrated by the Valencian painting cited above, in which the common ancestry of the two instruments is not blurred by the contrasting shape of their waists.

The idea that the smooth, guitar-shaped waists of the renaissance *vihuela* were introduced in order to distinguish it from earlier viol-like, plucked instruments, runs contrary to received opinion. Dart argued that 'in 1500 or so the viol still retained the hour-glass shape, with a flat back and belly, characteristic of the vihuela'. In the Kingdom of Aragon at least, the characteristic *vihuela* shape was established after that of the viol. A magnificent, guitar-shaped *vihuela de mano* of about 1500 with a very long neck is played by one of the angels in Rodrigo Osona's Ibiza retable (Plate 25). This instrument has several features in common with the Valencian *vihuela* mentioned above: the join between the neck and the body is several inches above the shoulders; the neck itself is patterned; there is a simple, lozenge-shaped ornament and a large soundhole in the upper part of the belly. Further examples of the early 16th-century plucked *vihuela* appear in an anonymous Valencian panel of the Virgin and Child[12] and in a retable by the Sardinian painter known as the Castelsardo Master in the parish church of that town (Plate 26).

At this point, a further complication must be considered, for there is some evidence that a bowed *vihuela* with guitar-shaped waists was popular for a time in Castille. An anonymous late 15th-century Castilian master working in Burgo de Osma depicted a 'bowed guitar' of this type (Plate 35) in two different paintings located in the cathedral of that city. In their general proportions these instruments closely resemble the Valencian pattern from which they undoubtedly derive. The appearance of this sub-species of the early viol merely confirms the closeness of the relationship that existed between bowed and plucked instruments at this period. Perhaps the most convincing demonstration of this relationship is a visual one. Readers may judge for themselves by examining four photographs of late 15th-century *vihuelas* placed side by side for comparison (Plates 32–35). (As we shall see in Chapter 7, the guitar-shaped viol enjoyed a certain vogue in 16th-century Italy.)

Despite the not infrequent appearance of the *vihuela* in early 16th-century Italian art, it was in Spain that the instrument made its most lasting impression. The first published collection of music for the *vihuela*, Luis Milán's *El Maestro* (1535) appeared, appropriately enough, in the city of Valencia. The illustration of a *vihuela* in this volume shows an instrument similar in most respects to the early 16th-century Valencian *vihuela*, but with its pegs inserted from the rear of a flat pegbox. This arrangement is confirmed by later *vihuela* publications such as Bermudo's *Declaración de instrumentos*[13] and by the surviving *vihuela de mano* in the Musée Jacquemart-André in Paris. This fascinating instrument has several features which clearly stem from the tradition of *vihuela* making established in the early 16th century.[14] It is well worth comparing it with the *vihuela* depicted by Rodrigo Osona; both instruments have a neck patterned with inlays of light and dark woods up to two or three inches immediately above the belly and a small, lozenge-shaped ornament at the top of the belly.

Having discussed the rôle of the *vihuela* in the early development of the viol, we can see now how close Dart's brilliant intuition led him to the truth about the origins of the viol. His argument is worth quoting in full:

Its origins lie in fifteenth-century Spain, home of the flat-backed *vihuela de mano*, the five- or later six-stringed guitar. This instrument was held and played much like the plectrum guitar of the present day; the cross-fertilization consisted of applying to it a playing technique which had always been associated with an entirely different family of instruments, the fiddles, in which there had never been any frets around the neck and the strings were always sounded with a bow.

In one important respect only was Dart inaccurate; the cross-fertilisation did not involve the medieval fiddle but the bowed *rabāb* played by the Moorish musicians of the Kingdom of Aragon. Nor should the impression be given that the cross-fertilisation leading to the 'birth' of the viol was an isolated development, for there are many indications in Aragonese art that the whole period was one of remarkable experiment and flux. There were indeed few rigid divisions between the characteristics of string instruments: some fiddles had

32   Madonna and Child with angel musicians: detail of an angel musician playing a *vihuela de mano*
(late 15th century, Aragonese school: Palacio Episcopal, Jaca)

33  Six angel musicians: detail of an angel musician playing a viol
(*c*1500, Sardinian school: Museo Nazionale, Cagliari)

34    Six angel musicians: detail of an angel musician playing a *vihuela de mano*; see also Plate 33 (*c*1500, Sardinian school: Museo Nazionale, Cagliari)

35  The Assumption of the Virgin: detail of an angel musician playing a viol
(*c*1500, Castilian school: Cathedral, Burgo de Osma)

36    The Coronation of the Virgin: detail of an angel musician playing a *vihuela de mano* (early 16th century, Valencian school: private collection, Valencia)

37   The Coronation of the Virgin: detail of an angel musician playing a viol; see also Plate 36
(early 16th century, Valencian school: private collection, Valencia)

smooth waists, others cornered waists; some fiddles reverse pegboxes with lateral pegs, others disc-shaped pegboxes with pegs inserted from the front; some *rabābs* frets, others no frets; some *rabābs* reverse pegboxes, other sickle-shaped pegboxes surmounted by a carved head; some *vihuelas* cornered waists, others smooth waists. The division between bowed and plucked instruments was particularly indistinct; so many bowed instruments were constructed like plucked instruments with a flat bridge or stringholder that it must have seemed a perfectly logical step to try bowing a new plucked instrument such as the *vihuela* (or indeed to pluck an old bowed instrument such as the fiddle!). Even lutes seem to have been bowed on occasion.[15] The early viol, therefore, was not so much the result of a unique experiment in combining the physical features of one instrument with the playing techniques of another, as the outcome of a long period of experiment.[16]

# 4

## The Valencian viol: its structure, playing techniques and music

A survey of the artists who first depicted the new viol or *vihuela de arco* points so unequivocally to the city and province of Valencia as the main centre of the instrument that the use of this geographical definition seems fully justified. The viol appears in the Marian paintings of the two most important schools of late-medieval and early-renaissance Valencian painting, those headed by Rodrigo Osona and the Perea Master.[1] It appears, too, in the works of artists active in Mediterranean islands such as Majorca and Sardinia which at that period enjoyed close cultural links with Valencia, and there are further examples from peripheral regions of the province such as the Maestrazgo and from locations just across the border such as Tarragona in Catalonia. In marked contrast, there is scant evidence of the bowed viol in nearby inland areas such as the province of Aragon where *rabāb* playing was still common, notably the Zaragoza district. Perhaps the relative isolation of the land-locked province of Aragon and the roughness of its terrain resulted in a greater conservatism than was possible in the more outward-looking, cosmopolitan life of a major Mediterranean port like Valencia. In fact, the eventual appearance of the viol in works of art executed in Zaragoza and Huesca was partly a result of the arrival of Valencian-trained artists such as the great sculptor Damián Forment. One of Forment's first commissions in Zaragoza was the magnificent high altar of El Pilar Cathedral, the centrepiece of which is the Virgin of the Assumption attended by an angel playing a viol of Valencian design (Plate 46).

The earliest depiction of a Valencian viol so far discovered is in San Felíu, a small church attractively situated just above the town of Játiva (Plate 38). Post,[2] suggesting a date of *c*1473 for the panel, which represents the traditional Madonna and Child with serenading musicians, ascribed it to a member of the Montolíu family who headed a group of artists active in the Maestrazgo region, a barren, mountainous area to the north of Castellón de la Plana on the northern borders of Valencia. The painting has been substantially restored in recent years, but its deplorable condition prior to renovation was recorded for posterity by the Mas Archive. Most illustrations of the early Valencian viol, however, date from a slightly later period than this example, *c*1485–1510. If due

38   Madonna and Child with angel musicians
(c1470-1480, Maestrazgo school: San Felíu, Játiva)

39   Madonna and Child with angel musicians: detail of angel musicians playing a viol and a
harp
(late 15th century, Valencian school: San Esteban, Valencia)

40    Madonna and Child with angel musicians: detail of an angel musician playing a viol (*c*1500, Sardinian school: Birmingham City Museum and Art Gallery)

41   The Coronation of the Virgin
(early 16th century, Majorcan or Valencian school: Museo de Bellas Artes, Valencia)

45   The Dormition of the Virgin: detail of angel musicians
(early 16th century, Valencian school: Museo de Bellas Artes, Barcelona)

42    Angel musician playing a viol: detail of Plate 41
(early 16th century, Majorcan or Valencian school: Museo de Bellas Artes, Valencia)

43   Angel musician playing a lute
(early 16th century, Valencian school: private collection, Barcelona)

44   Angel musician playing a viol; see also
Plate 43
(early 16th century, Valencian school: private
collection, Barcelona)

46   The Assumption of the Virgin: detail of an angel musician playing a viol
(*c*1509-1512, Damián Forment: El Pilar Cathedral, Zaragoza)

allowance is made for a short time-lag between new developments in instrument making and their regular appearance in works of art, then the Valencian
viol was at the height of its popularity during the last two decades of the 15th
century. To judge by the number of surviving paintings in which the instrument appears, there must have been a considerable, if brief, vogue for it.

In its general appearance the Valencian viol was a tall, slim instrument
with a long neck, thin ribs and an attractive, if rather plain, body design. A distinctive form quickly emerged which derived almost all of its physical characteristics from the plucked *vihuela de mano* (to which, as we have seen, it was very
closely related). An examination of the body proportions of this type confirms
the general impression that the instrument was indeed very tall and slim by
comparison with later viols. To illustrate this, it will be helpful to draw some

specific comparisons between the outlines of two individual instruments, an early viol depicted in a Sardinian painting of *c*1500 (Plate 33) and the well-known 17th-century viol pictured in Simpson's *Division Violist*[3] (Figure 5):

|  | viol *c*1650 | viol *c*1500 |
|---|---|---|
| i | overall length (a) about three times greatest breadth (b) | overall length (a) about five times greatest breadth (b) |
| ii | body length (c) just over one and a half times greatest breadth (b) | body length (c) just over twice greatest breadth (b) |
| iii | neck length including pegbox (d) less than body length (c) | neck length including pegbox (d) greater than body length (c) |
| iv | lower section of belly wider than upper | upper and lower sections of belly equally wide |
| v | large waists about a quarter of body length (c) | small waists no more than a sixth of body length (c) |
| vi | shoulders slope down to waists | shoulders curved forming a right angle with neck |
| vii | broad neck | slim neck |
| viii | deep ribs | shallow ribs |

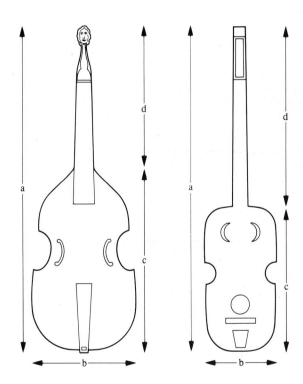

Figure 5   A mid 17th-century English viol depicted in Christopher Simpson's *The Division Violist* (London, 1659) and a *vihuela de arco* depicted in a Sardinian painting of *c*1500: scale drawing for the purpose of comparing proportions

These comparisons highlight the difference between the large, broad belly of the classic viol and the slender, small body of its early Valencian ancestor. Indeed, the relative proportions of the early viol differ so markedly from those associated with later instruments that the traditional nomenclature for viol sizes, treble, tenor and bass, is of doubtful value as a method of classification. In some ways, it makes best sense to think of the early viol as a tenor instrument with a rather small body, but an overall length verging on that of a bass.

The ribs of the early viol were so shallow that makers did not need to bend the top of the back inwards in order to join it to the neck; this practice was introduced later to cope with deeper-bodied viols. In fact, the ribs were often no deeper than the side of the neck. The neck itself was not 'set back' as on later instruments; the whole surface of the instrument from the fret nut to the bottom of the belly formed a single plane, a point clearly verified by the profile of Damián Forment's sculpted viol (Plate 46).

This very distinctive body outline was not adopted uncritically by all makers. Even at this early stage there were experiments with alternative designs, and some changes were made to the proportions of the body, waists and neck. An instrument with a shorter neck and longer waists seems to have become popular in the early 16th century and is depicted in several Valencian paintings of the period (Plates 37 and 44). Presumably the larger waists were introduced to help players draw the bow across the strings without it striking the side of the instrument. Angelic violists seem to have coped with the tiny waists without difficulty, not least the Sardinian player whose bow skilfully bisects the small indentations in the side of the instrument. However, this aspect of design may well have caused problems for mortal musicians.

It would be wrong to give the impression that there were only two types of Valencian viol, instruments with long necks and tiny waists and instruments with short necks and large waists. Some viols belong to neither category but derive features from both; an instrument with small waists and a very short neck may be seen in a Valencian painting of the Dormition of the Virgin in the Museo de Bellas Artes, Barcelona (Plate 45); a viol combining a long neck with large waists appears in a second Sardinian Madonna and Child in the Birmingham City Museum and Art Gallery (Plate 40). Makers were clearly continuing to experiment in an attempt to formulate the best possible design for the new instrument, as indeed they continued to do throughout the 16th century.

All the viols so far discussed had waists with well-defined corners like the early plucked *vihuelas* found in paintings throughout the Kingdom of Aragon during the second half of the 15th century. But, as was pointed out in the previous chapter, it was not long before the plucked *vihuela* began to develop an identity of its own, abandoning corners and reverting to the gently incurving, guitar-shaped waists that were to become characteristic of the instrument in the 16th century. This growing division between the bowed viol and plucked *vihuela* was obscured for a time by the brief appearance in Castille of a bowed *vihuela* with guitar-shaped waists. Although instruments of this type do not seem to have been popular in Valencia – both the examples I have so far located come from Castilian sources – their construction was undoubtedly influenced by the long-necked Valencian model. One need only compare the bowed viol illustrated in a painting from the Cathedral at Burgo de Osma (Plate 35) with a selection of instruments of the Valencian type (Plates 32, 33 and 34) to see the many similarities, the narrow body, the long neck and the slim ribs. The influence of the local Castilian school of instrument making may be discerned not only in the smoothly incurving waists, but also in the slight dip where the shoulders meet the neck, the ornaments decorating each corner of the belly and, in so far as it is visible, the method of stringing, all of which features recur on fiddles from the same area.[4]

To return to the Valencian viol, the commonest method of string-fastening was exactly that of contemporary plucked instruments such as the *vihuela de mano* and the lute, the strings being attached directly to a flat bar glued to the lower part of the belly. These stringholders were pierced horizontally to enable the strings to be looped round and fastened securely. The strings thus passed directly from fret nut to stringholder without the benefit of an arched bridge to raise them higher over the belly, a method of stringing that necessarily precluded both the raised fingerboard and the setting back of the neck (Plate 37). Readers may easily reproduce the general effect of this by trying to bow a modern guitar! This type of stringing, more than any other, illustrates how apt was the contemporary terminology *vihuela de mano* and *vihuela de arco*, which differentiated between the playing techniques rather than the construction of the two instruments. A popular alternative to this method of stringing was to turn the stringholder into a type of flat bridge and to fix the strings to a tailpiece (Plate 33). Arched bridges were exceptional at this period and so it is all the more curious that the earliest known depiction of a viol, the one from the Maestrazgo region (Plate 38), should show an instrument with a steeply arched bridge as well as a fingerboard. The remarkably advanced state of the viol – its bridge resembles one pictured over 40 years later by Raphael in his celebrated painting of *St Cecilia* in the Pinacoteca, Bologna (Plate 50) – raises a few suspicions that the panel may have been repainted. Yet the instrument must certainly not be rejected out of hand as spurious merely because it does not conform to our preconceived ideas about the development of the early viol. In other respects, notably its body outline with small, well-defined waists, it is absolutely typical of the period. Moreover, arched bridges, though still quite rare in Aragon, were gradually gaining acceptance even by some players of that most traditional of instruments, the *rabāb* (Plate 9).

One of the most variable aspects of the early viol was the number of its strings; some instruments had as few as three (Plate 35), but the majority were equipped with five or six (Plate 33). By modern standards, the strings of five-

and six-string viols were placed remarkably close together, so that they could all be depressed against the very narrow neck. Indeed, in some cases, most notably the Cagliari instrument (Plate 33), it is difficult to see how the violist could pick out individual strings at all. Perhaps, though, the most significant difference between the stringing of the Valencian viol and that of the instrument played today lies in the length of the strings relative to that of the body. On a viol of classic proportions the sounding length of the strings (i.e. from the fret nut to the bridge) is roughly that of the body, whereas the strings of a Valencian viol far exceed the length of the body, owing partly to the length of the neck and partly to the low position of the stringholder or bridge (Plate 39). This relationship between body length and sounding string length, the latter being about half as long again as the former, is characteristic of the guitar family. Many viols of the 16th century retained this arrangement, the long string length being achieved by means of a long neck, a low placement of the bridge or a combination of both features.

At this period the commonest type of pegbox was the simple, lute-like reverse pegbox placed at a sharp angle to the neck with the pegs inserted laterally (Plate 44). A small number of instruments were supplied with a sickle-shaped peg-box, sometimes with the addition of a carved animal head (Plate 39). The scroll was not yet in use, although the Sardinian painting from Cagliari shows a viol with a fairly close approach to one (Plate 33), a pegbox that curves back on itself but ends in an uncarved block of wood.

Frets were in common use on all string instruments of the period both bowed and plucked, and even the traditionally unfretted *rabāb* was more and more often to be seen with frets tied round the upper part of its neck (Plate 13). Valencian makers of the viol were no exception, and so frets quickly became established as an important characteristic of the instrument, emphasising still further the close links between the bowed and plucked *vihuela*. The number of frets varied considerably according to the length of the neck; both the long-necked Sardinian instruments are pictured with nine, giving a range of a major sixth above the open strings assuming that all the frets were placed at intervals of a semitone. The frets themselves seem to have been movable; in some instances each individual fret is formed from two very thin bands of material, presumably gut, tied together behind the neck (Plate 33). The 17th-century writer Mace described how to tie a fret round the neck of a lute 'after the old Fashion, *Viz*. Double' but recommended the more modern method of single fretting. Both methods were probably used by Valencian viol makers.

The size, shape and position of the soundholes or ornamental roses were determined, more than any other features, by the preference of individual makers rather than by adherence to the regional consensus. At this period the single central rose was still preferred to the paired c-holes (Plate 39). Even on very closely related instruments the soundhole was not always located in the same position; of the two otherwise almost identical viols played in a Majorcan angelic orchestra, one has a soundhole level with the waists while on the other instrument it is located in the upper segment of the belly (Plate 41). There seems to have been a fashion in some quarters for placing the c-holes quite high up on the belly; both the Sardinian instruments were made in this way. On the whole, the somewhat extravagant Moorish style of black and white geometric ornamentation which decorates the bellies of so many string instruments in the Kingdom of Aragon during the first half of the 15th century,[5] is not to be found in representations of the viol, the most ornamental viol belly being that of an instrument with a scheme of five diamond-shaped motifs (Plate 37).

Having surveyed the external features of the early viol, a much more problematic task must now be approached, that of its internal construction. As no Valencian viol survives from the late 15th century, any discussion of necessity verges on the purely speculative. The most likely hypothesis is one which takes into account the close relationship between bowed and plucked instruments of the period. If the external appearance of the Valencian viol or *vihuela de arco* was so like that of the *vihuela de mano* as to make the two instruments almost indistinguishable, its internal construction was perhaps also comparable with that of the plucked instrument. To be more precise, its flat belly was probably supported by some form of transverse barring. There are, in fact, three tiny shreds of evidence to support this notion. The only surviving *vihuela de mano* which is presumed to date from the 16th century and which may thus relate more closely to the Valencian *vihuela de arco* than any surviving viols, has two transverse bars supporting its belly. According to Prynne,[6] these are fixed 35cm. and 46.5cm. from the bottom. Then there is one early painting in which a viol does appear to have a transverse bar. This is none other than Grünewald's Isenheim Altarpiece. Fanciful though this instrument may be, a close examination of its c-holes reveals a thin strip of pale brown material crossing both holes at their halfway point, quite possibly a transverse bar attached to the under-side of the belly (Plate 60). Finally, there is the group of mid 16th-century Venetian viols discussed by Harwood and Edmunds[7] in *Early Music* (October 1978). Edmunds describes the soundboard of the earliest of these instruments, made by Francesco Linarol about 1550, as follows: 'On first inspection it looks very similar to the other viols but on closer investigation it turns out that the soundboard is made from a flat piece of quartered pine like a lute table, but supported by two transverse arched bars, one just above the top corners and one below the lower corners.' Later, Edmunds re-examined another 16th-century viol, a tenor by Ebert, and found that the insides of its ribs were clearly marked where there had once been transverse bars as on the Linarol instrument (Plate 70). This discovery fits in very neatly with the theory that the flat belly of the early Valencian viol was supported by transverse bars. At some stage, presumably in the early 16th century, makers began to arch the belly slightly over these bars in order to cope with the higher tension imposed on the belly by the introduction of the tall, arched bridge. (This subject will be dealt with more fully in Chapter 7.)

The first players of the viol copied both the downwards playing position and the underhand bowing techniques associated with the Moorish *rabāb*. Quite possibly some musicians simply transferred from the one instrument to the other, the traditional playing methods of the *rabāb* being well suited to the viol. With few exceptions, angel violists are shown holding their instrument vertically downwards, and on the few occasions when a variant posture is adopted, one suspects that the reason for its appearance is artistic rather than musical. To take an example, there are a few instances of a player raising a viol almost to eye-level, though still holding it downwards, in order to prevent it from being obscured by another player or an intervening object (Plate 39). Moreover, the desire for symmetry has led one artist to insist on the viol-playing member of a duo (Plate 44) copying exactly the posture of his lutenist colleague (Plate 43): the result is a rather improbable playing position. Yet most painters were careful to differentiate between the slanting position apt for plucked instruments and the vertical position better suited to the bowed viol. By comparison with *rabāb*-playing angels in mid 15th-century Marian paintings, few angel violists in late 15th-century Valencian art are actually seated with their instruments held *a gamba*. Once again, this is unlikely to reflect an actual change in the playing habits of real musicians, since it can be explained readily in terms of new developments in the field of artistic design. In the earlier part of the century it was customary to depict the Madonna and Child enthroned on a magnificent Gothic structure adorned with numerous pinnacles, turrets and ledges upon which minute angel musicians could be seated for the purpose of serenading the objects of their adoration. Under the growing influence of the Italian Renaissance, these elaborate thrones gave way to a much simpler type of chair, while at the same time the musical angels 'grew' considerably in stature, eventually being drawn on almost the same scale as the Madonna. These life-sized musicians were too large to be allocated a seat on the structure of the throne itself and so were usually grouped standing around, or kneeling before, the Madonna.

The variety of bow grips used by angelic viol players is remarkable, though not one adopts the overhand fiddle grip. The term 'underhand' is commonly used to describe viol bowing, since the hand is held under the bow. Most angelic violists of the period have their thumb and first finger 'fastned on the Stalk' in the manner advocated centuries later by Simpson (1659), but a very tight grip is sometimes pictured with all four fingers curved round the stick (Plate 37). An important aspect of underhand bowing is the management of the wrist, which should be relaxed. Simpson suggested that quick notes be played with the wrist. But the wrist also has an important function in longer bow strokes. If it is held completely relaxed, then towards the end of a pushed up-bow it will continue the momentum of the stroke after the arm has stopped, a movement which tends to turn the palm of the hand in towards the player's body. During the pulled down-bow the wrist is not cocked until the end of the bow stroke, when the momentum of the relaxed wrist again continues to move the bow after the arm has come to a halt. To an observer, the effect of this is that from the end of the pushed up-bow to the end of the pulled down-bow the player's wrist and bow form a single curve so that the hand appears to point in the same direction as the bow. At the end of the pulled stroke and during the pushed stroke the wrist appears to be cocked and forms an angle with the bow. The Sardinian panel in Birmingham illustrates the hand position during a pulled stroke when the wrist and bow point in the same direction (Plate 40). Unusual bow grips are most often encountered when the viol, for artistic reasons, is held in an awkward position, a fact that tends to confirm the unrealistic nature of such depictions. For example, a Majorcan painting which includes two viols shows one held low down and bowed quite normally, and the other held high up to ensure its visibility and hence bowed in a very cramped manner with the forearm almost vertical (Plate 41).

The physical characteristics and playing methods of the early Valencian viol are summed up in the list below, which presents the most typical features of the instrument including any important variations. With the assistance of this summary, Dart's theory of the origins of the viol may now be given the close attention that it fully deserves.[8]

*Features of the Valencian viol*

|     |                                                                                       |
| --- | ------------------------------------------------------------------------------------- |
| i    | tenor size                                                                           |
| ii   | long narrow body                                                                     |
| iii  | shallow ribs                                                                         |
| iv   | narrow neck                                                                          |
| v    | long *or* short neck                                                                 |
| vi   | flat belly                                                                           |
| vii  | neck not set back at an angle from belly                                             |
| viii | waists with corners                                                                 |
| ix   | small *or* large waists                                                              |
| x    | no fingerboard                                                                      |
| xi   | frets                                                                                |
| xii  | strings attached to a flat stringholder *or* passed over a flat bridge and attached to a tailpiece |
| xiii | reverse *or* sickle-shaped pegbox                                                    |
| xiv  | lateral pegs                                                                         |
| xv   | central rose *or* c-holes                                                            |
| xvi  | belly supported by transverse barring (?)                                           |
| xvii | played downwards 'a gamba'                                                           |
| xviii| bowed underhand                                                                     |

As was noted in Chapter 3, his basic assumption that the viol evolved as a type of bowed *vihuela* was accurate except that its bowed ancestor was the Moorish *rabāb* rather than the medieval fiddle. But for the last two items, the summary could just as easily have been compiled from late 15th-century paintings of the plucked *vihuela*, a striking testimony to the aptness of his characterisation of the early viol as a 'bowed guitar'. However, not all the arguments with which Dart supports his central thesis are valid, and his comments, especially on body shape and playing position, need to be revised. Concerning the former, Dart wrote that 'in 1500 or so the viol still retained the hour-glass shape, with a flat back and belly, characteristic of the vihuela, and preserved in a rather exaggerated manner by the present-day guitar'. The evidence of Valencian paintings contradicts the notion that the early viol had an hour-glass shape; by far the commonest type was the instrument with cornered waists. A more serious error resulted from Dart's attempt to derive the playing position of the viol from that of the *vihuela*: 'its playing position was identical with that of the vihuela, the instrument being held across the body, slantingly, and the bow being manipulated rather awkwardly from below, or, more conveniently, from above'. Veronese's *Marriage Feast at Cana*, cited by Dart as evidence, was painted well over half a century after the earliest viols had appeared in Valencia and can therefore be discounted immediately as evidence of the manner in which the first violists held their instruments. Hardly any Valencian depictions of the early viol illustrate this slanting, guitar-like hold. It is true that a group of northern Italian paintings of the 1540s and 1550s depict tenor viols being played in the horizontal position, but this would seem to have been a passing phase – one condemned, incidentally, by Ganassi in his treatise *Regola Ruber-tina* (see Chapter 9). These minor criticisms, however, do not detract from Dart's two main achievements in this field, the establishment of 15th-century Spain as the birthplace of the viol and the recognition of the organological links between the early viol and the guitar family.

The preceding discussion has left unanswered one question of considerable importance about the instrument; what was its musical rôle? If information could be uncovered about the music played by the earliest violists, this would undoubtedly help to explain why the instrument became popular so quickly and equally why in its original Valencian form it fell into disuse so soon, for the rise and fall of any instrument depends to no small extent on public reaction to its repertory. It had to be admitted in Chapter 2 that evidence concerning the repertory and performance practice of the *rabāb* in the Kingdom of Aragon during the 15th century was fragmentary and rather speculative in character, yet there are several reasons why it is very much more difficult to isolate hard facts about the music of the early viol. Whereas the *rabāb* was played over a period of many centuries, the Valencian viol enjoyed a short life of two or three decades at most, before being altered fundamentally by instrument makers working, it would appear, in Italy. The innovations of this second generation of craftsmen included the arched bridge, which transformed the musical potential of the instrument. The subsequent development of viol music in 16th-century Europe is thus of little value in determining the repertory of the early Valencian viol, since the flat bridge of this instrument would have prevented it from playing a single line in a polyphonic piece in the manner of later viols. Not only was the Valencian viol a relatively short-lived instrument, it was also not very widely distributed, restricting still further the possible field of inquiry. Furthermore, even when potential references are located, the lack of precision in the terminology often renders them useless for supporting a specific theory about the instrument. To take a single example of this, in Fernando de Rojas's *La Celestina*, published in 1499, reference is made to the value of a *vihuela* in soothing a toothache: 'e el mayor remedio que tiene es tomar una vihuela'. The use of the generic term *vihuela* without qualification excludes the possibility of an exact identification to the extent that it is not even certain whether this particular instrument was bowed or plucked, though Mabbe, an early 17th-century translator of the work into English, was not troubled by doubts on this point, rendering 'vihuela' as 'Vial de gamba'.[9] An agnostic viewpoint is often the only safe one. To repeat Boyden's vivid caution, the terminology of bowed instruments in the early 16th century can be a 'treacherous quicksand ready and eager to engulf those who mistake it for *terra firma*'.[10] But the question of what type of music the first violists played is important enough to merit some discussion even without much firm evidence.

Perhaps the most attractive explanation of the instrument's appearance is that it evolved as a late offshoot of the long-established traditions of *rabāb* playing in the Kingdom of Aragon. An interesting analogy may be drawn between this hypothetical development and the recent appearance of the Western violin in the traditional orchestras of North Africa, where it is not uncommon to see violinists imitating the playing methods of the *rabāb* by seating themselves on the ground with their instruments held downwards and bowed underhand.[11] The close proximity of Christian and Moorish culture in late 15th-century Valencia would no doubt have facilitated, possibly even stimulated, such a cross-fertilisation between an instrument from one tradition and a playing technique from another.[12] Centuries later, one can only guess at whether it was players of the *rabāb* who first expressed an interest in the waisted body of the *vihuela*, or whether it was players of the *vihuela* who copied the bowed instrument's playing techniques. In support of the idea that the viol was initially developed as an alternative to the *rabāb*, it is interesting to note that when it came to selecting which instruments were to appear in the hands of their music-making angels, Valencian artists never included both the *rabāb* and the viol in one painting, whereas the *rabāb* and the viol were both frequently pictured with other string instruments of the period, especially the fiddle, the gittern, the harp, the lute and the *vihuela de mano* (Plates 8, 13, 39 and 45). Apparently only one representative of the class of bowed string instruments played *a gamba* was considered necessary, almost as though the *rabāb* and the viol were, at least in the eyes of the artist, alternative manifestations of the one basic type.

The physical structure of the early viol supports the idea that, like the *rabāb*, it was a drone-playing instrument; its method of stringing with the strings attached directly to a flat stringholder would seem very appropriate for such a task. The only way to bow such an instrument in practice is to play all the strings together which, to judge by experiments with a modern guitar, produces a soft, rather nebulous sound. The strings run so close to the belly that bowing the outer strings individually produces rather unsatisfactory results. It is difficult to avoid the conclusion that the Valencian viol really was a most impractical instrument even for the relatively simple task of playing drones, and that its demise was fully deserved. It must not be forgotten, however, that a player of this type of *vihuela de arco* could turn his instrument into a *vihuela de mano* whenever necessary, simply by putting down the bow.

As was mentioned previously, the only late 15th-century theorist to deal with musical instruments was Tinctoris.[13] Because he served at the Aragonese court in Naples and visited Catalonia, his remarks, though tantalisingly brief, are of particular interest in the study of the early Valencian viol. He was well acquainted with instruments of the Mediterranean area, mentioning two invented on the Iberian peninsula, the 'viola sine arculo' (*vihuela*) and the 'ghittera' (*gittern*), and he was also aware of, though rather disgusted by, eastern instruments such as the three-string *tambura* played in Naples by captive Turks. As the date of compilation of his treatise *De inventione et usu musicae* is usually considered to be *c*1487, it is unlikely that Tinctoris would have been as familiar with the newly-emerging Valencian viol (if indeed he had yet come across it at all) as he was with the plucked *vihuela de mano* which had appeared a good deal earlier, in the mid 15th century. Nonetheless, his comments on other bowed instruments are of considerable interest in establishing the general performing customs of the period. Having dealt with the lute and the plucked *vihuela*, Tinctoris turns his attention to another 'viola', waisted in shape like the *vihuela* but tuned differently and played with a bow. Two tunings are given, one for an instrument with three strings (tuned in fifths), the other for an instrument with five strings (tuned in unisons and fifths). Tinctoris makes a point of describing the way the strings are placed so that the player can sound any one individually at will without touching the others ('unam tangens: juxta libitum sonitoris: alias reliquat inconcussas'), a clear reference to an instrument with an arched bridge. From the details given here, it would seem likely that Tinctoris was describing the medieval fiddle, which in the late 15th century often appears with an arched bridge.

Tinctoris later refers briefly to the music performed by players of the 'viola cum arculo'. He instances a performance at Bruges by two musicians, Jean and Charles Orbus, the former playing the treble line of some songs, the latter the tenor: in other words a performance of polyphonic music with one instrument to a part. It is unlikely, however, that the Valencian viol was played in this manner. Apart from the fact that it did not usually have an arched bridge, the instrument rarely appears in consorts of three or even two. Valencian artists seem to have followed a fairly well established convention, probably reflecting current musical usage, whereby singers and players of *haut* wind instruments such as the shawm could appear in unmixed groups, but players of *bas* string instruments were restricted to 'broken' consorts made up from a selection of various single instruments.[14] As well as playing polyphonic music, the 'viola cum arculo' was used, in Tinctoris's own words, to accompany the recitations of epic poetry ('ad historiarum recitationem'). Throughout this section on string instruments Tinctoris seems keen to appear well informed about the national origins and geographical range of instruments, making frequent observations about where instruments were invented, where they were best played and where they were most popular. It is therefore surely significant that, commenting on the use of the 'viola cum arculo' to accompany the recitation of epics, he should imply that the practice was an almost universal one, taking place over the greater part of the world ('in plerisque partibus orbis'). In Italy the development of the *lira da braccio* was a response to the demand for improvised accompaniments to vocal recitations, but in Spain, where the *lira* was apparently unknown, one must assume that other bowed instruments such as the fiddle, the *rabāb* and the viol met this need. Certainly of the two kinds of music played by Tinctoris's 'viola cum arculo', the provision of simple accompaniments for epics and other recitations would have suited the flat-bridged Valencian viol much better. (It has often been suggested that the 15th-century Spanish traditions of improvising accompaniments for the recitation of epic or lyric poetry left an imprint upon music for the *vihuela de mano* published in the mid 16th century, particularly some of the romance settings and variations on romance tunes. As always, however, it is impossible to draw any specific conclusions about earlier oral traditions from later, possibly refined and stylised published versions. In any case the bowed *vihuela de arco*, our concern here, would have been limited to a far simpler style of accompaniment than would have been possible on the plucked *vihuela*. Even the relatively undemanding chordal reciting-patterns known to have been used by players of the *lira da braccio* in Italy would not have been easily playable on a flat-bridged instrument like the *vihuela*.) The vagueness of this conclusion will, no doubt, be frustrating to readers keen to know what music was played by the immediate ancestor of the viol, and yet it is inevitable given the brevity of the bowed *vihuela*'s existence, the limited geographical range in which it was played and the insuperable difficulties of string instrument terminology at the beginning of the century.

In view of the general assessment of the Valencian viol as a late offshoot of the old medieval tradition of using bowed instruments to accompany the human voice, an offshoot of the *rabāb*-playing tradition, some may well question the use of the term 'viol' to denote such an instrument, since its techniques and musical capabilities differed so radically from those of later viols. But the choice is justified not so much by the instrument itself, which clearly owes much to medieval tradition, but by the extent of its influence on the subsequent development of the early 16th-century Italian renaissance viol.

# 5

## The introduction of the viol into Italy

After an initial success in the late 15th century, the *vihuela de arco* declined rapidly in the city of its origins. By the second decade of the 16th century, the instrument was rarely depicted in Valencian art, and there is hardly any trace of it in the works of Valencian painters of the 1520s and 1530s.[1] It is difficult to avoid the conclusion that the *vihuela de arco* was a late and unimportant offshoot of medieval traditions of string playing which, despite a brief period of popularity, ultimately failed to supplant the long-established *rabāb*. The crucial importance of the instrument's speedy migration eastwards across the Mediterranean to Italy is therefore easy to understand. It may indeed be no exaggeration to suggest that its very survival depended on this, since Italian instrument makers were responsible for developing the instrument into the form that was to enjoy lasting popularity.

As one of the two major coastal cities of the mainland Kingdom of Aragon, Valencia was at this period an important commercial centre, an indispensable trading link between inland cities such as Zaragoza and the whole Mediterranean area from the Balearic Islands to the Kingdom of Naples. In view of the city's dominant position in the western Mediterranean, it is hardly surprising that her artistic links should have been at least as strong with the islands on the main trading routes, such as Majorca, as with other provinces on the mainland. Certainly, to judge by surviving paintings, the new Valencian *vihuela de arco* spread to the east much more quickly than it did to the west; the instrument appears at an early date in the works of both Majorcan and Sardinian artists, whereas its westward advance into the heart of Castille seems to have been relatively sluggish. The tendency of Valencian instruments to spread to the east was undoubtedly reinforced by the city's political links with the Italian mainland, by far the most significant of which was the election of two Popes from the most influential Valencian family of the period, the Borgias.

The homeland of the Borgia dynasty lay to the south of the city of Valencia around the small towns of Játiva and Gandia. Here the family lived in relative obscurity until in 1455 Alonso Borgia, Bishop of Valencia, was chosen as a compromise candidate in the papal enclave and elected as Pope Calixtus III.

Following his elevation, the new Pope installed a large number of his Catalan-speaking countrymen (many, no doubt, from Valencia) in the papal household, thereby prompting the inevitable accusations of nepotism. 'Everyone expected an invasion of grasping Catalans and they were not to be disappointed', wrote Mallett.[2] Shortly before his death in 1458 Calixtus, once again favouring a member of his own family, appointed his nephew Rodrigo Borgia as Bishop of Valencia. Rodrigo, however, remained for many years an absentee in Italy, and it was not until 1472 that he belatedly visited his diocese, entering the city in a splendid procession to the accompaniment of trumpets and drums.[3] In 1492, to the surprise of many observers, Rodrigo was chosen as the new Pope and took the title Alexander VI. As his uncle had done before him, Rodrigo immediately began to fill the papal household with his own countrymen, Catalan speakers, many of whom had previously served him as a cardinal in Rome. Once again there was controversy over the Spanish Pope's supposed nepotism, and the number of Catalans in positions of authority caused resentment.[4]

The years of Alexander VI's papacy (1492–1503) marked a high point of Spanish influence in Rome and the Papal States. Significantly, this was exactly the period during which the new Valencian *vihuelas* first began to appear in these areas. The conclusion to be drawn from this coincidence of dates is that the Borgia family played a vital, if inadvertent, rôle in the dissemination of these instruments on the Italian mainland. Both iconographic and archival evidence, as I shall show, confirm that the *vihuela de mano* and *vihuela de arco* first appeared in cities and states ruled by, or at least closely connected with, the Borgia family. There is also some evidence of another 'port-of-entry' further south in Aragonese-dominated Naples; on the other hand, the new Valencian instruments took appreciably longer to establish themselves in the three major Italian powers – Venice, Milan and Florence – that were comparatively untouched by Spanish influence.

With its large Catalan-speaking community, the city of Rome under Alexander VI must have provided employment for many musicians from the Kingdom of Aragon. A performance given by one group of Spanish musicians from Rome was reported to Isabella d'Este by the Ferrarese chancellor, Bernardino Prospero.[5] Writing on 6 March 1493, he described a celebration in Vigevano near Milan to mark the birth of an heir to Ludovico Sforza, at which there was a musical performance by 'the Spanish players sent from Rome by the Most Reverend Monsignor Ascanio' ('quelli sonadorj spagnoli che mandò el Reverendissimo Monsignore Ascanio da Roma'). These musicians, the report continued, played 'viols almost as large as myself' ('viole grande quasi come mj'), but their playing of these instruments was considered 'sweet rather than artful' ('il sonare suo è più presto dolce che de multa arte'). Brief though it is, this report highlights the manner in which the new Spanish instruments were introduced, first into Rome and then into other regions of

Italy. Having arrived in Rome, this particular group of Spanish 'viola' players came to the attention of Cardinal Ascanio Sforza, whose support for Rodrigo Borgia the previous year in the papal enclave had ensured the Spaniard's victory. They may even have been in the employment of Ascanio himself who, as recent research has shown, was by no means as indifferent to music as he was once made out to be.[6] Whether in his service or not, their journey north-wards was arranged by Ascanio to coincide with the celebrations attending the birth of his brother's heir. Considerable surprise was expressed by Isabella's correspondent at the size of the instruments played by these Spaniards, a fact that supports the idea that their 'viole' were *vihuelas* of the elongated Valencian type and therefore probably new to him. A later report of musicians from Aragonese Naples playing in Rome dates from 1505, when the Venetian diarist Sanuto recorded that at the Roman abode of Cardinal Grimaldi two musi-cians from Palermo in Sicily had played 'two large viols with the greatest sweetness giving universal pleasure' ('due viole grande da archetto, con gran-dissime suavità et gratitudine di tutti').[7] As in the earlier report, the large size of the instruments was noted and the 'sweetness' of their sound.

These reports are complemented by the iconographic evidence of Spanish instruments in Rome during the Borgia papacy; indeed one of the earliest re-presentations of the plucked *vihuela* in Italy can be found in the very rooms in-habited by Rodrigo Borgia in the Vatican. Immediately following his election in 1492, the new Pope invited the painter Pinturicchio to supervise the decora-tion of a suite of apartments to be used by the Borgias. In one of these lavishly decorated rooms, now known as the Borgia Apartments, is a fresco on the sub-ject of music which clearly depicts a *vihuela de mano* (Plate 47). The exceptional length of the instrument's neck and its well-defined waists with corners betray the presence of an instrument from the Kingdom of Aragon. Indeed, it is well worth comparing its body with that of a Valencian *vihuela de arco* (Plate 37). Another Roman plucked *vihuela* with corners to its waists appears in Peruzzi's *Incoronazione della Vergine* of *c*1505 in the church of San Pietro in Montorio (Plate 48). In the same painting is an excellent depiction of a bowed *vihuela*, one of the few early 16th-century Italian viols that still merit this description. Viols with arched bridges were depicted by Roman artists in the second decade of the 16th-century. One example is in the Vatican itself, an *intarsia* on one of the doors of the Stanze della Segnatura (Plate 49). Almost contem-porary with this is Raphael's *St Cecilia*, in which the saint stands with a portative organ in her hands gazing at her vision of the celestial choir, while at her feet lies a pile of broken terrestrial instruments including a viol (Plate 50).

The new Spanish instruments soon spread beyond the immediate environs of Rome. Within a few years *vihuelas* both bowed and plucked began to appear elsewhere in the Papal States, notably in cities directly under Borgia control. The best-known early 16th-century Italian depiction of the classic *vihuela de mano* with guitar-shaped waists is to be seen in a fresco painted by Signorelli at

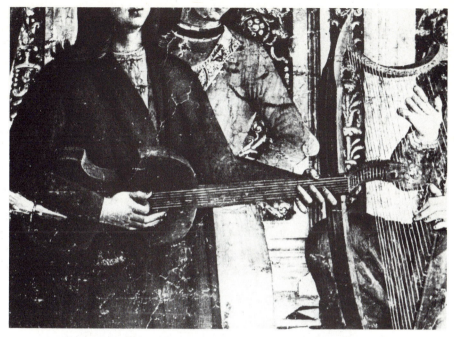

47   Music as a liberal art: detail of a musician playing a *vihuela de mano*
(*c*1492, Pinturicchio: Borgia Apartments, Vatican)

48   The Coronation of the Virgin
(*c*1505, Peruzzi: San Pietro in Montorio, Rome)

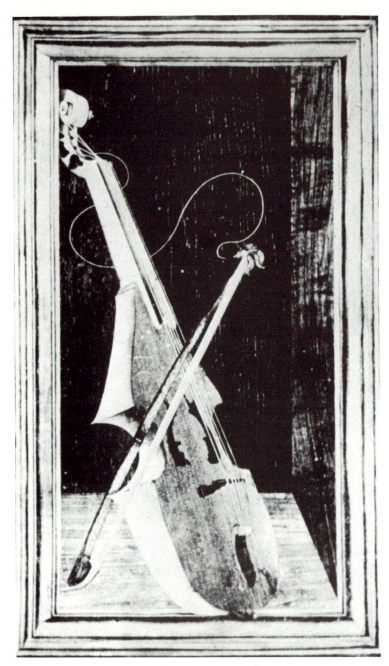

49    *Intarsia* depicting a viol
(*c*1510-1515: Stanze della Segnatura, Vatican)

50  *St Cecilia*: detail of a viol lying at the feet of the Saint
(*c*1514, Raphael: Pinacoteca, Bologna)

51  The Calling of the Elect: detail of an angel musician playing a *vihuela de mano*
(*c*1500-1505, Signorelli: Cathedral, Orvieto)

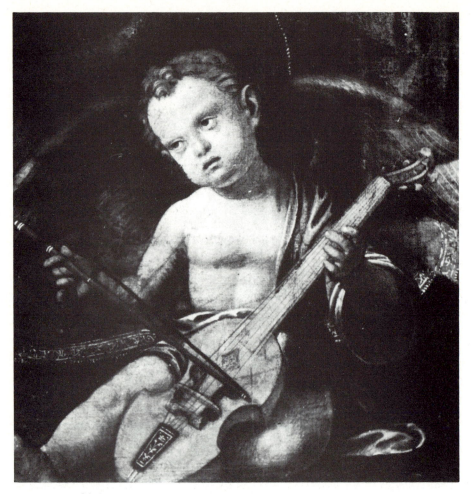

52    Madonna and Child: detail of a child playing a viol
(c1501-1505, Timoteo Viti: Brera, Milan)

Orvieto Cathedral c1500 (Plate 51). Orvieto, an important Borgia stronghold, was used by Alexander VI himself as a refuge when French troops were approaching Rome in 1495.[8] Furthermore, in line with the Borgia policy of retaining personal control over their key fortresses, Cesare Borgia was appointed governor of the town and commander of the garrison for life.[9]

Further north, Urbino was also receptive to the new Spanish instruments. Under the rule of the Montefeltro family the Duchy of Urbino had become one of the most important cultural centres in the Papal States. In 1502, however, the city fell to Cesare Borgia's army after a surprise attack during his campaign to subdue dissident elements in the Papal States. It is surely no coincidence that the viol first appeared in the art of Urbino about the time of the Borgia occupation. Timoteo Viti, for example, included a viol in one of his earliest commissions in that city, a painting of the Madonna and Child completed before *c*1505 (Plate 52). Vasari singled out Viti's young viol player for special praise: 'there is a little child angel sitting on the ground who plays the viol with a truly angelic grace and childlike simplicity' ('dove è un Angeletto sedente in terra, che suona la viola con grazie veramente angelica e con semplicità fanciullesca').[10] The continuing popularity of the viol at the court of Urbino is attested to by Castiglione, whose *Il Libro del Cortegiano*, a wonderfully evocative, if idealised, record of life at a Renaissance court, was largely based on his experiences at Urbino.[11] He praised the music of a consort of viols in glowing terms: 'And no less delightful is the music of four bowed viols which is very sweet and artful' ('Et nò meno diletta la musica delle quattro viole de arco, la qual' è soavissima & artificiosa').

Perhaps the most important centre of the new Spanish instruments in the Papal States was the court of Ercole d'Este at Ferrara.[12] Ercole's personal contact with the Aragonese can be traced back to his youth, when he studied in Naples during the years immediately following the Aragonese conquest. He subsequently married Eleanor of Aragon. As Duke of Ferrara, Ercole was widely regarded as one of the most powerful and independent of the papal vicars. In 1501, Alexander VI, perceiving the value of a dynastic alliance with the influential d'Este family, negotiated the marriage of his daughter Lucrezia to the Ferrarese heir, Alfonso d'Este, thereby ensuring that Ferrara would remain loyal to the Borgia camp. With its long-standing Aragonese connections as well as its dynastic alliance with the Borgias, the Ferrarese court was almost certain to encounter new Spanish instruments at an early date. One of the first depictions of a bowed viol in Italian art does indeed occur in the work of a Ferrarese artist, an altarpiece dated 1497 by Lorenzo Costa in the Church of San Giovanni in Monte at Bologna (Plate 53). In 1500 Costa's friend Francesco Francia depicted another viol, rather curious in shape (Plate 54). The appearance of the plucked *vihuela de mano* in Ferrarese art confirms the importance of the d'Este court as a centre for newly imported Valencian instruments. An excellent depiction of a *vihuela* of the older cornered variety appears in a painting by Pisano, one of Costa's colleagues at Ferrara (Plate 55). The shape of this instrument's body is almost identical to that of a *vihuela* illustrated in a Valencian painting of about four decades earlier (Plate 20).[13]

In 1499 Alfonso d'Este himself began to take an interest in the viol. Lorenzo da Pavia, Isabella d'Este's instrument maker, wrote to her on 19 March that her brother was in Venice and that he had requested five 'viole da archo' to be made, as he was intending to learn to play the instrument. By 1502 he had become proficient enough to perform in public. Sanuto, reporting the lavish celebrations that followed his marriage to Lucrezia Borgia, wrote that during the third act of the festivities there was a performance by six 'viole', one of which was played by the bridegroom himself ('una musica de sei viole, fra

53    Madonna and Child: detail of two viol players
(1497, Costa: San Giovanni in Monte, Bologna)

54   Madonna and Child: detail of angel musicians playing a viol and a lute
(1500, Francesco Francia: Hermitage, Leningrad)

quale vi era il Signor don Alfonso').[14] A portrait medallion of Lucrezia Borgia
struck shortly after her marriage to Alfonso depicts on its obverse side a viol-
shaped instrument with a bow, an obvious allusion to her husband's instrument.[15] The personal interest shown by Alfonso d'Este undoubtedly helped to
establish Ferrara as a leading centre of viol playing in early 16th-century Italy.
This is borne out by the frequency with which the viol appears in Ferrarese
paintings of the period. A fine example is a wall painting of *c*1510 in the church
of Santa Maria della Consolazione at Ferrara; four groups of angel musicians
are visible, one of which includes two large viols as well as a *vihuela de mano*.[16]
Viols also appear on several occasions in the work of the Ferrarese artist
Benvenuto Tisi ('Il Garofalo'); a single viol is played by an angel in his *Vision of
St Augustine* (Plate 56) while a viol duo serenades one of his Madonnas (Plate
57). That other members of the d'Este family took an interest in the viol and
the plucked *vihuela* is demonstrated by an inventory of instruments (dated

55    Madonna and Child: detail of an angel musician playing a *vihuela de mano* (*c*1512, Pisano: Brera, Milan)

56   *Vision of St Augustine*: detail of angel musicians
(early/mid 16th century, Il Garofalo: National Gallery, London)

57    Madonna and Child: detail of two angel musicians playing viols
(early/mid 16th century, Il Garofalo: Estense Gallery, Modena)

1520) in the possession of Cardinal Ippolito d'Este, Ercole's brother, which included the following: '1 viola da mano [one *viola da mano*]; 7 viole da archo nove
di piu sorte [seven new bowed viols of various kinds]; 1 viola grande da archo
nova [one large new bowed viol]; 1 violone grande da archo [one large bowed
*violone*]'.[17]

A short distance away from Ferrara was the city of Mantua, the home of
Alfonso's sister Isabella d'Este, a celebrated patron of poets and musicians.
Thanks to recent research by Prizer, there is now detailed documentary
evidence of the popularity of Spanish string instruments at the Mantuan
court at about the time of their appearance in nearby Ferrara.[18] The correspondence between Isabella and her agents, notably Lorenzo da Pavia her
instrument maker, includes many requests for Spanish instruments to be
made or purchased, in most cases string instruments such as the 'viola
spagnola', the 'viola a la spagnola', the 'liutto a la spagnola' or even simply the
'spagnola'. Though it is notoriously difficult to equate archival references such
as these with specific instrumental types, the Mantuan documents are sufficiently numerous and detailed to enable some fairly firm identifications to
be made. From the evidence of this correspondence, it seems fairly certain
that both the bowed viol and the plucked *vihuela* were established in Mantua
by the early years of the 16th century. The latter instrument, it should be

58   The Coronation of the Virgin
(c1500, Cristoforo Scacco: Museo di Capodimonte, Naples)

pointed out, appears in an *intarsia* of the period in one of Isabella's own rooms.[19]

Isabella's interest in bowed instruments can be traced back to 1495 when she ordered three or four 'viole' from an instrument maker in Brescia. These instruments, called 'viole ovver lire' by one of her correspondents, were almost certainly bowed viols of some kind.[20] They were evidently made in different sizes, as in 1499 she requested a further 'viola grande' from the same maker to be made 'the size of the larger ones'. In the same year Isabella attempted to obtain a set of three perfect 'viole' from Casale Monferrato and another set from her brother Alfonso in Ferrara. In 1503 the terminology used in the correspondence changed, and henceforth bowed viols were referred to as 'vyoloni de archetto' or 'violoni', the large size of the instruments now being reflected by the augmentative form of the word 'viola'. In 1507, for example, Piero Gonzaga, wishing to learn to play his favourite instruments the 'violoni', wrote to Isabella to ask if he might borrow one of the set made in Brescia, of which he had heard good reports. This reference, incidentally, confirms that Isabella's Brescian 'viole' were in fact viols, the term 'violone' being a standard one for the instrument in the early 16th century. Having equipped herself with a set of viols, Isabella turned her attention to an instrument called the 'viola spagnola' or the 'viola a la spagnola' which was sometimes simply designated 'spagnola'. She was very eager to have the instrument made from ebony, and Lorenzo da Pavia was put to a good deal of trouble to find a suitable piece of wood. A letter dated 6 December 1503 draws a clear distinction between instruments of this type and bowed viols by classifying them separately as 'tri vyoloni de archetto e doi spagnoli'.[21] The supposition that the 'viola spagnola' may have been a plucked *vihuela* is strengthened by the fact that most references to it are in the singular, whereas the 'violoni' usually appear in groups of three or four, as might be expected with bowed viols. Isabella did not import her 'Spanish' instruments directly from Spain; instead she ordered instruments from her own Italian craftsmen to be made 'in the Spanish manner' ('a la spagnola'). Prizer cites one instance in which a request for a 'liutto a la spagnola' caused problems because Venetian instrument makers could only make lutes 'all'italiana'. The appearance of all these Spanish string instruments at the Mantuan court in the 1490s and early 1500s confirms the evidence of Italian paintings that the *vihuela* and the viol were firmly established in northern Italy before the end of the Borgia papacy in 1503.

In stressing the significance of the Borgias in the introduction of Spanish instruments into Italy, it must not be forgotten that the Spanish were extremely influential in another area of southern Italy, the Kingdom of Naples. The growing influence of the Kingdom of Aragon in the Mediterranean area reached its climax in 1442 with the fall of Naples to Alfonso V, an event of major political significance which was officially recognised by Pope Eugenius IV the following year in the Treaty of Terracina. The seizure of Naples by the forces of the Kingdom of Aragon was bitterly disputed by the French, but their attempt to recapture the territory in 1494 ended in abject failure. Not surprisingly, the presence of the Spaniards in Naples throughout the second half of the 15th century resulted in an inflow of instruments from the Spanish mainland. Writing in Naples *c*1487, Tinctoris informed his readers about the *vihuela*, an instrument 'invented by the Spaniards which both they and the Italians call the *viola*': a clear indication that the instrument was known in Italy by the mid 1480s.[22] Neapolitan musicians sometimes travelled northwards, thereby contributing to the spread of Spanish instruments throughout Italy. Sanuto, the Venetian diarist, described a performance given by two players of 'viole grande da archetto' from Palermo which took place at the Roman abode of Cardinal Grimaldi in 1505.[23] Other Spanish instruments were purchased in Naples by visitors from the north; for example, one of the two 'spagnoli' mentioned in 1503 in a letter to Isabella d'Este had apparently been brought back to Mantua by Francesco Gonzaga after a visit to Naples. Neapolitan string instruments, moreover, appear on several other occasions in Isabella's correspondence, where they are referred to as 'viole a la napoletana'. Icono-graphic evidence confirms the presence of Spanish instruments in Naples. To take but one example, a plucked *vihuela* with cornered waists appears in Cristoforo Scacco's *Incoronazione* of *c*1500 kept in the Museo di Capodimonte, Naples (Plate 58). Finally it should be noted that one influential 16th-century Italian theorist, Vincenzo Galilei, believed that the viol had actually origi-nated in the Kingdom of Naples.[24] Though his arguments now seem spuri-ous, the mere fact that Naples was specified at all may reflect a contemporary tradition associating the south of Italy with the early viol.

The circumstances of the viol's appearance in Italy are reflected in the terminology which Italians applied to the new arrival. Using the standard Italian word for a string instrument, 'viola', many different modifying terms were tried out, most of which can be seen to have derived from contemporary perceptions of how the new viol differed from other instruments of the time.[25] One obvious way to define any instrument is by the country of its origin, but, as I have already suggested, the evidence of Isabella d'Este's correspondence with her instrument maker is that the definition 'Spanish' was usually reserved for the viol's close relative the plucked *vihuela*. Terms such as 'viola spagnola', 'viola a la spagnola' or 'viola napoletana' normally referred to the *vihuela de mano* – understandably so, since this instrument retained its close association with Spain throughout the 16th century,[26] and remained to some extent a peripheral, 'exotic' instrument, whereas the viol, having been very quickly as-similated into the very centre of Italian musical life, soon lost any association it may once have had with its Spanish ancestor.

By far the most popular method of defining the viol in early 16th-century Italy was by making reference to its large size. To Italian string players of the late 15th century, used to playing the rebec, the fiddle and the *lira da braccio*, the tall Valencian *vihuela de arco* must have seemed abnormally large, and so the frequent use of the modifying adjective 'large' ('grande') is not unexpected. One early 16th-century source refers to 'viole grande da archetto',[27] another to a 'viola grande da archo nova'.[28] Also possible was the adjective 'grosso'. Folengo uses it – admittedly for poetic reasons – in his *Orlandino* (1526) when describing the music of three lutes and 'two large viols' ('due viole grosse').[29] More common, however, was the use of the augmentative form 'violone' with its plural 'violoni'. And, as if to reinforce the impression made by the viol's large size, one inventory even lists a 'violone grande da archo'.[30] Just as in Germany the term 'grosse Geigen' (lit. 'large fiddles') came to refer to viols as a class – whether large or small – so in Italy 'violoni' soon acquired the force of a generic term. Thus, a reference to the 'violone il soprano' in 1544 is not really a contradiction in terms,[31] nor the use of the seemingly redundant 'bassi di violoni' (rather than 'bassi di viuole') to describe a consort of bass viols in 1568.[32]

The observant reader may already have noticed that in the early 16th century the identification of viols solely by their large size was often considered insufficient. Some additional modifying phrase such as 'da archo' or 'da archetto' was often given. The classification of string instruments by means of their playing techniques had earlier been sanctioned by Tinctoris in his treatise *De inventione et usu musicae* (c1487) in which the bowed 'viola' ('viola cum arculo') and the plucked 'viola' ('viola sine arculo') were discussed almost as though they were two manifestations of the one basic type. In the late 15th century this method of classification was obviously useful in helping to distinguish the *vihuela de mano* from its near relative the *vihuela de arco*. Even after the viol had developed its own identity, quite distinct from that of the plucked instrument, the terminological distinction between different playing methods remained useful, since the unmodified 'viola grande', especially in the singular, could still be applied to the plucked *vihuela* in Italy. Only in the latter part of the 16th century, with the decline of the *vihuela de mano* in Italy, did the term 'da archo' gradually become redundant.

To distinguish the viol from its new competitor the violin, documents from the 1530s onwards increasingly refer to the viol as the 'fretted viol'. In 1530 Andrea di Verona is mentioned as a player of both the 'viola con tasti' and the 'viola senza tasti'.[33] This method of classification was also used by important theorists. Lanfranco (1533) writes of the 'violoni da tasti & da arco' and the 'violette da arco senza tasti' – whether his fretless, bowed *violette* are rebecs or violins is not certain. Ganassi, too, makes this distinction. The title-page of *Regola Rubertina* promises the reader a method for learning to play the 'viola darcho Tastada', that of *Lettione Seconda* 'il violone d'arco da tasti'. Later, when discussing the tuning of three-string viols, Ganassi mentions the 'viola da brazo senza tasti'.

One method of classification not regularly in use during this early period was that of playing position. A Ferrarese inventory of 1511 lists the following: 'Viole da gamba, numero sei, con sei archetti'. This, however, is fairly unusual; not until the mid 16th century was the word 'gamba' applied to the viol in order to distinguish it from instruments played *a braccio* like the violin. (See, for example, Troiano's descriptions of the 1568 Bavarian wedding, cited in Chapter 12).

Why was the *vihuela de arco*, an instrument with obvious limitations, so immediately successful in Italy? In attempting to answer this question, it must be pointed out that the flat-bridged, drone-playing form of the instrument popular in the city of Valencia was quickly rejected. Instruments of this type are rarely depicted in early 16th-century Italian art, the bowed *vihuela* in Peruzzi's *Incoronazione della Vergine* being a notable exception. The failure of this type of bowed *vihuela* is easy to understand; no instrument constructed to provide a drone accompaniment could have expected to make much of an impact in Italy at this late date, since the tradition of improvising accompaniments for vocal recitations on the indigenous *lira da braccio* was by then well established. With its slightly arched bridge, moreover, the *lira* could provide a much more versatile accompaniment than any flat-bridged instrument, which would be restricted to chords involving all the strings simultaneously. Yet despite their rejection of the instrument in its original form, Italian musicians evidently recognised that a large, bowed string instrument played *a gamba* might be very useful in a different sphere of music-making, the performance of polyphonic music. Accordingly, they modified the bowed *vihuela* by supplying it with an arched bridge, thereby equipping it for the much broader range of musical activities open to an instrument capable of sustaining an individual line in a polyphonic composition. Whether or not this transformation occurred exclusively in Italy is hard to determine, but iconographic evidence certainly supports the view that Italian makers played the major rôle, since most Spanish sources illustrate the flat-bridged *vihuela de arco*, most Italian sources the viol with an arched bridge. Having made this transition, the viol was an instant success and spread rapidly throughout the Italian peninsula.

This view of the *vihuela de arco*, as an instrument borrowed to perform music for which it was not originally destined, rather implies that there was a repertory already in existence for which the instrument was perceived to be potentially suitable. In late 15th-century Italy there were two important genres of polyphonic secular music that might have been played on viols, Franco-Netherlandish chansons and Italian frottole. A large number of chansons by northern composers working in Italy survive in late 15th-century Italian sources, almost invariably copied out without text, or at most with a short text incipit for the purposes of identification. The almost universal tendency of Italian scribes to omit the text is probably an indication of instrumental performance.[34] Some of the most popular chansons of the time were arranged by northern composers working in Italy with additional parts featuring fast-moving, ornamental figurations.[35] These may well have been composed specifically for instrumental performance. A pair of viols could have been used to good effect in one such piece, Josquin's four-part setting of 'De tous bien plaine' in which the lyrical duet between the upper two voices is accompanied by two incongruously jerky lower parts which hop and skip around in close canon. Viols may also have been used in performances of late 15th-century secular music with Italian text, the quiet, homogeneous tone of a group of viols being well suited to new genres such as the frottola. With its low tessitura, its relatively large compass and its ability to sustain a melodic line, the viol was probably welcomed as a very useful addition to the rather limited number of late 15th-century instruments capable of performing the whole range of secular music of the period.

The success of the viol in Italy was so immediate and lasting that the instrument soon came to be regarded throughout Europe as an instrument of Italian origin. Its Spanish antecedents were quickly forgotten, and its immediate precursor the *vihuela de arco* vanished into obscurity.[36]

# 6

## The viol in early 16th-century Germany

Having established itself firmly in Italy during the early years of the 16th century, the viol was now ready for the second important stage in its dissemination throughout Europe – its migration northwards across the Alps. The first regions to encounter the viol during this phase of its development were areas of southern Germany and Austria under the rule of Maximilian I. By the second decade of the 16th century, there is much evidence to suggest that the viol was being played across a broad band of German-speaking, south-central Europe from Basle to Vienna.

The growing popularity of the viol throughout this area is shown not only by the frequent depictions of the instrument in woodcuts and paintings but also by the number of published works in which the instrument figures. These range from the general surveys of Virdung and Agricola to the more specific instrumental tutors of Judenkünig and Gerle. There survives, in addition, one important manuscript. The sources are:

| | | |
|---|---|---|
| 1511 | Virdung | *Musica getutscht* (Basle) |
| *c*1518 | Judenkünig | *Utilis et compendaria introductio* (Vienna) |
| 1523 | Judenkünig | *Ain schone kunstliche underweisung* (Vienna) |
| 1523/4 | Munich University Library 4° Cod. ms. 718 | |
| 1528 | Agricola | *Musica instrumentalis deudsch* (Wittenberg) |
| 1532 | Gerle | *Musica Teusch* (Nuremberg) |
| 1545 | Agricola | *Musica instrumentalis deudsch* (Wittenberg) (a much revised edition of the 1528 print) |
| 1546 | Gerle | *Musica und Tabulatur* (Nuremberg) (a revised edition of *Musica Teusch*) |

Germany was, in fact, the only country to produce a substantial number of publications concerning the viol during the first four decades of the 16th century.

The terminology of bowed string instruments that evolved in German-speaking lands during the early 16th century adopted size as its main method of classification. The generic term 'Geigen' ('fiddles') could be modified in one of two ways: 'grosse Geigen' (lit. 'large fiddles') for viols; 'kleine Geigen' (lit. 'small fiddles') for violins or rebecs. Some theorists felt the need to qualify these terms further. In the revised edition of *Musica instrumentalis deudsch* (1545) Agricola leaves no room for doubt about the identification of his rebec

99

consort: 'Vier kleine Geigen one bünde und mit dreien Seiten' ('four small fiddles without frets and with three strings'). Relative size was used as a method of classifying families of instruments, even though, individually, the bass of a consort of 'kleine Geigen' may well have been larger than the treble of a consort of 'grosse Geigen'.

Agricola (1545), referring to the viol consort, uses an additional modifying term 'grossen welschen Geigen'. His use of 'welsch' deserves comment. 'Welsch' can mean foreign, but it has a more specific meaning – Italian. It is, therefore, an appropriate term for the viol, which, as I have shown, originated in southern Europe and spread initially along a southern Mediterranean 'axis': Valencia–Majorca–Sardinia–Naples–Rome, and thence across the Alps into Germany. Though encountered less frequently than the simple 'grosse Geigen', the term 'welsch' remained in use throughout the 16th century. In 1565 the Weimar Hofkapelle[1] paid two 'welscher Geiger'; in 1571 a chest of 'grosse welsche geigen' was made by the Bassanos in London.[2] Confirmation that the term 'grosse Geigen' referred specifically to viols may be found in the Ambras inventory of 1596 which gives both the German and the Italian: 'viole de gamba oder die grosz geigen'; 'viole de praz [braccio] oder cleine geigen'.[3]

The first published depiction of a viol in a German source is the woodcut of a *gross Geigen* in *Musica getutscht*,[4] a bizarre instrument with huge waists and awkwardly projecting shoulders. It has the remarkable number of nine strings attached to a lute-like stringholder. One of the 1511 editions of *Musica getutscht*, however, has a title-page woodcut, the border to which illustrates a number of miniature musical instruments including a *gross Geigen* with only five strings.[5] This suggests that the nine-string version in the text may have been intended as an instrument with four lower courses of two strings in unison and a single top string, in the manner of a five-string lute. Whether Virdung's *gross Geigen* should be regarded as a type of viol has long been a matter for debate. Few scholars have been willing to commit themselves more definitely than Sir John Hawkins, who cautiously labelled the instrument 'a species of Bass Viol'.[6] That Virdung's image of the *gross Geigen* proved an enduring one – it reappeared in subsequent translations and, in a modified form, in all the editions of Agricola's treatise – does not of course prove its initial validity. Yet the most frequently voiced objections to this woodcut as an accurate depiction of a contemporary instrument, that its method of stringing is totally impractical and that its shape is unrealistic, are not as strong as is sometimes suggested. To take the method of stringing first, iconographic evidence from late 15th-century Spain shows conclusively that the early Valencian *vihuela de arco* was commonly strung in just this fashion with the strings attached directly to a stringholder (see Chapter 4). A short-lived German vogue for bowed instruments of this type is by no means out of the question before the final ascendancy of the viol with raised fingerboard and arched bridge. There is, too, independent iconographic confirmation of the ungainly outline of Virdung's

*gross Geigen*. In the Schweizerisches Landesmuseum at Basle there is a table
made in 1515 for Hans Baer and his wife Barbara Brunner of Basle. Its surface
is decorated with a vast collection of objects including a number of musical instruments: a xylophone (one of the earliest known depictions of this instrument), a lute, a recorder, a marine trumpet, bagpipes and a *gross Geigen*.[7] The
*gross Geigen* certainly resembles the Virdung instrument with its amazingly
long waists and almost hook-like projections above and below, and yet it is not
a direct copy; it has only three strings and its c-holes are low down on the belly.
There are many other examples of this shape in early 16th-century German
art, and also a few in Italian sources.[8]

In the first edition of *Musica instrumentalis deudsch* Agricola published a
woodcut of four *grossen Geigen* labelled discantus, altus, tenor and bassus.[9]
Their derivation from *Musica getutscht* is obvious at a glance. Agricola's
draughtsman copied Virdung's body shape almost exactly and also his placing
of the c-holes and central rose. A few alterations were made; the neck was
narrowed down and the number of strings and pegs reduced to four (notwithstanding the fact that in the text Agricola gives tunings for five- and six-
stringed viols). But one significant change was not made; Agricola's *grossen
Geigen* were not fitted with arched bridges. Even in the revised 1545 edition in
which the text makes it abundantly clear that Agricola considered the *grossen
Geigen* to be viols with arched bridges, the same quartet of instruments with
stringholders appears (Plate 59). Thus, whatever the truth about Virdung's
*gross Geigen*, it seems more than likely that in Agricola's treatise the instrument
remained bridgeless only by an oversight.

Viols with fingerboard, arched bridge and tailpiece begin to appear regularly in German art after the first decade of the 16th century. In his celebrated Isenheim Altarpiece (c1515) Grünewald depicted a pair of extraordinary bass viols, grotesque in appearance, with waists so deeply cut into the
body that they all but meet behind the fingerboard (Plate 60). It is hard to
credit these instruments with being trustworthy representations of contemporary viols. The bowing method, too, looks suspiciously unworkable.[10] Yet
some of the smaller details seem genuine enough. The arched bridge is very
clearly drawn, as is the tailpiece. Equally well known are the viols that appear
in Hans Burgkmair's woodcuts for *The Triumph of Maximilian I* (c1518). Like
many German viols of this period, they display a certain angularity about the
shoulders, which dip away from the neck before returning to a point.[11] Other
features worth noting are the frets tied behind the neck and the fluted scrolls
(Plate 61). Two other theorists of the period print woodcuts of viols in their
treatises. Judenkünig has a rather crude woodcut of a viol on the title-page of
his instruction books (Plate 62), and Gerle illustrates his tutor with a woodcut
of two rather more conventional viols showing a plan of the neck and belly
with the string names and frets.

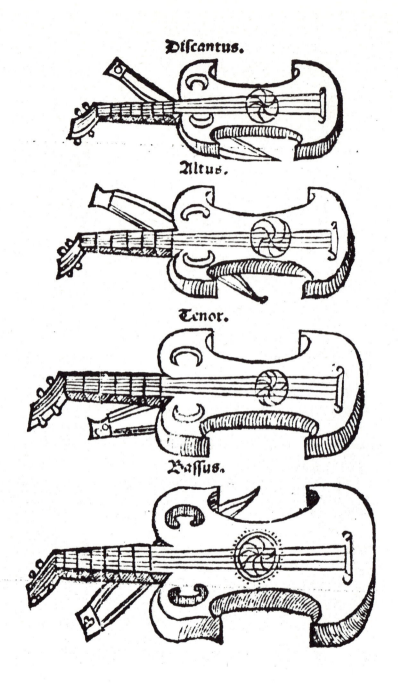

59   *Grossen Geigen*
(woodcut from M. Agricola: *Musica instrumentalis deudsch*, Wittenberg, 1545)

60 Isenheim Altarpiece: detail of angel musicians playing viols (c1515, Grünewald: Museum, Colmar)

61    *The Triumph of Maximilian I*: a cart transporting three lutenists and two viol players (*c*1518, Hans Burgkmair)

It is fairly clear from the variety of shapes depicted in early 16th-century German art that there was as yet no generally accepted pattern for making viols in this area. However, a number of distinctive types recur often enough to justify the use of the term 'school'. The most typical features of this German school are, of course, the *gross Geigen* body shape and the predilection for angular, rather pointed shoulders. The sickle-shaped pegbox with the beginnings of a small scroll is also fairly characteristic. In the general construction of the body, though, there is little evidence as yet of the influence of the second generation of Italian viol makers. The deep ribs, the bend in the top of the back and the sloping shoulders which were being developed by the Italians hardly appear at all. Most German viols of the period still have fairly shallow ribs. All the viols depicted in German art at this period are quite large in size: either tenor, bass or large bass. This reflects the early 16th-century preference for consorts of large viols. The small treble viol had not come into general use.[12]

From the point of view of the 16th-century student of the viol, the most helpful German publication of the period would have been Gerle's *Musica Teusch* of 1532, which contains a substantial amount of practical advice for

62    A lutenist and a viol player
(woodcut from H. Judenkünig: *Ain schone kunstliche underweisung*, Vienna, 1523)

beginners.[13] *Musica Teusch* was in fact the first publication in any language to merit the description 'viol tutor'.[14] No other German work of the period quite matched its scope, though in both editions of *Musica instrumentalis deudsch* Agricola made some interesting, if tantalisingly brief, comments.

Gerle's instructions on the playing position of the viol and its bowing and fingering methods are succinct.[15] The reader is simply advised to take the neck of the viol in the left hand, the bow in the right hand, to sit down and hold the instrument between the legs, but not so low down that the bow is impeded. The bow should be drawn across the strings in a 'straight and even' ('gerad unnd eben') manner, and the player should take care not to sound two strings instead of one. The bow itself should not be allowed to become greasy. If it does become too smooth, the hair should be scraped carefully with a knife and then smeared with colophony or English resin, which may be obtained from apothecaries. On the subject of fingering, Gerle advocates half position, with the forefinger on the first fret, the middle finger on the second and the ring finger on the third.[16] For the higher frets such as the fifth and the seventh the little finger is used, but no clues are given about how to change into these higher positions.

Gerle gives valuable advice on the maintenance of the viol. He explains at some length the procedure for replacing broken strings.[17] If a string snaps, a 'little bundle' ('buntlein') of the correct size of string should be taken and a length measured out, equal to the distance between the bridge and the highest fret. This should then be pulled taut and plucked with the ring finger of the right hand. If the string vibrates cleanly giving the appearance of two strings, then it is satisfactory; if it vibrates in a confused manner giving the appearance of many strings, then it is of no use, and some more string must be pulled out of the little bundle until a good result is obtained (Ganassi recommends a similar procedure: see Chapter 8). When a satisfactory length of string has been found, a little more should be added and the string fastened. This explanation is accompanied by an illustration showing the difference between a good and a bad length of string when stretched and plucked. The 'little bundle' mentioned in the text is also clearly illustrated. Viol strings were evidently not sold in predetermined lengths but in reels from which a player could cut a suitable length. In view of the lack of standardisation of viol sizes at this period, this was a sensible procedure.

Concerning the replacement of frets, Gerle states that if one breaks it should be replaced by a piece of string the same size as the previous fret.[18] If all the frets need to be replaced, Gerle refers the reader to the chapter on rebecs in which he explains how to calculate the position of the frets by using a pair of dividers. To derive from these instructions the exact temperament used by early 16th-century German viol players would be to misunderstand the nature of Gerle's treatise. *Musica Teusch* was not written for experienced players, for whom most of its information would have been completely redundant, but for beginners. By providing the inexperienced with a simple mathematical method of positioning the frets, Gerle was hoping to ensure that even the musically illiterate would play approximately in tune. Agricola, who also recommends a pair of dividers and a mathematical scheme for placing the frets, is quite specific about this. He justifies his method by observing that many people place their frets badly and thus play out of tune.[19] More advanced players could still make use of a mathematical scheme such as Gerle's, but they would no doubt effect fine tuning by ear in the manner advocated by Ganassi (see Chapter 8).

A substantial section of *Musica Teusch* is devoted to the notation of viol music. Like the compiler of the Munich manuscript, Gerle makes use of the German lute tablature system. He begins with the basic information, the number of strings and frets on the instrument. Immediately there are complications, for, as Gerle points out, some viols have five strings and others six. The names of the five strings are given as follows, the nomenclature again being derived from the lute: 'quint sait' (fifth string); 'gesang sait' (melody string); 'mittel sait' (middle string); 'klein Bomhart' (small buzzer); 'mittel Bomhart' (middle buzzer). (The labelling of the top string 'quint sait' or 'fifth string' suggests that the system was originally intended for a five-string instrument.) The sixth string is named 'gross Bomhart' or 'ober Bomhart' (large buzzer). The number of frets was likewise variable; the smaller sizes of viol had seven, but only five were apparently necessary on the bass viol. The German tablature system (shown below) was a simple alphabetical one. Gerle sensibly points out possible areas of confusion such as the common errors of mistaking *i* for 1 or *z* for 2. The rhythm signs are the standard ones.

*German viol tablature*

|              | Fret 1 | Fret 2 | Fret 3 | Fret 4 | Fret 5 | Fret 6 | Fret 7 |
|--------------|--------|--------|--------|--------|--------|--------|--------|
| (top string) 5 | e | k | p | v | ꝯ | e̅ | k̅ |
| 4            | d | i | o | t | ≠ | d̅ | i̅ |
| 3            | c | h | n | s | z | c̅ | h̅ |
| 2            | b | g | m | r | y | b̅ | g̅ |
| 1            | a | f | l | q | x | a̅ | f̅ |
| (sixth string) | 1 | 2 | 3 | 4 | 5 | 6 | 7 | 8 |

*Rhythm signs*

□ = •

◇ = |

◊ = ⌐

♦ = ⌐ (with flag)

♦ = (with double flag)

At first sight, German lute tablature with its alphabetical system using a different letter for each fret position on each string seems unnecessarily cumbersome. And it certainly did not meet with universal approval, even in early 16th-century Germany. Agricola, for example, much preferred instrumentalists to learn to read from mensural notation. Yet the system was probably not as difficult to use in practice as is sometimes made out. Although the number of symbols to be memorised seems formidable, a viol player performing the repertory of transcribed vocal music for which the system was envisaged would have encountered relatively few. A random glance through some of the musical examples in *Musica Teusch* reveals that even in the more elaborate pieces only nine or ten symbols appear in each part, and some of the less adventurous alto and tenor parts make use of only six letters.

The earliest source of German viol tunings is not in fact *Musica Teusch* but the manuscript of German viol tablature in the Munich University Library (4° Cod. ms. 718) which is dated 1523.[20] Munich 718 includes a series of twelve charts correlating tablature letters with the notes of the scale, thereby indicating nominal pitch.[21] Two basic tunings are given for each size of viol, and assuming that the compiler of the manuscript was intending to use five-string viols – there is certainly no evidence to suggest otherwise – the two systems may be summarised as follows, the first being in essence an *a–d–a* and the second a *d–g–d* consort tuning:

|  | 1 |  |  |  |  | 2 |  |  |  |  |
|---|---|---|---|---|---|---|---|---|---|---|
| Discantus | a' | e' | b | g | d | d" | a' | e' | c' | g |
| Altus | | d' | a | e | c | G | g' | d' | a | f | c |
| Tenor | | | | | | | | | | | |
| Bassus | a | e | B | G | D | d' | a | e | c | G |

Below the tables for the second tuning are written several captions: 'darnach auff die quartt her ab so der discanttus zu hoch gelt'; 'auff die quartt so der tenor zu hoch gelt'. These explain – albeit in a somewhat cryptic manner – that the alternative tuning is a fourth 'lower' to help the instruments cope with parts that would otherwise go too high.

It must be emphasised that these charts were aimed not at players tuning their instruments but at musicians transcribing mensural compositions into tablature for viol consort using the German system. This whole section of the Munich manuscript is, in fact, devoted to a fairly comprehensive set of instructions for the transcriber: a solmization chart; a list of mensural note values with their tablature equivalents; a table of common ligatures; a chart of clefs; and finally charts equating pitches with tablature letters. Equipped with these guidelines, it would be a relatively simple task for an early 16th-century viol player to borrow a set of partbooks in mensural notation and copy out the music in tablature. A transcription of the celebrated 'Cum sancto spiritu' from Josquin's *Missa De Beata Virgine* will serve to show how the copying process worked and why the two 'tunings' were considered necessary.[22] Having noted the high tessitura of Josquin's superius line, the transcriber of Munich 718 would have rejected the normal level of pitch equivalents (i.e. the 'low' *a–d–a* tuning) on the grounds that the discant viol player would be compelled to play well above the frets and indeed beyond the normal scope of the tablature notation itself. By making use of the alternative charts, however, in which all the tablature letters are re-aligned with nominal pitches a fourth higher (i.e. the

'high' *d–g–d* tuning), the piece could be played without difficulty in first position. The absolute pitch of a viol consort playing the piece would have been of
little significance, since tablature notation only specifies the physical position
of each note on the neck of the instrument. If, however, the strings were tuned
to the nominal pitch levels given, the transcription of the piece in the 'high'
tuning would sound a fourth lower than its original written pitch – hence the
seemingly paradoxical comment in Munich 718 that the high *d–g–d* tuning is a
fourth lower. To put it another way, this was both a transcription system and,
when necessary, a transposition system.

   This dual consort tuning system was first published in *Musica Teusch*. Like
the compiler of the Munich manuscript, Gerle provides a set of charts align-
ing tablature letters with pitches.[23] His first charts give the normal pitch relationship of the low *a–d–a* tuning. Next there is an explanation of the alternative charts giving the high *d–g–d* tuning which is for use 'when you wish to
transcribe a melody into tablature and it goes so high that you do not have
enough frets on the viol' ('Wan du ein gesang in die Tabulatur setzen wolst /
und er ging so hoch / das du nit so viel bund auff der Geygen hettest'). Thus,
as in the Munich manuscript, the high tuning is reserved for pieces which, if
transcribed in the low tuning, would force violists to play above the frets.
Gerle gives tablature symbols for seven frets so that in his notation the top
note of a discant viol (in the low tuning) would be *e″*. His discourse on tuning
ends with the rather superfluous warning to viol players to make sure that all
four viols are in the one tuning!

   In all of his tuning charts and tables, Gerle (like the compiler of Munich
718) deals exclusively with five-string viols. Yet the introductory remarks to
*Musica Teusch* clearly imply that a six-string viol was sometimes needed – the
sixth string being added below the other five. To play the repertory of transcribed vocal music envisaged by Gerle, the additional sixth string might
occasionally be required by the bass viol player. If, for example, the overall
range of a vocal composition were *F–f″*, the transcriber would need to use the
*d–g–d* tuning, because the *f″* in the discant part would be too high for the instrument in the low tuning. The bass viol would, therefore, need a low *C*
(written *F* in the mensural original) for which a sixth string would be required
(the lowest string of a five-string bass viol in the high tuning being *D*). The
strange bass viol tunings given by Agricola in the 1545 edition of *Musica instrumentalis deudsch*, *b♮ g d A F* and *a e c G F*, certainly seem to confirm that low *F*
was a note in fairly frequent use.[24] (Ganassi, too, makes sure that a low *F* is
available in his tuning for a four-string bass viol: *g d A F*.) If a six-string viol
were not available, the bass part would then need to be revised, but in most
cases this would entail little more than putting the final note up an octave.[25]

   The popularity of this dual tuning system for viol consorts in early 16th-
century Germany may be attributed to two factors. First, it was of great benefit
to unskilled amateur players as it avoided high positions. Secondly, as
Morrow points out, it enabled viol consorts to play for most of the time on the

upper strings of the viol, resulting in a better-focused sound, a tone 'crisper, brighter, with possibly more of a rebec-like clarity of articulation than that which we are accustomed to hear today'.[26] One other point worth noting is that it was ideally suited to the consorts of large viols prevalent in the early 16th century, an *a*-tuned tenor being the top member of the consort. That the system eventually failed was due to the expanding range of vocal music. When Gerle published *Musica Teusch* in 1532, the system was still just about workable; many pieces would still fit the low *a–d–a* tuning, and if a discantus part did go too high, the piece could easily be transposed down a fourth using the *d–g–d* tuning.[27] As the 16th century progressed, however, the system became more and more anachronistic, since with the expanding range of vocal music notes such as *f″*, *g″* and *a″* became increasingly commonplace.[28] Moreover, the German practice of copying out viol music in tablature which enabled the system to function smoothly was not widely adopted.

The viol tunings published in the 1545 edition of Agricola's *Musica instrumentalis deudsch* reflect the growing problem of range. A plan of the neck of a four-string discant viol appears with the standard low *a* tuning: *a′ e′ b g*. Agricola, however, goes on to explain that another tuning is worth consideration:[29]

> Dieweil man im gsang selden spürt
> Das der Discant das G. berürt
> Und offt ins dd / ee geht
> Mocht man ihn zihn wie alhie steht

('As one seldom finds in the music that the discant goes down to a *g* but often ascends to a *d″* or an *e″*, one may tune it as follows.') This alternative is, not unexpectedly, the *d* tuning: *d″ a′ e′ c′*. Agricola's justification for this tuning is that its range is better suited to the music for which it would normally be required, the discant viol, as he points out, rarely requiring a low *g* but frequently ascending to *d″* or *e″*. Moreover, in a significant little appendix to these remarks, he goes on to argue that even if the low tuning were retained, it might still be worth adding a fifth string to the discant viol tuned *d″*, so that the notes *e″* and *f″* could be played more easily.[30] By resolving the problem of the discant viol's range with the simple addition of a higher string, Agricola avoids having to transpose any music. He is therefore advocating, at least for the discant viol, an actual *d* tuning of the type favoured by many Italian authorities of the 16th century and, by implication, a small treble viol.

The 1528 edition of *Musica instrumentalis deudsch* is the only early 16th-century German source of viol tunings not to give the dual system outlined above. Instead, it advocates a unique tuning system based on a single series of intervals for the whole consort as follows:

| Discantus | *c″* | *g′* | *d′* | *a* | *f* | | |
|-----------|------|------|------|-----|-----|---|---|
| Tenor | | *g′* | *d′* | *a* | *f* | *c* | |
| Bass | | *g′* | *d′* | *a* | *f* | *c* | *G* |

The major third upon which this tuning is based (*a–f*) is that of the standard *g*-tuned lute or *vihuela de mano*. This tuning thus serves to emphasise once again how close the relationship was between the viol and plucked instruments of the period.

Whether Gerle's *Musica Teusch* of 1532 should be considered the earliest published music for viols depends on our view of Judenkünig's two treatises, *Utilis et compendaria introductio* (*c*1518) and *Ain schone kunstliche underweisung* (1523). The title-page woodcut of both works depicts a lute–viol duet (Plate 62) and the introductory remarks state quite unambiguously that the reader is to be instructed how to play both the lute and the viol. On fol. Ai of the earlier work Judenkünig promises to teach 'both the lute and the instrument popularly known as the Geygen' ('& Lutine & quod wulgo Geygen nominant'). Whereas Judenkünig clearly expected his readers to know what a lute was, he seemed to feel the need to define the *Geygen* rather more precisely. Thus on fol. Aii he again promises to teach both instruments, 'the lute and the instrument which is popularly known as the Geygen which is very similiar to the lira' ('& Lutine & quod Lyrae simillimum est, quodque wulgo Geygen vocant'). In the later German work he simply refers to the 'Lautten und Geygen' perhaps because the latter instrument was by this time better known. Curiously enough, after these opening allusions to the *Geygen*, the instrument disappears completely from view; both treatises are in fact devoted exclusively to the lute, Judenkünig's own instrument. So why was the viol mentioned at all?

Perhaps the reason for Judenkünig's inclusion of the viol – apart from the obvious commercial advantages of expanding the potential market for his publications – lay in the fact that viol players could have performed without difficulty some of his musical examples. German lute tablature would have been readily understood by viol players in this area of southern Germany; it is the notation used both by the compiler of Munich 718 and by Gerle in his publications. A viol player, it goes without saying, could only have performed a single line at a time, but some of Judenkünig's material would have facilitated this. *Utilis et compendaria introductio*, for example, begins with a series of two-part pieces which could well have been performed as a viol duet, one instrument reading each line from the same copy. Alternatively, a lutenist could have played one or both parts with a viol player accompanying, as illustrated on the title-page woodcut. Yet another alternative would have been to perform these pieces as accompanied songs with a vocalist singing the discantus line – presumably from the mensural original – and a lutenist or two viol players using Judenkünig's intabulations of the tenor and bass parts. This method of performance (with the alto line of the original omitted completely) was sanctioned by Schlick.[31]

The Munich manuscript of viol tablature makes a very interesting comparison with Judenkünig's two publications. It was compiled by Jorg Weltzell, perhaps while he was a student at the University of Ingolstadt (which, like Vienna – Judenkünig's home town – is on the river Danube). During the course of the manuscript's compilation, Weltzell on several occasions made a note of the year: 1523 appears twice and 1524 four times.[32] This dates the manuscript precisely to the year of Judenkünig's second publication *Ain schone kunstliche underweisung*. In essence the manuscript is a scrapbook collection of parts for viols of different sizes copied out in an apparently haphazard manner. At the end are five pieces for lute dated 1524. One of these, 'Maduna Katerina', also appears in Judenkünig's *Utilis et compendaria introductio* which enables a direct comparison to be made (Example 1). The similarities are

Ex. 1    'Maduna Katerina' (two versions for g-tuned lute)

Ex. 2     'Unnser maydtt' (parts for tenor viol and g-tuned lute from Munich 718)

obvious at a glance; both are simple two-part settings with the melody in the tenor. The Munich version is the more elaborate of the two with some divisions in the upper part. The idea that simple two-part lute pieces such as this were also performed as viol duets is certainly confirmed by the Munich manuscript which contains a number of pieces of this type for tenor and bass viols. Moreover, for one song, 'Unnser maydtt', there are parts for a possible duet between lute and tenor viol (Example 2). Disregarding one or two slapdash errors with the rhythm signs – the manuscript is full of these – it seems likely that the upper part of the lute version and the tenor viol part were copied from the same mensural source. This is exactly how Judenkünig's two lute treatises might have been used by viol players.

   Apart from the lute pieces and the viol duets, Munich 718 contains a substantial selection of music for a viol consort of up to five members. For the five-part pieces the additional viol labelled 'vagantus auf der Geygen' is tuned like the alto and tenor viols. Except for a pair of dances, 'Hoff Dantz' and 'Hupff auff', a two-part 'Benedictus' and the 'Cum sancto spiritu' from Josquin's *Missa De Beata Virgine*, the repertory consists of secular music, predominantly German *Tenorlieder*. These instrumental arrangements differ little from their vocal originals. The most significant changes are rhythmic ones; dotted rhythms are usually written out, so that a dotted crotchet – quaver rhythm becomes a crotchet and two quavers. This practice of simplifying dotted rhythms, probably to assist inexperienced players, was widely adopted by early 16th-century German musicians, but it often worked to the detriment of the original composition. Carefully contrived syncopated passages such as the concluding measures of Josquin's 'Cum sancto spiritu' were all too often transformed into a dull 'on-the-beat' rhythm (Example 3).

Ex. 3    'Cum Sancto Spiritu' from Josquin's *Missa De Beata Virgine* (the closing measures of the vocal original with a transcription for discant viol from Munich 718)

As a source Munich 718 is of poor quality and full of errors, yet it is invaluable as evidence of what German viol consorts of the early 1520s were playing. Changes in taste during the following decades are reflected very clearly in Gerle's two publications for viols. The music published in the earlier treatise is not unlike that of the Munich manuscript, mainly *Tenorlieder* by composers such as Hofhaimer and Senfl. In the 1546 edition, however, there is a change of emphasis, and four-part Parisian chansons are included, showing Gerle to be sensitive to changes in musical taste. A few alterations to the text of Gerle's treatise in its second edition also reflect the growing predominance of the four-part Parisian repertory. When discussing how to tune a viol consort in *Musica Teusch*, Gerle mentions both four- and five-part consorts. As in Munich 718, the fifth part is to be taken by the 'vagrant' viol which must be tuned like the alto and tenor viols. In *Musica und Tabulatur* this passing mention of the five-part viol consort was omitted, presumably because Gerle no longer believed it to be necessary.[33]

In his transcriptions of vocal music for viol consort Gerle's policy was to leave the original pieces unornamented. However, he clearly approved of the practice of adding divisions to vocal pieces. Both *Musica Teusch* and *Musica und Tabulatur* include instructions on how to add ornaments to ensemble pieces.[34] These are of great interest because they are the earliest published examples of how viol players were supposed to ornament vocal compositions, predating Ortiz's much more extensive treatment of the subject by two decades.[35] Gerle gives the consort player a choice of two types of ornamentation. The first evidently stems from the aforementioned German habit of splitting up dotted rhythms. Gerle quite simply transforms these dactyls into runs of semiminims by inserting an extra note (Example 4). Confirmation of this practice comes

Ex. 4     Ornaments (*Musica und Tabulatur*, 1546, fol. L<sup>v</sup>)

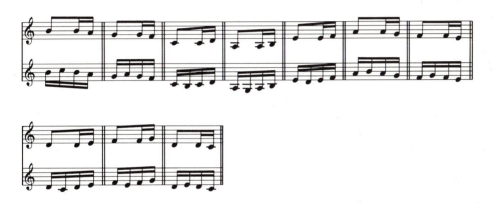

from one of the few pieces in Munich 718 to have written-out ornaments, the closing measures of Josquin's 'Cum sancto spiritu' (Example 3). The judicious application of these ornaments to the discantus viol part produces quite a florid finish. The second type recommended by Gerle was a cadential ornament usually to be found in the discantus but occasionally also in the alto or tenor (Example 5). One of the most interesting features of Gerle's musical examples of this ornament is the conscious application of *musica ficta* to the ornamented cadences where it was not given in the original. When intabulating vocal pieces, Gerle was much more sparing in his use of added accidentals in German *Tenorlieder* than in Parisian chansons, presumably in deference to divergent practices in his mensural sources. These cadential ornaments, however, seem to indicate that his personal preference was for sharpened leading notes.

The published treatises of Judenkünig and Gerle, together with the Munich manuscript, present a fairly clear picture of the type of music played by early 16th-century viol consorts. Summing up their evidence, it is possible to say that the repertory consisted largely of transcriptions of secular vocal

Ex. 5    Ornaments (*Musica und Tabulatur*, 1546, fol. K)

music with the occasional addition of an excerpt from a well-known mass or motet. The choice of music was determined by current musical taste, and a popular new genre such as the four-part Parisian chanson was quickly incorporated into the viol player's repertory. At least in southern Germany, it was customary to copy out the chosen pieces in tablature, arranging the music for an *a–d–a* consort of tenor and bass viols. In copying out the vocal originals few alterations were made, the chief exception being the regrettable habit of smoothing out syncopations and dotted rhythms. In performance and occasionally in written-out parts a little light ornamentation would be applied, especially at cadences. It is clear, then, that the musical diet of viol consorts was still largely a reflection of contemporary vocal music. Of a repertory of music specifically, let alone idiomatically, conceived for viols, there was as yet no sign.

   The publication of a tutor for beginners such as Gerle's *Musica Teusch* shows that in Germany at least the art of playing the viol was no longer restricted to professional musicians and their aristocratic patrons. The popularisation of the viol outside the immediate confines of courtly life was, of course, a major step in establishing the instrument as one of the leading bowed string instruments of renaissance Europe. With its new 'amateur' status – 'an instrument played by gentlemen, merchants and other men of virtue' as Jambe de Fer put it – the viol was henceforth ensured an even wider distribution.[36]

# 7

## The structural development of the Italian viol in the 16th century

Mention was made in Chapter 5 of the crucial importance of Italian craftsmen in the development of the physical structure of the viol. But a detailed examination of their work is sadly hampered by the lack of surviving instruments. Until recently very little was known about any of the few renaissance viols that have survived to the 20th century. Thanks to the pioneering researches of Harwood and Edmunds, however, our knowledge of the structural design of the renaissance viol has increased considerably.[1] In particular, a number of mid 16th-century Venetian viols, some of them in a relatively unaltered condition, have now been identified and described. Yet the comparative wealth of viols from the mid 16th century onwards only serves to highlight the lack of authenticated examples from the earlier period. To my knowledge, there is not a single extant viol that can be dated convincingly to the formative years of the instrument's development, *c*1490–1520. Once again, therefore, a study of the iconographic evidence is essential.

Before discussing in detail the evolution of the structure of the viol, it will be helpful to summarise in general terms the most significant developments. The first stage of the transformation of the *vihuela* into the viol – the application of the bow to the plucked *vihuela de mano* – had already been accomplished on the Iberian peninsula. Italian makers were thus confronted with a potentially very useful low-pitched bowed string instrument, but one which would need considerable modification if it were to be of practical value in ensemble playing. Their initial reaction was to equip the hitherto flat-bridged *vihuela de arco* with an arched bridge and a fingerboard so that it would henceforth be of use in polyphonic ensemble music. Iconographic evidence certainly suggests that this fundamental alteration to the instrument's nature was quickly accomplished, as the old flat-bridged *vihuela de arco* hardly survived a decade in Italy. The next phase of the viol's development, however, was a much more protracted one and stemmed directly from the change in method of stringing. The internal construction of the old flat-bridged *vihuela de arco* was in all probability akin to that of its twin the *vihuela de mano*, that is with a completely flat belly supported by light transverse barring. This method would have been well suited to the *vihuela de arco*; the low, flat bridge found on some instruments

(Plate 33) would have exerted very little pressure on the belly. But as soon as the downwards pressure was increased by the tall arched bridge, the flat belly would have been less practical as it would tend to collapse under the additional stress. Clearly a new method of construction was required, and a satisfactory solution to this problem must have been one of the chief concerns of early Italian viol makers. During the course of the 16th century many different methods were tried out: continued use of transverse barring to support the under side of the belly; arching the belly itself; increasing the thickness of the belly; carving an integral, longitudinal 'spine' to the belly to increase its resistance. But the evidence of surviving 16th-century viols is that the solution which eventually achieved widespread acceptance – an arched belly supported by a bass-bar and soundpost – had yet to be implemented. As well as their differing responses to the basic problem of belly construction, early 16th-century Italian craftsmen naturally had their own ideas about other aspects of design such as the choice of woods, and of course each individual had his own particular mannerisms in the fashioning of minor details such as the shape of the soundholes. So the early 16th century was a period of considerable variety, both in fundamental aspects of construction and in less significant external details. Not until the middle of the century did certain dominant types, most notably the Venetian viol, begin to emerge from the wealth of different models available.

One additional factor to be considered is that of size. The bowed *vihuela* was never intended for use in polyphonic music and so remained essentially a single-sized instrument. But the logical consequence of fitting the instrument with an arched bridge to enable it to participate in polyphony was the need to develop a range of sizes suited to the high, middle and low parts that a group of viols playing in consort would have to perform. Experimenting with different sizes to find the best string length and body size for each member of the consort was thus another important concern of early 16th-century viol makers, adding still further to the bewildering variety of sizes current at that period.

The earliest form of viol found in Italian art, an instrument closely resembling the Valencian *vihuela de arco*, may be seen in Peruzzi's *Incoronazione della Vergine* (*c*1505) in the Chiesa di San Pietro in Montorio (Plate 48). Many of its features betray an affinity with the Valencian *vihuela* of the late 15th century: the long, thin, narrow neck, the slim ribs and above all the attachment of the strings to a flat stringholder. Examples such as this, however, are most unusual, since in its original form the bowed *vihuela* suffered a rapid decline in Italy, probably for the reason mentioned in Chapter 5: namely that it could not compete with the *lira da braccio* as an instrument of vocal accompaniment and was thus musically redundant.

Viols with arched bridges begin to appear in Italian art even before 1500. The best-known example from the late 15th century is an altarpiece by Costa dated 1497 in the Bolognese church of San Giovanni in Monte (Plate 53).

Beneath an enthroned Madonna and Child are two youthful viol players, set against an attractive landscape. Their instruments are clearly strung in the Italian manner with a raised fingerboard, an arched bridge and a tailpiece. At first glance there are a number of points about these instruments that could easily have stemmed from a knowledge of the Valencian *vihuela de arco*, notably the extremely thin, narrow neck and the very shallow ribs. And yet they are unmistakably the work of an Italian rather than a Spanish craftsman, since their body shape is that of the *lira da braccio*, an instrument never, to my knowledge, encountered in late 15th-century Spanish art. The Italianate physical appearance of these viols, however, is not at all surprising. From the evidence of Isabella d'Este's correspondence with her instrument maker, it is clear that it was quite normal for an Italian patron to rely on compatriot craftsmen to provide instruments of foreign design. Isabella commissioned both 'viole a la spagnola' ('viols in the Spanish manner') and 'liutti a la spagnola' ('lutes in the Spanish manner') from her own trusted Italian makers (see Chapter 5). So the earliest viols to appear in Italian art, while still owing something to the general conception of the Valencian *vihuela*, tend to reflect rather more openly the instrument-making traditions of their own country.[2]

The next stage in the evolution of the Italian renaissance viol is a particularly fascinating one. It took place during the two decades after about 1510 when, following their earliest efforts, Italian makers gradually began to experiment with, and ultimately to incorporate into their designs, features that were subsequently to become standard. In their external appearance these 'second generation' instruments, as they may be termed, have already left behind the direct legacy of the *vihuela de arco*, and indeed the most advanced of them come remarkably close to the 'classic' viol outline established much later. Any developments in internal construction during this period can still only be guessed at in the absence of authenticated instruments. The most significant innovations in external appearance were the following: the introduction of the deep ribs and the bend in the upper part of the back; sloping shoulders; large waists; the development of the scroll. The end product of these changes was an instrument altogether bulkier, more substantial in appearance than the slender *vihuela de arco*. A good early example of a viol with deep ribs is the instrument which lies among the wreckage at the feet of the saint in Raphael's *St Cecilia* (c1515). The bend in the back just above the waists, clearly visible in this painting, was introduced as a direct result of the considerable increase in rib depth, so that the back could more easily be joined to the base of the neck (Plate 50). Sloping shoulders – that is shoulders which fall away from the neck rather than make a right angle with it at the join – are well illustrated by an *intarsia* of a viola da gamba in the Vatican (Plate 49). Both the aforementioned instruments have large, fairly deep waists, as do the two bass viols in a Ferrarese wall painting of c1510 in the church of Santa Maria della Consolazione.[3] Italian makers abandoned the tiny waists of some earlier *vihuelas*. No

63   *The Concert*
(*c*1510, Titian: Pitti Palace, Florence)

doubt these were impractical on instruments with arched bridges which would need to allow much more room for bow clearance on the outer strings.

Though of no structural significance, the development of the viol scroll by Italian makers proved an important addition to the instrument's visual appearance. The pegbox of the *vihuela de arco* was usually one of three types: the reverse lute-like pegbox (Plate 40); the sickle-shaped pegbox ending in an uncarved block (Plate 33); the sickle-shaped pegbox surmounted by a carved animal head (Plate 39). The earliest Italian viols normally made use of one or other of these types, but experiments with scrolls were quickly initiated. Interestingly enough, the viols depicted by Costa in 1497 each have a different scroll; the smaller instrument has the normal forward scroll, the larger a type of reversed scroll. An early example of the scroll with projecting 'ears' may be seen on the viol in the Vatican *intarsia* (Plate 49). More common, however, was the flat-sided scroll with a spiral groove, well illustrated by the viol in a paint-

64    Madonna and Child: detail of a child playing a viol
(*c*1535 Pordenone: Madonna di Campagna, Piacenza)

65   Viol by Francesco Linarol
(mid 16th century: Kunst-
historisches Museum, Vienna)

66   Viol by Francesco
Linarol: side view
(mid 16th century:
Kunsthistorisches
Museum, Vienna)

67   Viol by Francesco Linarol:
rear view
(mid 16th century: Kunst-
historisches Museum, Vienna)

ing by Titian of about 1510. The back of this particular scroll is carved with a
decorative floral motif, and its pegs, like those of several other early viols, are
key-shaped rather than round (Plate 63).

By the 1530s some viols were being made which combined all the features
discussed above. A painting of the Madonna and Child of about 1535 by
Pordenone depicts one such instrument which is viewed from behind (Plate
64). Clearly visible are the deep ribs, the bend in the back, the sloping
shoulders and the scroll with the spiral groove. Instruments like this formed
the basis for the development of the most important viol type of the mid 16th
century, the Venetian viol.

The surviving instruments of the 16th-century Venetian school of viol making have recently been described by Edmunds in an article for the *Galpin Society Journal* entitled 'Venetian Viols of the Sixteenth Century'. The following discussion of these very important instruments is much indebted to this piece of work. Possibly the earliest surviving Venetian viol is the tenor by Francesco Linarol in the Kunsthistorisches Museum, Vienna (Figure 6).[4] Francesco's

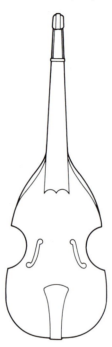

Figure 6  A viol by Francesco Linarol

dates are not known exactly, but since his son Ventura is reported to have been over 60 in 1601, it seems reasonable to assume that he (Francesco) was making viols by the 1540s.[5] The label of this viol reads *Franciscus Linarolus Bergomensis Venetiis Faciebat*. In its general characteristics – sloping shoulders, large waists, deep ribs, bend in the back – the instrument follows the pattern being developed by Italian makers of the early decades of the 16th century (Plates 65–67). But it also displays a number of highly characteristic features of the mid 16th-century Venetian school of viol making, and for convenience these are listed as follows:

*Characteristics of the mid 16th-century Venetian viol*

i    The scroll is flat-sided with fluting on the top and back and a deep spiral groove carved in the side.

ii    The pegbox sits fairly upright and is S-shaped.

iii    The join between the neck and the ribs slopes forwards. (This can best be seen on a profile of a Venetian viol, for example Plate 66.)

iv   The neck is quite thick and not tilted back.
v    The thick fingerboard is arched, hollowed out underneath and shaped at the end in the form of a double semicircle.
vi   The shoulders slope inwards from the back so that the belly is smaller and slimmer than the back at the upper end of the body.
vii  The waists have a distinctive shape with the curve inwards sharper at the upper end and more gentle towards the lower end.
viii The upper corners are more sharply pointed than the lower ones.

Some of the most interesting facts about this instrument concern its internal construction. Edmunds notes that the belly is in fact a flat plate of wood (such as might be used for the front of a plucked instrument) which has been bent into a transverse arch.[6] This arch is supported underneath by two arched transverse bars, one above and one below the corners, and the bars are in turn supported by small blocks fixed to the ribs. One consequence of this method of construction (transverse bending of a flat plate) is that the ribs have had to be made deeper at the lower end of the belly where they meet the transverse ridge at its highest point. Francesco Linarol's use of a flat plate as the basis of this viol's belly accords perfectly with the proposition that the construction of the mid 16th-century Italian viol was still being influenced by that of its plucked ancestor the *vihuela de mano*. His response to the problem of the extra tension on the belly from the arched bridge was a good one. By arching both the belly and its supporting bars transversely, Linarol was able to counteract the downwards pressure of the bridge. The force exerted by the bridge of this viol on its belly would in any case have been a relatively small one because its neck was not tilted back (Plate 66). There are no markings to indicate that a soundpost was ever used, and the back is not fitted with a plate to support one.

The second Venetian viol maker to merit consideration is Hainrich Ebert who, according to Witten, appears in Venetian documents during the 1560s. A tenor viol in the Brussels Conservatoire (M.1402) has this maker's printed label (Plate 69). The instrument is similar to the Linarol viol and thus probably dates from the same period, the mid 16th century (Plate 68). There are a few extra decorative features, notably a small carved flower at the centre of the spiral groove on the scroll, purfling round the edge of the belly and a geometric motif on the fingerboard. Again the internal construction is of interest. Although the present top is carved, Edmunds notes that the ribs are marked where blocks have at some stage been removed from the very places where there are still blocks on the Linarol viol to support the transverse bars, and, moreover, that the lower ribs are slightly arched.[7] The conclusion to be drawn from this is that the original belly of the Ebert viol was a flat plate, arched transversely and supported, like the belly of the Linarol instrument, with arched transverse barring. This top presumably collapsed at a fairly early stage in the instrument's life and had to be replaced by the carved belly. If this speculation is well-founded, then the Ebert viol remains an eloquent testimony to the problems faced by early 16th-century Italian viol makers trying to

68    Viol by Hainrich Ebert
(mid 16th century: Conservatoire, Brussels)

70    Viol by Hainrich Ebert with
belly removed

69    Label of viol by Hainrich Ebert

71  Viol by Antonio Ciciliano
(mid 16th century: Kunst-
historisches Museum, Vienna,
C.75)

72  Viol by Antonio
Ciciliano: side view
(mid 16th century:
Kunsthistorisches
Museum, Vienna,
C.75)

73  Viol by Antonio Ciciliano:
rear view
(mid 16th century: Kunst-
historisches Museum, Vienna,
C.75)

adapt the flat belly of the *vihuela* to withstand the arched bridge of the viol.
Evidently the transverse bending of a flat plate did not always work. One
further point about the Ebert viol noted by Edmunds is that its neck has been
shortened. In its original form it would have appeared as a very tall, slim instrument with a string length comfortably in excess of its body length, another
legacy from the viol's elongated Valencian ancestor.

   To judge by the number of their instruments that have survived, the most
prolific Venetian viol makers of the second half of the 16th century were the
Cicilianos, Antonio and his son Battista. The first member of the Ciciliano
family to achieve a widespread reputation, however, did so as a player rather
than a maker.[8] In his *Ragionamenti* Cosimo Bartoli refers to an excellent player

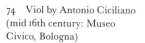

74   Viol by Antonio Ciciliano
(mid 16th century: Museo
Civico, Bologna)

75   Viol by Battista Ciciliano
(late 16th century: Conservatoire,
Brussels, M.1424)

76   Viol by Battista Ciciliano
(late 16th century: Conservatoire,
Brussels, M.1425)

of the 'viola' called 'Il Siciliano' who, he recalls, was in the service of Cardinal
Ippolito de' Medici (*d*1535). 'Il Siciliano' was evidently one of the outstanding
players of his generation, and several commentators of the 1540s and 1550s
refer to his talents with approbation. Writing in 1543, Ganassi praises the skill
of 'un Messer Ioanbattista Cicilian', ranking him as one of the most expert viol
players of his acquaintance. Vasari records that in 1546 Titian's son Orazio
painted one 'Messer Battista Ciciliano. . . an excellent player of the viol'
('eccelente sonatore di Violone'). Then in 1553 in his *Dialogo Secondo della Musica*
Luigi Dentice refers to four musicians of whom 'M. Battista Siciliano' was
one. Whether this outstanding violist was related to the two viol makers of the
same name must remain an open question, though it would seem quite likely.[9]

77   Viol by Battista Ciciliano
(late 16th century: Conservatoire, Brussels, M.1426)

78   Label of viol by Battista Ciciliano
(Conservatoire, Brussels, M.1426)

79    Parchment lining of viol by Battista Ciciliano
(Conservatoire, Brussels, M.1426)

The elder of the two makers, active around the mid 16th century, was Antonio
Ciciliano, who, according to Witten, is mentioned in Venetian documents of
1566, 1569 and 1581.[10] Four of Antonio's instruments survive: three are in the
Kunsthistorisches Museum, Vienna, a tenor (C.75), a bass (C.76) and a large
bass (C.77); one is in the Museo Civico Medievale, Bologna (1761). Four bass
viols survive by Antonio's son Battista Ciciliano: three in Brussels (M.1424,
M.1425 and M.1426) and one in Yale University. Battista Ciciliano signed his
instruments 'Battista son of Antonio Ciciliano in Venice' ('Batista fiol đ antº
cicilian in Vª'); see Plate 78.

    Antonio's extant viols conform in almost every respect to the mid 16th-
century Venetian model. Like Hainrich Ebert, Antonio incorporated a carved
floral motif in the centre of the spiral groove of his scrolls, and his fingerboards
display a geometric pattern (Plate 74). One of his surviving tenor viols makes
a minor departure from the usual body outline by having slightly pointed

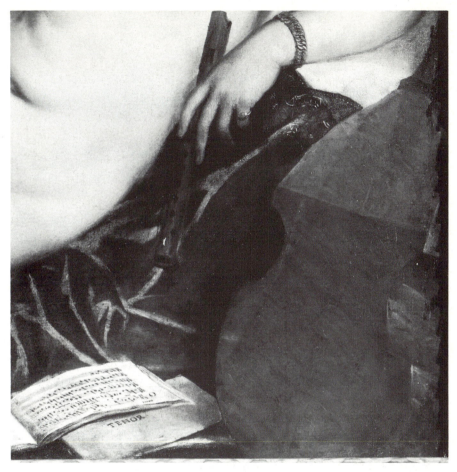

80  *Venus and Cupid with a Lute Player*: detail of a viol
(*c*1565, Titian: Fitzwilliam Museum, Cambridge)

corners to its waists (Plate 71). Battista's bass viols, while obviously modelled
on the standard mid 16th-century Venetian pattern, differ from his father's instruments in their rather broader body outline (Figure 7). Other points worth
noting are Battista's preference for nicked c-holes and less sharply sloping
shoulders, and his different approach to carving the scroll, which has no floral
decoration and fluting only over the top. The Ciciliano viols have carved
rather than bent tops, reflecting the growing preference for this type of construction, but the top of Antonio's large bass, though carved, was apparently
also bent to increase its arching.[11] Of the eight extant Ciciliano viols, two are
tenors, five are basses and one is a large bass. This distribution is no accident
of fate. Rather it reflects the marked preference in Italy, as elsewhere in
Europe, for consorts of large viols. Even in the mid 16th century the tenor–
bass–bass grouping was still preferred to the treble–tenor–bass consort (see
Chapter 11).

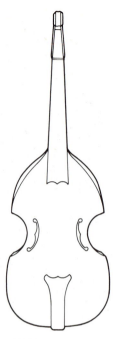

Figure 7    A viol by Battista Ciciliano

The importance of the mid 16th-century Venetian school of viol making is reflected not only in the comparatively large number of surviving instruments, but also in the appearance of Venetian viols in Italian art. The viol depicted by Pordenone in the mid 1530s has already been cited as an example of the prototype of the Venetian viol (Plate 64). Two features in particular are reminiscent of the Venetian model: the way in which the bend in the back is positioned low down just above the waists and the shape of the waists themselves with the sharper angle and corner at the upper end. But the best contemporary representation of a Venetian viol must surely be the instrument in Titian's *Venus and Cupid with a Lute Player*, in the copy owned by the Fitzwilliam Museum (Plate 80). The date of the painting is usually given as *c*1565, that is, during the working lifetime of most, if not all, the Venetian viol makers discussed above. The body of the instrument is viewed from the rear, but the scroll is unfortunately not visible. So close in appearance is this instrument to Francesco Linarol's viol that it might almost be regarded as a portrait of one of this maker's instruments. The shape of the shoulders, the position of the bend in the back and the shape of the waists all point towards this identification. Another mid 16th-century instrument closely allied to the Venetian school is the bass member of the quartet of viols depicted by Aurelio Luini in the monastery of San Maurizio at Milan (Plate 95): the shoulders slope forwards; the back is clearly larger than the belly; the neck joins the ribs at an angle; the end of the fingerboard is shaped. Readers of *Early Music* will already have had

81  *Hermes, Herse and Aglauros*: detail of a viol
(mid/late 16th century, Veronese: Fitzwilliam Museum, Cambridge)

a chance to study a further example, a drawing of a young lad playing a bass
viol (attributed to Bartolomeo Cesi).[12] Once again the characteristics of the
Venetian school are self-evident: the sloping shoulders; the back wider than
the belly; the characteristic waists and sharp upper corners; the very thick
fingerboard with double semicircle shaped end; the S-shaped pegbox; the
scroll with a spiral groove. Finally, a viol depicted by Paolo Veronese at a most
unusual angle – flat and almost head-on – illustrates a rather attractive fluted
scroll of the Venetian pattern (Plate 81).

Detailed lists of features of viols in works of art may make rather tedious
reading, but an analysis of them is nonetheless a very necessary exercise, for it
serves to strengthen confidence in the iconographic evidence upon which so
much of this study is necessarily based. If the instruments of this unquestion-
ably important mid 16th-century Venetian school of instrument making had
left no trace in works of art of the period, we should then have to suspect either
that surviving depictions of viols have left us with a distorted view of reality, or
that the extant instruments themselves do not represent a true cross-section of
the work of contemporary makers. By testing the evidence of the one against

82    Portrait of a viol player
(*c*1540, Zacchia: Louvre, Paris)

83   Viol by Gasparo da Salò
(late 16th century: Ashmolean
Museum, Oxford)

84   Copy by Ian Harwood of a mid 16th century Italian viol in the
Dolmetsch Collection

the evidence of the other, however, the true importance of the Venetian school
emerges with much greater clarity.[13]

The rise of the dominant Venetian school of viol making took place against a
background of considerable variety. Even in the mid 16th century numerous
experiments were still being made with the shape, size and construction of the
viol, and if the resulting models did not gain wide acceptance at the time, let
alone exert much influence on subsequent generations of makers, they are
nonetheless of considerable historical interest. Faced with the task of developing a relatively new instrument, it was understandable that many 16th-century
instrument makers should have drawn upon the knowledge and expertise that

85    Treble viol by Gioan Maria
(late 16th century: Ashmolean Museum, Oxford)

they were building up in the manufacture of other instrumental types and
then applied them to the viol. This approach accounts for many of the variant
forms encountered in the 16th century, and in extreme cases it produced
hybrid instruments which are difficult to classify in any of the major families.

    The most highly regarded bowed instrument in Italy at the time of the
*vihuela de arco*'s arrival was the *lira da braccio*, and so, almost inevitably, some
Italian viol makers copied its characteristic body shape with two lower corners
and smoothly rounded upper belly (Figure 8). Though no viols of this type
have survived, there are several depictions of them in early 16th-century
Italian art. A number of *lira*-shaped viols seem to have been in use at Ferrara.
In addition to the well-known pair of instruments depicted by Costa in 1497
(Plate 53), there are two *lira*-shaped viols in a Ferrarese painting of the 1530s by
Benvenuto Tisi ('Il Garofalo') in the Galleria Estense at Modena (Plate 57). A
further example of the *lira*-shaped viol may be seen in an early Titian drawing
in Christ Church, Oxford (*c*1510–1515).[14] The use of *lira*-shaped viols at Ferrara
in the early 16th century is hinted at in a report of an entertainment given in
1506. On 5 February Prospero wrote from Ferrara to Isabella d'Este describing

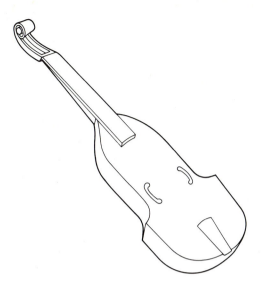

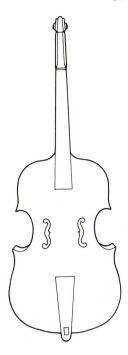

Figure 8 An early 16th-century *lira*-shaped viol depicted in a
painting by Il Garofalo

Figure 9 A late 16th-century violin-shaped
viol by Gasparo da Salò

the *intermedii*. The first of these had consisted of 'lire grande sonate da octo
persone', ('large liras [i.e. viols] played by eight people').[15] After the first few
decades of the 16th century viols of this type gradually disappear from view, no
doubt a reflection of the diminishing popularity of the *lira* itself.

The rise to importance of the violin in the 1520s and the 1530s affected many
Italian viol makers profoundly. Features of the new instrument began to be incorporated quite regularly into viol designs. The characteristic violin outline
with the pointed, slightly turned-out corners to the waists was often copied
(Figure 9). The title-page woodcut of Ganassi's *Fontegara* (1535) depicts three
viols all with pointed corners hanging on a wall. A rather crude-looking viol
with its corners turned out (though not pointed) is the instrument belonging
to the musician whose portrait by Zacchia hangs in the Louvre (Plate 82).
Even a well-established maker like Antonio Ciciliano with his own distinctive
design was not immune from this trend (Plate 71). The overhanging edges
(Plate 100) and even the arched back of the violin were also sometimes
copied.[16] By the mid-16th century the cross-fertilisation between the viol and
the violin families was sometimes so marked that genuinely hybrid instruments were produced. A mid 16th-century painting that I know only from a
photocopy from the Kunsthistorisches Institut of Florence shows one such
cross-breed, an instrument with the body of a violin but the frets, six strings
and playing position of the viol. The influence of the violin on the viol was a
lasting one. For the remainder of the 16th century and well into the 17th cen-

tury viol makers made use of the violin's outline and continued to experiment with features such as its arched back. In his *Division Violist* of 1659, for example, Simpson illustrated a violin-shaped viol, its belly 'digged out of the Plank', with the comment that its sound was 'quick and sprightly'.

The one plucked instrument to influence the form of the viol in the 16th century was the guitar. It will be remembered that by the early 16th century Valencian makers of *vihuelas* were beginning to reserve smoothly incurving waists for their plucked instruments, leaving the cornered outline for the *vihuela de arco*; early 16th-century Italian viol makers followed this practice. Yet, from time to time, Italian craftsmen, especially those working in Brescia, experimented with the curved outline. Several 16th-century viols of this pattern have survived. Two are by Zanetto di Montichiaro, who is mentioned in Lanfranco's *Scintille di Musica* (1533) as one of two makers (the other is Giovanni Giacopo dalla Corna) whose string instruments were worthy of praise. Both his surviving viols – one is in the Brussels Conservatoire and the other is in the Witten collection – are labelled, the former 'Zanetto in Bressa', the latter 'Zanetto da Bressa'. Other 16th-century guitar-shaped viols have the characteristic flat-sided Venetian scroll. One example is the anonymous tenor in the Dolmetsch collection (Plate 84); another is the treble viol by the Brescian maker Gioan Maria (labelled 'Juan Maria da bressa: fece in Venecia') who, according to documents cited by Witten, was a long-standing resident of Venice from c1560 to 1591 (Plate 85). The length of Gioan Maria's residence in Venice probably accounts for his use of the Venetian scroll and also for the pattern of the c-holes which resemble those of his contemporary Battista Ciciliano.

The internal construction of two of these guitar-shaped viols adds to our knowledge of how some 16th-century viol makers responded to the problems of belly construction. The belly of the Italian tenor viol in the Dolmetsch collection is strengthened by having central thickening in the form of a spine carved on its under side. The belly of the Zanetto viol in Brussels is strengthened with an integral bar. An alternative to the spine or bar was to carve the curves of the belly so that the whole of its central section was very much thicker than the outer edges (on a carved top it is usually slightly thicker anyway). Interestingly enough, the belly of the viol depicted in Raphael's *St Cecilia* may have been made in this fashion. The wood round the edge of the c-hole on the bass side is markedly thicker than the wood round the edges of the belly as revealed by the carefully depicted cracks (Plate 50). Devices such as the central spine or the thicker belly would certainly tend to increase the resistance of the belly to the pressure of the bridge and prevent the collapse of the top.

As will by now have become very clear, Italian art of the 16th century, to say nothing of surviving instruments, reveals a remarkable kaleidoscope of viols of different shapes and sizes, clear evidence of the amount of experiment still taking place.[17] Much work remains to be done on the extant viols of the next generation of Italian viol makers active in the late 16th and early 17th centuries, Ventura Linarol, Gasparo da Salò, Antonio Brensio and others. When this has been done, it may be possible to put the earlier Italian viols of the second and the third quarters of the 16th century into a clearer perspective. It has already become clear, however, that it was the central Venetian tradition of the mid 16th century that more than any other gave rise to the 'classic' viol of English and north European craftsmen of the 17th and 18th centuries. It was to be many years, though, well into the 17th century indeed, before this shape, in its final form, had gained sufficiently widespread acceptance to merit the term 'classic'. Even then hybrid instruments influenced by the violin or the guitar continued to appear in substantial numbers.

# 8

## Italian viol tunings

An early manuscript source of a bass viol tuning has been discovered on a single leaf bound in with two treatises in the Biblioteca Marciana, Venice (ms. Lat. 336, coll. 1581). In his discussion of the fragment, Harrán proposes a date of *c*1470–1480, but this seems rather early for an Italian to have recorded a viol tuning.[1] An early 16th-century date, soon after the viol's arrival in Italy, is more probable. The tuning is set out in the form of a plan of a fingerboard with the strings named and frets marked:

|             | 1 | 2 | 3 | 4 | 5 | 6 | 7 | 8 (frets) |
|-------------|---|---|---|---|---|---|---|-----------|
| Cante       | D |   | e | f |   | G |   |           |
| Sottanelli  | A | ♭ | ♮ | c |   | D |   |           |
| Tenorcelli  | E | f |   | g |   | A |   |           |
| Tenor       | C |   | d |   | e | f |   |           |
| Bordon      | Γ |   | a | ♭ | ♮ | C |   |           |
| Contra      | D |   | e | f |   | Γ |   |           |

The anonymous scribe's terms for the strings are similar to those used by Lanfranco ('canto, sotanella, mezzanella, tenore, bordone, basso') and Ganassi ('canto, sotana, mezana, tenor, bordon, basso'). The first published source of Italian viol tunings is Lanfranco's *Scintille di Musica* (1533) which gives tunings for the whole consort: the tenor viol is tuned exactly like the lute (*a′ e′ b g d A*); the treble is pitched a fourth higher (*d″ a′ e′ c′ g d*) and the bass a fifth lower (*d′ a e c G D*); an alternative is to tune the bass a fourth lower than the tenor (*e′ b f♯ d A E*) so that the treble is a seventh above the bass.

An important source of Italian viol tunings of the 1530s has been found on a manuscript leaf at the back of a copy of Michele Savonarola's *De tutte le cose che se manzano comunamente* (Venice, 1515).[2] This leaf can probably be dated to *c*1536, since a note in the same hand refers to an earthquake which occurred on 16 August 1536. The instructions on viol tunings are in two sections: the first is headed 'il modo de sonar il violon segondo alfonso de la viola' ('the method of tuning the viol according to Alfonso della Viola'); the second, 'il modo d'accordar li violoni seccondo il detto authore' ('the method of tuning viols according to the said author'). Alfonso della Viola, whose method of tuning

140

viols is described in this passage, was one of the foremost viol players of his generation, and no less an authority than Ganassi (1543) praises his skill. The explanation of how to tune a set of viols together begins thus; first 'the viol playing the bass line should be tuned well' ('accordar bene quel violone col quale s'ha a sonnare il basso'); next the tenor is tuned a fourth above the bass; finally the treble is tuned a fourth above the tenor. Alfonso della Viola thus confirms Lanfranco's alternative consort tuning with the treble a seventh above the bass.[3] The remaining comments concern the location of the clefs on each size of viol. An interesting fact emerges; two different tunings are given, one for use in keys with *b* naturals ('per b♮'), the other a tone lower, for use in keys with *b* flats ('per b mol'):

| | | | | | | | | | | | |
|---|---|---|---|---|---|---|---|---|---|---|---|
| *d"* | *a'* | *e'* | *c'* | *g* | *d* | | *c"* | *g'* | *d'* | *b♭* | *f* | *c* |
| *a'* | *e'* | *b* | *g* | *d* | *A* | | *g'* | *d'* | *a* | *f* | *c* | *G* |
| *e'* | *b* | *f♯* | *d* | *A* | *E* | | *d'* | *a* | *e* | *c* | *G* | *D* |

This seems to betray a concern that the strings of a set of viols should be matched as closely as possible to the key of the piece to be performed, probably as a means of ensuring maximum resonance. The *b* flat and *f* strings of the second tuning would be ideal for pieces in *f* but less so for pieces in *g*.

The most complete coverage of viol consort tunings in the mid 16th century is found in the celebrated two-volume viol tutor *Regola Rubertina* published in Venice by the Venetian instrumentalist Sylvestro di Ganassi. Apart from the fact that he was born in 1492 at Fontego near Venice, nothing is known about Ganassi's early life. By 1535, however, he was in the employment of the Signoria of Venice. In 1542 he published the first volume of his viol tutor under the title *Regola Rubertina*, and this was followed in 1543 by the sequel *Lettione Seconda*. The title *Regola Rubertina* (the 'Rubertine Rule' or the 'Rubertine Method') is something of an enigma. The first volume is dedicated to Ruberto Strozzi and the title may have been intended as a compliment to him, but another candidate for the actual derivation of the word 'Rubertina' is the celebrated violist mentioned by Ganassi in Chapter 20 of *Lettione Seconda*, Rubertino Mantoano. (Prizer plausibly argues that Rubertino Mantoano was Roberto d'Avanzini, the long-serving Mantuan lutenist and singer.)[4] The word 'regola' clearly refers to the four rules of tuning ('regole'), the description of which occupies a substantial part of the first volume. The aforementioned manuscript explanation of Alfonso della Viola's tuning method (*c*1536) also uses 'regola' in this sense: 'questa sia la regola del soprano' ('which is the rule [of tuning] of the treble'). The 'Rubertine Rule' could, therefore, have been the method of tuning taught by, or at least associated with, Rubertino of Mantua.

Ganassi's method of presenting these rules of tuning is that of many 16th-century theorists: a series of scales with their tablature equivalents, giving the position of the notes on the fingerboard (Plate 88). In all, there are four rules of tuning ('regole'), and each rule has three 'orders' ('ordini'): the first 'ordine' consists of a scale without accidentals; the second has *b* flats; the third, described by Ganassi as appropriate for 'musicha finta', has *b* flats and *e* flats. Thus, like Alfonso della Viola, Ganassi recognises the importance of giving a different tuning for use in key signatures with flats (though unlike Alfonso he reserves his alternative for keys with two flats). The first rule of tuning presents the standard *d–g–d* consort tuning still in use today:

Regola Prima

| Ordine Primo | | | | | | | Ordine Secondo | | | | | | | Ordine Terzo | | | | | |
|---|---|---|---|---|---|---|---|---|---|---|---|---|---|---|---|---|---|---|---|
| *d"* | *a'* | *e'* | *c'* | *g* | *d* | | *d"* | *a'* | *e'* | *c'* | *g* | *d* | | *c"* | *g'* | *d'* | *b*♭ | *f* | *c* |
| *g'* | *d'* | *a* | *f* | *c* | *G* | | *g'* | *d'* | *a* | *f* | *c* | *G* | | *f'* | *c'* | *g* | *e*♭ | *B*♭ | *F* |
| *d'* | *a* | *e* | *c* | *G* | *D* | | *d'* | *a* | *e* | *c* | *G* | *D* | | *c'* | *g* | *d* | *B*♭ | *F* | *C* |

The first two 'ordini' give the conventional tuning. The third 'ordine', however, needs some further explanation. For music that has a key signature of two flats, Ganassi realigns the tablature symbols to notes that are a tone lower. There are two possible interpretations of this. If, like Gerle and the compiler of Munich 718, Ganassi is addressing the viol player primarily as a transcriber of mensural notation into tablature, the use of the third 'ordine' is quite logical. When intabulating a piece with a key signature of two flats, the transcriber simply realigns the mensural pitches with the tablature symbols by a tone. On a bass viol middle *c* becomes the open top string instead of the third fret of the *a* string. The result is twofold. First, there is an upward transposition of a tone; the piece is played a tone higher than it would have been if the transcriber had used either of the first two 'ordini'. Secondly, much greater use is made of the resonance of the open strings. Brown gives a practical explanation of this. If, for example, a piece is in the Dorian mode twice transposed with a key signature of two flats and final of *c*, the third order will ensure that the final of the mode, or to put it another way the 'tonic' key of *c*, makes the maximum use of open strings.[5] Alternatively, Ganassi's third 'ordine' could have been used by viol players reading from mensural notation. For a piece with two flats the viols might have to be retuned a tone lower (if playing with instruments of fixed pitch). However, even if there were no need to retune the viols, the players would still have had the very difficult task of relearning the position of the notes on the instrument, a mental adjustment that is far from easy.

Of these two procedures the first is simplicity itself. The viol players can use one set of instruments, and there is no need to retune or learn new fingerings. In the act of transcribing the music into tablature, the pitches are realigned so that the music is better suited to the viols. The alternative is cumbersome. Not only might the players have to adjust their instruments to cope with a lower pitch level – altering the position of the bridge and using thicker strings are two methods suggested by Ganassi – they would certainly have to relearn completely the fingering patterns on the instrument. It is no wonder, then, that the tablature system of notation was so popular with viol players in the first half of the 16th century. German theorists used it, and Ganassi himself either gives both mensural and tablature versions of his examples as in *Regola Rubertina* or tablature versions only as in *Lettione Seconda*. Yet tablature notation, suitable though it was for amateur players, had some limitations. A professional violist playing in an *intermedio* orchestra, for example, would almost certainly have needed to be flexible enough to read from mensural notation, to retune up or down to fit in with other instruments and voices, even to transpose at sight. In his discussion of *barré* fingerings in *Lettione Seconda* (Chapter 20) Ganassi implies that a violist playing in an ensemble with other instruments tuned a semitone or a tone higher can instantly 'retune' his own instrument by laying his first finger flat across several strings at the first or second fret, thereby effectively shortening the string length. To use a device such as this certainly requires a flexible cast of mind!

In Ganassi's second rule of tuning the tenor viol is tuned a fifth above the bass in the manner advocated by Lanfranco (1533):

Regola Seconda

| Ordine Primo | | | | | | Ordine Secondo | | | | | | Ordine Terzo | | | | | |
|---|---|---|---|---|---|---|---|---|---|---|---|---|---|---|---|---|---|
| *d″* | *a′* | *e′* | *c′* | *g* | *d* | *d″* | *a′* | *e′* | *c′* | *g* | *d* | *c″* | *g′* | *d′* | *bb* | *f* | *c* |
| *a′* | *e′* | *b* | *g* | *d* | *A* | *a′* | *e′* | *b* | *g* | *d* | *A* | *g′* | *d′* | *a* | *f* | *c* | *G* |
| *d′* | *a* | *e* | *c* | *G* | *D* | *d′* | *a* | *e* | *c* | *G* | *D* | *c′* | *g* | *d* | *Bb* | *F* | *C* |

The third rule of tuning involves retuning the treble viol a tone lower so that it is a fourth above the tenor viol and a seventh above the bass viol; it is thus the disposition recommended by Alfonso della Viola for keys with *b* flats ('per b mol'):

Regola Terza

| Ordine Primo | | | | | | Ordine Secondo | | | | | | Ordine Terzo | | | | | |
|---|---|---|---|---|---|---|---|---|---|---|---|---|---|---|---|---|---|
| *c″* | *g′* | *d′* | *bb* | *f* | *c* | *c″* | *g′* | *d′* | *bb* | *f* | *c* | *bb′* | *f′* | *c′* | *ab* | *eb* | *Bb* |
| *g′* | *d′* | *a* | *f* | *c* | *G* | *g′* | *d′* | *a* | *f* | *c* | *G* | *f′* | *c′* | *g* | *eb* | *Bb* | *F* |
| *d′* | *a* | *e* | *c* | *G* | *D* | *d′* | *a* | *e* | *c* | *G* | *D* | *c′* | *g* | *d* | *Bb* | *F* | *C* |

Ganassi points out one drawback of this tuning, namely that in the first 'ordine' the effect of the treble viol is 'a little odd' ('un puoco stranio') because one of its strings is tuned to a *b* flat in a key signature without flats. He therefore recommends an alternative in which the bass is retuned. (Again, this corresponds exactly with Alfonso della Viola's tuning, in this case his tuning for keys with *b* naturals, 'per b♮'.)

Regola Terza

| Ordine Primo | | | | | |
|---|---|---|---|---|---|
| *d″* | *a′* | *e′* | *c′* | *g* | *d* |
| *a′* | *e′* | *b* | *g* | *d* | *A* |
| *e′* | *b* | *f♯* | *d* | *A* | *E* |

Ganassi's comment about the adverse effect of the *b* flat string in the first 'ordine' of this rule confirms that the basic justification for all the varied and seemingly over-elaborate tuning systems devised by viol players at this period was a very practical one: to ensure the best possible match between the key of a piece to be performed and the tuning of the consort, thereby making the best use of the 'ring' of the open strings and achieving the best resonance. This is in marked contrast to the attitude of present-day consorts who tend to use one set of instruments tuned at one pitch, regardless of key.

Taken together, then, these three rules of tuning present a comprehensive selection of variant consort tunings centred around the basic pitch levels of the standard *d–g–d* consort tuning. At the end of *Regola Rubertina* are four ricercars 'in various modes' ('di modi variati'), and since Ganassi supplies both mensural and tablature versions, it is possible to observe the practical application of his first three rules of tuning. The first ricercar is for treble viol tuned according to the first order of the first rule of tuning. The second ricercar, also for treble viol, makes use of the second order of the first rule of tuning, that is with a key signature of one flat. The third ricercar is for bass viol. Its key signature of two flats requires the use of the third order of the first rule of tuning, the one appropriate for 'musicha finta'. The fourth and final ricercar is for tenor viol tuned, because of the key signature of two flats, to the third order of the second rule of tuning. But this highlights one of the more pointless aspects of Ganassi's system, because the tenor in the third 'ordine' of the second rule of tuning is no different from the *g*-tuned tenor in the first 'ordine' of the first rule of tuning.

Later Italian advocates of the high consort tuning include Aurelio Marinati in *Somma di tutte le scienze* (Rome, 1587) and Cerreto in *Della prattica musica* (Naples, 1601). In his section on the tuning of viols ('Delle Viole et Violoni') Marinati, like Cerreto, opts for the *d–a–d* consort tuning with both the tenor and 'contralto' viols tuned to *a*. In his *Harmonie Universelle* (Paris, 1636) Mersenne, one of the last sources of Italian viol consort tunings, also cites the *d–a–d* tuning upon the authority of an unnamed informant from Rome. He remarks, however, that the tenor viol ('taille') may be tuned a fourth above the bass (to *g*) and the alto viol ('haute-contre') a fourth above the tenor (to *c*). This marks a departure from renaissance tradition, in which the two middle instruments of the four-part consort, however named, are always given one tuning.

Ganassi's fourth rule of tuning is quite unlike the others. He introduces it with the following somewhat surprising statement: 'And since most players play the viols a fourth higher than in our first rule of tuning, I would like to show you this method' ('E perche il piu di sonatori si sona le viole una quarta piu alta de la prima regola nostra: pero' voglio insegnarti il ditto modo'). The tuning is in fact for five-string viols:[6]

Regola Quarta

| a' | e' | b | g | d |
| d' | a | e | c | G |
| a | e | B | G | D |

In *Regola Rubertina* (Chapter 21) Ganassi points out that the position of the clefs is changed in the fourth rule of tuning. A glance at the tuning charts confirms that this is indeed the case. The note *d'* is the open top string of the bass viol in the first rule of tuning, but in the fourth rule it becomes the fifth fret of the top string. This is probably what Ganassi means when he writes that most players play 'a fourth higher'. Any given note is physically a fourth higher on the instrument than it was in the first rule of tuning.[7] Ganassi's fourth rule of tuning is in fact the exact equivalent of Gerle's *a–d–a* consort tuning for five-string viols, and so players using it would presumably have needed to make use of the German system of transposition for any music that exceeded the compass of the top *a*-tuned instrument. To help the viol player gain familarity with the new positions of the notes on the fingerboard in the 'quarta regola', Ganassi gives some exercises: these are entitled 'a method of practising on the fingerboard' ('Modo del pratichar il manico');[8] see Plate 91.

In the tuning system for five-string viols, described in Ganassi's 'regola quarta' and earlier used by the compiler of Munich 718 and Gerle, lies the origins of the low consort tunings of the late 16th century, so long a puzzle to musicologists.[9] The low tuning simply resulted from the addition of a low sixth string, a fourth below the others. Though he never uses it himself, Gerle mentions the possible addition of this low sixth string which he calls 'gross Bomhart'. In the late 16th century the lower string became a regular addition. Compare Ganassi's five-string bass viol tuning (*a e B G D*) with one given by Praetorius (*a e B G D A'*). By tuning the bass a tone lower as in two of Praetorius's examples (*g d A F C G'* or *g d A E C G'*), an even deeper sonority could be obtained. Indeed, Italian advocates of the low tuning such as Zacconi (1592) and Banchieri (1609) have the whole consort at this lower pitch (a *g–d–g* consort tuning). Banchieri, for example, gives the following consort tuning and for good measure includes a double-bass viol:

| quarta viola in soprano | *g'* | *d'* | *a* | *f* | *c* | *G* | |
|---|---|---|---|---|---|---|---|
| viola mezana da gamba | *d'* | *a* | *e* | *c* | *G* | *D* | |
| violone da gamba | *g* | *d* | *A* | *F* | *C* | *G'* | |
| violone in contrabasso | *d* | *A* | *E* | *C* | *G'* | *D'* | |

Interest in deep sonorities, as exemplified by this tuning, was a characteristic of the age. (Further on the low *a–d–a* consort and on the double-bass viol, see Chapter 12.)

The existence of a low consort in the late 16th century focuses attention on the problem of the terminology of the viol consort itself. In 20th-century usage, the term 'bass viol' immediately suggests an instrument of a particular size and tuning. In the 16th century, however, this terminology did not have a similar precision. In his first three 'regole' alone, Ganassi gives tunings for tenor viols in *a*, *g* and *f* and bass viols in *e*, *d* and *c*, and by the late 16th century the nominal pitch of any given 'size' of viol could vary from one authority to another by as much as a fifth. The conclusion to be drawn from this is that

86   *Madre de Deus* Retable: The Adoration of the Shepherds: detail of angel musicians
(early/mid 16th century, Portuguese school: Museu Nacional de Arte Antigua, Lisbon)

87   Violone by Hanns Vogel
(1563: Germanisches Nationalmuseum, Nuremberg)

terms such as 'treble', 'tenor' and 'bass' referred not to instruments of a particular size or tuning, but to the position of any given instrument in the hierarchy of the consort. Thus, an instrument tuned *d' a e c G D* might have been played as a 'tenor' in a low consort one day, and the next as a 'bass' in a high consort. In the words of Marcuse, 'one man's bass was simply another man's tenor'.[10] So the terminology used by any theorist of this period should be regarded as a matter of personal preference or local custom, not as evidence of an internationally accepted standard.

The evolution of viol tunings in the 16th century was closely related to the development of different sizes of viol. The early 16th-century German system – an *a–d–a* consort tuning with music that was too high transposed down a fourth – was well suited to the earliest consorts of viols which, adopting the characteristics of the elongated Valencian *vihuela de arco*, tended to be quite large in size. At this period the *a*-tuned 'tenor' viol – to use modern termi-

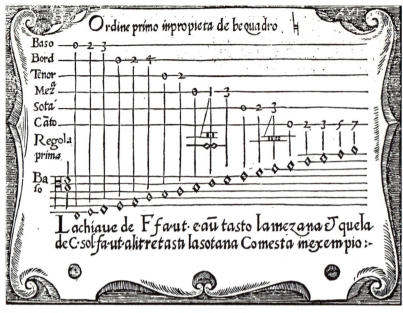

88   *Regola Prima*: the first rule of tuning for the bass viol
(woodcut from S. di Ganassi: *Regola Rubertina*, Venice, 1542)

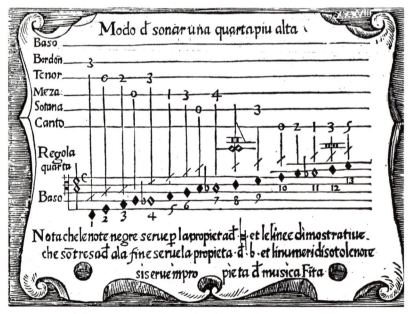

89   *Regola Quarta*: the fourth rule of tuning for the bass viol
(woodcut from S. di Ganassi: *Regola Rubertina*, Venice, 1542)

90  An illustration of a string of poor quality
(woodcut from S. di Ganassi: *Lettione Seconda*, Venice, 1543)

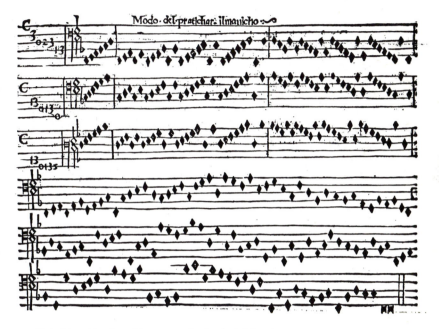

91  *Modo del pratichar il manicho*: an exercise for the left hand
(woodcut from S. di Ganassi: *Regola Rubertina*, Venice, 1542)

nology – was the highest instrument of the consort and thus played parts
labelled 'discantus' or 'superius'. The remaining parts of the consort would
naturally be taken by larger bass viols. Theorists such as Gerle gave their viol
consort tuning at three levels: the top part to be played on an *a*-tuned instrument; the two inner parts to be played by *d*-tuned instruments; the lowest part
by a low *a*-tuned instrument. Ideally, this disposition would involve instruments of three sizes: tenor; bass; large bass (to use modern terminology again).
But this need not necessarily have been the case. The parts could have been distributed as follows: tenor-sized viol (tuned *a' e' b g d*) playing the discantus part;
tenor- or bass-sized viols (tuned *d' a e c G*) playing the alto and tenor lines;
bass-sized viol (tuned *a e B G D*) playing the bass line. In other words, two sizes
of viol coping with three part-ranges, just as later three sizes of viol sometimes
had to cope with four part-ranges. There is a good deal of evidence, both

pictorial and from written records, that in the mid 16th century the four-part viol consort often consisted of only two sizes of instrument, for example, a tenor and three basses. (The 16th-century viol consort will be discussed further in Chapters 11 and 12.)

Performing a four-part composition on a consort of only two sizes would produce a satisfactory result only if the overall range were fairly limited. Any composition exceeding the limits of this rather narrow compass would immediately cause difficulties. Ganassi recognised this problem and in Chapter 11 of *Regola Rubertina* discussed how to tune a consort of four or more viols if the size of the instruments was unsuited to the range of the music. The first step is to try the consort tuning of the 'prima regola', that is, with the tenor and alto a fourth above the bass and a fifth below the soprano. If the relative sizes of the viols make this difficult, then the consort should adopt the system of transposition practised by Gombert, who, Ganassi explains, was expert at arranging music to suit the vocal compass of his singers. If a composition lay too high in the vocal register of the singers of the upper parts, he would transpose the piece downwards into a more comfortable register and, if necessary, rewrite the bass part to avoid the extremes of the bass register. A viol consort should follow Gombert's advice. If the viols playing the upper parts are too large to be tuned according to the 'prima regola', the bass viol should be tuned down. There are two ways in which the pitch of a bass can be lowered; the strings may be lengthened by moving the bridge closer to the tailpiece ('con longar la corda, con movere il scagnello appresso il cordiero'), or thicker strings may be fitted ('& ancora metter corde piu grosse'). If the pitch has to be raised, the bridge may be moved further away from the tailpiece or thinner strings fitted. Ganassi concludes the chapter by describing the benefits of Gombert's method which he sums up with the maxim 'it is better to tune a tone too low than a semitone too high' ('& piu tosto peccar ad incordarlo un tono piu basso che uno semitono piu alto'). For the viol consort there are two advantages, one practical, one aesthetic. Tuning down to a lower pitch means that the strings are less likely to snap and will last longer ('che non crepano & piu durano'); it also enables the consort to produce a sweeter tone ('l'armonia piu dolce').

A consort of viols headed by a *d*-tuned treble – Ganassi's primary recommendation – would probably never have needed to use this method of transposition. A small *d*-tuned viol could easily have coped with high superius parts. The Gombert method is thus obviously intended for those consorts – apparently still a majority in Ganassi's day – which were made up of large-sized viols only. For such a consort many superius lines would ascend far beyond the normal compass of the leading instrument. The music would thus have to be transposed downward to a more suitable pitch and the bass member of the consort adjusted, if necessary, to cope with a lower than usual bass part. The Gombert method of transposition, as applied to the viol consort by

Ganassi, is best viewed as a flexible alternative to the system of transposition advocated by early 16th-century German theorists. Instead of the automatic transposition of high parts down a fourth, a viol consort could select the lower pitch level best suited to an individual piece, say a tone or a minor third lower.

In their advocacy of the high *d*-tuned viol, Lanfranco and Ganassi were progressives, for, although the small *d*-tuned viol – by far the best solution to the problem caused by the upward extension of the range of music – ultimately gained widespread acceptance, it was not commonly played in Ganassi's day. In his own words, most players ('il piu di sonatori') used the fourth rule of tuning. Indeed, the title-page woodcut of his own treatise illustrates three viol players who seem to be making use of the 'quarta regola'. The consort consists of a very large tenor and two basses, one of which has the five strings appropriate for the fourth rule of tuning. The relative scarcity of the small *d*-tuned treble viol in the first half of the 16th century is reflected in works of art. Paintings which include small viols, such as the *Madre de Deus* Retable in Lisbon (Plate 86), are exceptional, and the majority of viol consorts depicted by mid 16th-century artists consist only of tenor and bass viols (see Chapter 11). Surviving instruments, too, reflect the lack of small viols in the 16th century.[11]

Having discussed at length a range of consort tunings in *Regola Rubertina*, Ganassi turns in the second volume of his tutor to the important subject of viol temperaments. As might be expected from a working instrumentalist, his overriding concern is not the theoretical perfection of his system, but its practical value for players. There are three stages in his method: (i) the frets are placed in position using a pair of dividers and an exact, easy-to-follow mathematical scheme; (ii) fine adjustments are made by ear following a carefully worked out scheme comparing stopped notes with open strings; (iii) further *ad hoc* adjustments are made by the player if he still considers the instrument out of tune. For Ganassi, then, the mathematical scheme is merely a convenient point of departure.

Before discussing his method of fret placement, Ganassi spends three chapters on a related topic, the quality of gut strings.[12] If a viol is strung with poor-quality strings, any attempt to tune the instrument or make adjustments to the frets will be rendered almost useless. Ganassi therefore advises his readers how to test the quality of a string. It should be taken between the two hands, stretched taut, and then plucked near the end which is to be attached to the tailpiece. If it vibrates cleanly producing two arches, the string is a good one. If, however, it 'trembles like a paralytic' ('tremante . . . al modo del paralitico'), then the string is a false one. (This is essentially the method advocated by Gerle in 1532.) As a practical musician, Ganassi also felt it necessary to describe the results produced by a string of average quality, one that is not perfect but still usable. When plucked, a string of average quality will produce

more than two arches, but the vibrations will still be fairly clean. In the mid
16th century really true gut strings seem to have been the exception rather
than the rule, and so to avoid undue expense, if for no other reason, Ganassi
accepts that less than perfect strings will sometimes be used.

Having checked the quality of the strings and tuned them to one or other of
the 'regole' given in *Regola Rubertina*, the viol player is now in a position to
embark upon the adjustment of the frets. The first stage, the positioning of the
frets according to a mathematical scheme, involves the following steps: [13]

i   Divide the sounding string length into nine equal parts and place the second fret at
    the first division from the nut.
ii  Place the first fret half-way between the nut and the second fret.
iii Measure the distance between the first and second frets and place the third fret at the
    same distance from the second.
iv  Divide the sounding string length into four equal parts and place the fifth fret at the
    first division from the nut.
v   Place the fourth fret half-way between the third and fifth frets.
vi  Divide the sounding string length into three equal parts and place the seventh fret at
    the first division from the nut.
vii Place the sixth fret half-way between the fifth and seventh frets.
viii Measure the distance between the fifth and sixth frets and place the eighth fret at the
    same distance from the seventh.

In effect, this process places the second, fifth and seventh frets at the pure
intervals of a whole tone, a perfect fourth and a perfect fifth.

Once the frets are in position, fine tuning by ear can commence. Ganassi
explains in some detail his system of fret adjustment which involves checking
stopped notes (i.e. the frets) against open strings. He works upwards from the
lowest string using only unisons or octaves for comparison. When comparing
two notes the player is advised to bow both strings equally so that a true comparison may be obtained. The stages in Ganassi's system may be summarised
as follows:

i    Check the fifth fret of the sixth string (*G*) against the open fifth string (*G*).
ii   Check the fifth fret of the fifth string (*c*) against the open fourth string (*c*).
iii  Check the seventh fret of the fifth string (*d*) against the open sixth string (*D*).
iv   Double check the second fret of the fourth string (*d*) against both the open sixth string
     (*D*) and the seventh fret of the fifth string (*d*).
v    Check the fourth fret of the fourth string (*e*) against the second fret of the sixth string
     (*E*).
vi   Check the open third string (*e*) against the fourth fret of the fourth string (*e*).
vii  Check the first fret of the third string (*f*) against the fifth fret of the fourth string (*f*).
viii Check the third fret of the sixth string (*F*) against the first fret of the third string (*f*).
ix   Check the open second string (*a*) against the fifth fret of the third string (*a*).
x    Check the sixth fret of the third string (*b* flat) against the first fret of the second string
     (*b* flat).
xi   Check the eighth fret of the third string (*c'*) against the open fourth string (*c*).
xii  Check the open first string (*d'*) against the fifth fret of the second string (*d'*).

The result of all these adjustments is that the second, fifth and seventh frets
remain as close to the pure intervals as the player's ear will allow. The first,
third, sixth and eighth frets are now on the flat side, while the fourth fret

which gives the major third is sharp. Even now, writes Ganassi, further adjustments to the frets may be necessary either because the player's ear is not acute enough, or because the nature of the music requires it. An experiment with the first ricercar of *Regola Rubertina* played on a bass viol fretted according to the instructions in *Lettione Seconda* shows that Ganassi's system does indeed have some defects. The problems of intonation are more acute still when such a viol is played in an ensemble with other instruments. The inherent difficulties of unequal temperaments on fretted instruments led to the widespread adoption in the late 16th century of equal temperament, notwithstanding the problems that this caused when fretted instruments performed with keyboard instruments in meantone temperament.[14] By leaving the final adjustment of the frets entirely to the player's own discretion, however, Ganassi does leave open the possibility of a move to a more equal temperament. Indeed, it is worth noting that his system of transposing music up a semitone or a tone by means of a *barré* fingering can only really work in a fairly equal temperament.

At the end of *Lettione Seconda* Ganassi returns to the subject of viol consort tunings and gives tunings for viols with only four or three strings. A consort of four-string viols is to be tuned as follows:

| | | | |
|---|---|---|---|
| a′ | e′ | b | g |
| d′ | a | e | c |
| g | d | A | F |

If the instruments of the consort are of an unsuitable size for this disposition, the reader is referred back to the discussion of Gombert's method of transposition in *Regola Rubertina*. For three-string viols Ganassi recommends a completely different approach; the whole consort is to be tuned in fifths throughout:

| | | |
|---|---|---|
| a′ | d′ | g |
| d′ | g | c |
| g | c | F |

This is the tuning used by players of the 'viola da brazo senza tasti' (the violin). Since all the strings are tuned a fifth apart, a different system of fingering is needed, and Ganassi illustrates this by supplying the scales in the tuning charts with fingering marks. The fourth finger is used to a much greater extent and becomes a vital part of basic fingering technique rather than a refinement for use in avoiding awkward string crossings. The one example of three consecutive whole tone steps on a single string (*F–G–A–B* in the first tuning scale for bass viol) is given the curious fingering 0–1–3–4.

The overriding impression given by *Regola Rubertina* is that a considerable variety of tuning systems were current in the mid 16th century. Moreover, even Ganassi's extensive treatment of the subject is not completely comprehensive; he does not, for example, mention the French 16th-century consort tuning system, five-string viols tuned in fourths throughout (see Chapter 13). Towards the end of the 16th century there was a growing consensus in favour of the high *d–g–d* or *d–a–d* and the low *a–d–a* or *g–d–g* consort tunings, yet a glance at Praetorius's tuning charts will confirm that even in the early 17th century a large number of variant tunings were still considered worth recording.

# 9

## Viol-playing techniques in 16th-century Italy

The mid 16th century in Italy may fairly be described as the first Golden Age of virtuoso viol playing. The growing perfection of the viol at the hands of Italian craftsmen was matched by the appearance of performers of outstanding ability. These Italian virtuosi were responsible for the advancement of viol playing techniques to a standard of perfection hitherto unknown. Indeed, many of the techniques perfected at this period remained in use throughout the viol's history and have been revived in the present century.

Although one or two prominent viol players from the early years of the 16th century are known by name – on 26 July 1513, for example, the celebrated Jewish lutenist Zoanne Maria is reported to have directed a concert of viols ('la musica di violoni') for Leo X which lasted a long time ('la qual durò molto')[1] – it is not until the 1530s and 1540s that large numbers of named Italian virtuoso violists appear on the scene. In the second volume of his viol tutor (1543) Ganassi commends six players for their talents: he seeks the approbation of two worthy players ('duoi Valenti') Iuliano Tiburtino and Lodovico Lasagnino; and four violists, Alfonso da Ferrara, Ioanbattista Cicilian, Francesco da Milano and Rubertino Mantoano, are praised for their skill at playing in high positions above the frets ('alla estremita del manico'). The following year Doni mentions others, Giovaniacopo Buzzino and Matteo Romano, the former for his graceful playing of divisions on the soprano 'violone' (presumably a treble viol).[2]

Travelling groups of Italian violists also played a very important part in the dissemination of the viol throughout Europe at this period. A consort of six Italians (possibly Jews of Iberian origin, see Chapter 14) were employed at the court of Henry VIII from 1540 as viol players: Alberto da Venezia, Vincenzo da Venezia, Alexander da Milano, Ambroso da Milano, Romano da Milano and Joan Maria da Cremona. In 1543 'six Italians with their *vihuelas de arco*' ('seys ytalianos con sus biguelas de arco') in the employ of the Duke of Medina Sidonia took part in the celebrations attending the arrival of the Portuguese princess in Castille for her marriage.[3] Another band of Italian violists were reported in Antwerp in 1545 seeking employment in England (see Chapter 14).

The excellent reputation enjoyed by the best of this new generation of viol players did not pass unrecorded by contemporary artists, and a number of portraits of viol players have survived from the 1530s and 1540s.[4] A portrait attributed to Parmigianino shows a young musician playing a tenor viol in the horizontal position condemned by Ganassi in 1542.[5] A portrait of a viol player by Zacchia shows a musician pointing to his instrument which is lying on a table nearby (Plate 82). Of especial interest is the portrait of a viol player by Domenico Brusasorzi in the Museo Civico, Verona. Brusasorzi depicts a musician holding a bow; his viol stands behind him against a curtain which is partly drawn aside to reveal a viol consort seated round a table making music. At least one portrait of a viol player has perished. As has been noted, Vasari informs us that Battista Ciciliano, an excellent player of the violone ('eccelente sonatore di violone') was painted by Titian's son Orazio in 1547.[6]

From the point of view of the 20th-century historian of the viol, the most significant member of this new generation of viol players was Sylvestro di Ganassi. His two-volume tutor *Regola Rubertina*, to which I have already referred, presents an exceptionally detailed and thorough examination of almost all aspects of viol playing. It far exceeds all other 16th-century instrumental tutors in the breadth and depth of its coverage and is thus our primary source of information about the viol-playing techniques of the mid 16th-century Italian virtuosi.

*Regola Rubertina* begins with a chapter devoted to the playing position of the viol, an aspect of performance about which Ganassi held strong views. The viol, he writes, should be held between the knees quite firmly so that it will not fall if the left hand is withdrawn, and so that the bow can be drawn across the strings without being impeded by the knees. The viol itself should slope a little to one side ('tenirla che la penda un puoco da la banda stanca'). The title-page woodcut of *Regola Rubertina* clearly demonstrates the direction of this slope; the gentleman violist in the centre holds his viol slanting over his left shoulder (Plate 93). The player should be seated upright ('dritta') yet not in too rigid a fashion ('de maniera sforzata'). He should not need to move his body but should be able to move the neck of the instrument away from or back towards his chest with a free arm and a graceful hand ('con il braccio pronto & la mano leggiadra'). In his discussion of posture Ganassi's main concern is the development of a graceful deportment and, in his view, the individual movements of the arms, hands and legs all contribute to the poise of the body. He therefore warns the viol player not to make any 'Moorish gesture' ('atto di moresca'). Italian readers of Ganassi's day would no doubt have recognised in this passage an allusion to the *moresca* or Moor's dance which was still quite often performed at that period. Contemporary representations of the dance usually emphasise its bizarre and grotesque character and the contorted gestures of the limbs of the participants. No hint of this outlandish deportment was to sully the viol player's posture! Completely convinced of the merits of his own playing position, Ganassi concludes with some criticism of another method of holding the viol in vogue during his day. Playing the viol horizontally ('per traverso') cannot in his view be recommended, first because the player requires twice as much room, and secondly because it tends to prevent the player sitting in an upright posture and even leads to a humpbacked ('gobo') one.

Most viol players will recognise in Ganassi's remarks the playing position that is almost universally accepted today, and yet his derogatory comments about the horizontal method adopted by some of his contemporaries show that at least one alternative position was in use in the mid 16th century. This is corroborated by the only other mid 16th-century treatise to discuss the subject, Jambe de Fer's *Epitome Musical* (Lyons, 1556). In discussing the derivation of the term 'viola da gamba', Jambe de Fer briefly mentions three ways in which it was customary to hold viols: (i) between the legs; (ii) on some seat or stool; (iii) on the knees. The first option clearly refers to the standard playing position. The second – supporting a viol on a piece of furniture of convenient height – is self-explanatory.[7] The meaning of the third alternative is not made entirely clear, but playing the viol on the knees is very probably the horizontal method rejected out of hand by Ganassi. This method, observes Jambe de Fer, is very popular with the Italians but hardly ever used by the French. Confirmation of the popularity of the horizontal playing position with Italian violists of the mid 16th century comes from a number of pictorial sources, and from these it is apparent that the tenor viol was considered the size best suited to a horizontal grip. There are in fact three mid 16th-century depictions of viol consorts in which only tenor viols are held crossways.[8] In Paolo Veronese's celebrated *Marriage Feast at Cana* two scallop-shaped tenor viols are held in the slanting position while the huge contrabass viol is played resting on the ground. The angelic quartet of viols depicted by Aurelio Luini consists of three large viols held downwards and a smaller instrument held horizontally across the lap (Plate 95). Similarly, in Nicolò dell'Abate's picture of a domestic concert there is a tenor–bass viol duo in which only the smaller instrument is held crossways (Plate 94). Dart[9] and others have expressed the view that this slanting, guitar-like hold represents a legacy from the viol's plucked ancestor, the *vihuela de mano*, but this seems improbable, since the vertical *a gamba* playing position was almost invariably used by players of the viol's bowed ancestors, the Moorish *rabāb* and the *vihuela de arco* itself. Only in the 1540s and 1550s did the horizontal method gain a following. One possible explanation for its popularity at this period could be the fact that many lutenists were taking up the viol. For long-standing players of the lute, holding the tenor viol like a plucked instrument probably seemed very natural.

In his discussion of the bass *violon da braccio* Jambe de Fer mentions a small device by which players could support the weight of the instrument while standing up. This consisted of a small hook worn by the player which could be fitted into an iron ring attached to the back of the instrument. The weight of

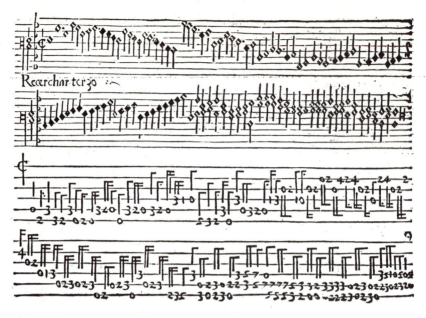

92   *Recerchar terzo*
(woodcut from S. di Ganassi: *Regola Rubertina*, Venice, 1542)

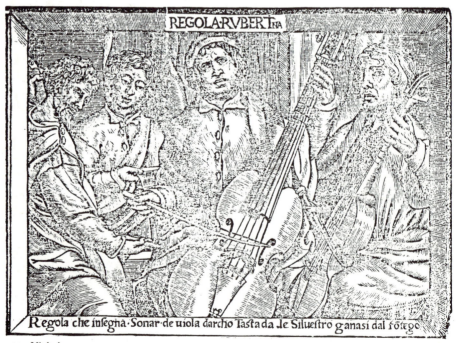

93   Viol players
(title-page woodcut from S. di Ganassi: *Regola Rubertina*, Venice, 1542)

94   *The Concert*
(mid 16th century, Nicolò dell'Abate: Estense Gallery, Modena)

96   Angelic viol quartet
(mid 16th century, attributed to G. Francia: Bologna)

95   Angelic viol quartet
(mid 16th century, Aurelio Luini: S. Maurizio, Milan)

the instrument would be supported by the hook leaving the player free to move about while playing. Some such device may have been used by bass viol players if the occasion required. There are certainly many 16th-century pictures of standing viol players performing with their instrument apparently unsupported.[10]

Chapter 4 of *Regola Rubertina* is the first of several devoted to the art of bowing. The viol bow, writes Ganassi, should be held by the thumb, index and middle fingers. More specifically, it should be gripped between the thumb and middle finger, while the index finger supplies sufficient pressure to ensure that it remains on the string in the position chosen by the player. This grip, it should be noted, is slightly different from the one advocated by the 17-century English authority Christopher Simpson and generally used today. In the *Division Violist* (1659) Simpson writes thus: 'Hold the Bow betwixt the ends of your Thumb and two foremost fingers, near to the Nut. The Thumb and first finger fastned on the Stalk; and the second fingers end turned *in* shorter, against the Hairs thereof; by which you may poize and keep up the point of the Bow.' To be of practical use, any underhand bow grip must do two things; it must support the bow from underneath to prevent it from falling and it must apply pressure from above so that the bow grips the strings. In Simpson's method the thumb and forefinger support the bow while the middle finger (and the ring finger if necessary) put pressure on the *hairs* of the bow, but in Ganassi's method it is the thumb and middle finger that support the bow while the index finger applies pressure to the *stick* of the bow. The art of underhand bowing was one of great antiquity and both the aforementioned grips were known to medieval Europe.[11] No great significance can thus be attached to Ganassi's own particular preference. The title-page woodcut of *Regola Rubertina* (Plate 93) clarifies one further point not discussed in the text; the players are shown gripping their bows at the nut. The fashion for holding the bow well down the stick away from the frog grew up much later in the 17th century, partly as a result of longer bows.[12]

Having described his method of gripping the bow, Ganassi then proceeds to discuss the bowing action. The bow should be drawn across the strings at a right angle, about four fingers breadth from the bridge, depending on the size of the instrument. The bow-stroke itself should be made 'with a free arm and a graceful and steady hand' ('con lo braccio pronto e mano leggiadra e firma') so that the sound is 'articulate and clean' ('spicata e netta'). If the bow is drawn too close to the fingerboard the sound will not be firm enough, but if, on the other hand, it is drawn too close to the bridge, the sound will be 'rough' ('cruda'). The middle way is therefore to be recommended, although should the music itself require a sad or a harsh tone quality, the bow may be moved in the appropriate direction. In Chapter 6 Ganassi discusses the various types of bow stroke appropriate for different note lengths. Note values such as the long, the breve, the semibreve and the minim are to be played with a single stroke of the bow from the arm; this should produce 'a splendid tone' ('uno sonar soperbo'). Shorter note values are better played with the wrist. Concerning the choice of up- or down-bows (in the present study 'up-bow' is always used to denote a forwards or pushed bowstroke, 'down-bow', a backwards or pulled bowstroke), Ganassi states that passages of short notes should be started with an up-bow. Yet he advises the reader to practise both ways. Using the analogy of a sword-fighter who has injured his right hand and must henceforth rely exclusively on his left, Ganassi points out that certain types of ornaments containing uneven numbers of notes (gropetti') sometimes have to be started with a down-bow, especially if they are repeated several times in quick succession. At this point in his treatise Ganassi moves on to a different topic, leaving the discussion of the use of up- and down-bows in a rather inconclusive state. However, in *Lettione Seconda* he returns to the subject and even includes some musical illustrations with the bowing marked in. These provide a very useful test of the validity of his sometimes garbled verbal instructions. Ganassi's system of notating the direction of the bow stroke is a simple one: a dot underneath a tablature symbol indicates a down-bow, the absence of a dot an up-bow. Unfortunately, this system leaves plenty of room for error; a dot is a very easy symbol for a printer to forget – there are in fact several bars in which the dots appear to have been omitted by accident – and conversely a single spurious blob of ink in the wrong place can easily wreck the sense of an entire passage.

Four ricercars are supplied with bowing marks and these divide neatly into two groups; two feature fast-moving passagework, runs and cadential divisions; two exploit the potential of the viol as a chordal instrument. The two solo voice pieces illustrate Ganassi's bowing method for virtuoso passagework; even-numbered groups of fast notes are started with an up-bow and are fully bowed out with alternating up- and down-bows. Sometimes two consecutive up- or down-bows have to be taken so that an ensuing passage of fast notes can be started with an up-bow, as in Example 6. In Chapter 15 of *Lettione Seconda*

Ex. 6     Three measures from the *Recercar Primo* for bass viol (*Lettione Seconda*, 1543, Chapter 20)

Ganassi explains how to do this. The bow should not be lifted from the strings, but the player should stress ('calcare') the second note a little. So two bow strokes in one direction do not (in Ganassi's notation) imply a true legato; both notes are to be articulated. On this subject Ganassi differs from his contemporary Diego Ortiz. In his *Trattado de glosas sobre clausulas* (1553) Ortiz implies that there are sometimes groups of two or three semiminims in which only the first note is articulated, the others not being marked by the bowing hand, or in modern terminology 'slurred' ('quando ay dos o tres semiminimas en una regla que no se nonbre sino la primera y las otras pasen sin herir la mano del arquillo'). In Chapter 18 Ganassi states that it is not possible to take two consecutive up- or down-bows during fast passages and for most of the time he follows his own advice. In his discussion of fingering, however, he gives a scale with five different fingerings; the first four are bowed conventionally starting with an up-bow and alternating throughout, but in the fifth version two consecutive down-bows are taken at the same point in both the ascending and the descending scales (see Example 7). The effect of this exceptional procedure is to place the accented bow strokes off the beat.

Ex. 7     A scale with five different fingerings for bass viol (*Lettione Seconda*, 1543, Chapter 17)

Unlike the solo ricercars which are bowed fairly consistently according to the principles outlined in the text, the chordal ricercars and the accompanied madrigal are bowed with considerable freedom. As Ganassi points out, his viol accompaniment to the madrigal 'Io vorei Dio d'amore' is an imitation of the style of playing associated with the *lira da braccio*. Realising that the chordal style is not ideally suited to the viol, Ganassi recommends several modifications to the instrument. He suggests using a longer bow than normal with slacker hair and fitting the viol itself with a bridge and fingerboard less highly arched than usual, all this to help the player execute chords with greater freedom. Though he does not mention the matter in the text, Ganassi also seems to expect the viol player to emulate the bowing technique of the *lira da braccio*. All three chordal pieces in *Lettione Seconda* begin with a down-bow, the stressed bow stroke of instruments played *a braccio* like the *lira*. This attempt to copy the style of bowing associated with the *lira da braccio* may account for the fact that these chordal pieces are bowed so inconsistently. Substantial sections of the viol accompaniment to the madrigal are, when repeated, bowed back to front.

This should not be taken as evidence of a somewhat cavalier attitude to bow-ing in general, for Ganassi, notwithstanding the obscurity and imprecision of some of his writing, was something of a pedant at heart, but it does indicate that he had not fully worked out the implications of adapting the *lira*'s chordal style to the viol.

In Chapter 5 of *Regola Rubertina* Ganassi briefly outlines his basic method of left-hand fingering. He recommends that the first finger be placed on the second fret, the second finger on the third fret, and so on.[13] In *Lettione Seconda* he returns to the subject in much more detail, and in this part of his treatise the musical examples are supplied with fingering marks. The symbols devised by Ganassi to denote fingering are as follows: a dot to the upper left for the first finger; a dot to the lower left for the second finger; a dot to the upper right for the third finger; a dot to the lower right for the fourth finger. This system of notation, albeit somewhat confusing in practice, is invaluable to the historian of the viol for the amount of detailed information that it presents about mid 16th-century fingering techniques.

Ganassi begins his discussion of advanced fingering techniques in Chapter 17 of *Lettione Seconda* in which a simple scale of a ninth is supplied with five different fingering patterns (Example 7). The first of these is the conventional fingering which involves a single change of position on the top string. The second is designed to allow the player to change position while playing an open string. The first three notes of the scale are played on the *a* string followed by an open *d'* string, which gives the player time to move his left hand up ready to resume the scale with an *e'* on the *a* string. Ganassi could have used a fourth finger on the *a* string for the *d'* and moved directly into a higher position, but he preferred to reserve the fourth finger for the highest note in any given pas-sage. The third fingering pattern is identical to the second in the ascending scale, but makes use of a high position on the *e* string for the descending scale. The fourth and fifth alternatives illustrate how by using a higher position with the first finger on the fifth or seventh fret, the whole scale can be played in one position. In some of his solo ricercars Ganassi ascends even higher than he does in this scale. A passage towards the end of the first ricercar in Chapter 20 of *Lettione Seconda* illustrates how high passages are to be fingered (Example 8). The first change of position occurs while the open *d'* string is being played; the second is effected by means of a direct shift with the first finger. Once the first finger has been established on the high *b'*, Ganassi makes use of all four fingers in the final cadential flourish, a method not practicable in a lower position because of the wider stretches that this would entail. A comparable passage in the other ricercar, one tone lower, does not employ all four fingers in succes-sion (Example 9), which suggests that Ganassi considered a major sixth with the first finger above the open string the lowest place in which all four fingers could be used consecutively in a diatonic scale.

At the other end of the fingerboard, Ganassi is well aware of the possibilities

Ex. 8      Five measures from the *Recercar Primo* for bass viol (*Lettione Seconda*, 1543, Chapter 20)

Ex. 9      Four measures from the *Recercar Secondo* 'a sola voce' for bass viol (*Lettione Seconda*, 1543, Chapter 20)

of half position. In *Lettione Seconda* (Chapter 22) he gives a tuning for a consort of four-string viols, and the scales with which he demonstrates this tuning are fingered in half position. In each case, half position is maintained until the top string is reached when the first finger is shifted up to the second fret. Half position is also sometimes introduced into the solo ricercars and the accompanied madrigal to improve the fingering. In Example 10 the musical sense of the passage is clarified by staying in half position for the first *d*.

On the important topic of string crossings Ganassi advises the viol player to avoid unnecessary movement from one string to another during fast passage-work. To illustrate this point he gives several standard cadential trills with both the correct and the incorrect fingering (Example 11).

An alternative method of fingering described by Ganassi in Chapter 20 of *Lettione Seconda* involves the use of a *barré*, that is, one finger laid flat across several strings. Ganassi indicates this with a vertical line, the length of which shows the number of strings over which the *barré* is to extend. One practical application of the *barré* is in transposing music at sight. By laying the first finger flat across several strings in the manner of a *capo tasto*, the player can transpose any given piece of music up a semitone or a tone. This necessitates the use of the extended position in which two consecutive whole-tone steps are fingered 1–2–4, the second finger being placed a semitone higher than usual.

Ex. 10    Two measures from the bass viol accompaniment to the madrigal 'Io vorei Dio d'amore' (*Lettione Seconda*, 1543, Chapter 16)

Ex. 11    Two cadential trills for bass viol with incorrect and correct fingerings (*Lettione Seconda*, 1543, Chapter 19)

Ex. 12    A scale of *e* flat minor for bass viol using a *barré* fingering (*Lettione Seconda*, 1543, Chapter 20)

Ex. 13    Two parallel thirds with fingerings for bass viol from the *Recercar Primo* (*Lettione Seconda*, 1543, Chapter 15)

Ex. 14    A three-part chord with a fingering for bass viol from the accompaniment to the madrigal 'Io vorei Dio d'amore' (*Lettione Seconda*, 1543, Chapter 16)

Ganassi gives two examples of the *barré* fingering; in each case the *barré* is terminated before the final cadential flourish, which is played in a higher position to avoid string crossings (Example 12).

The double-stopping used by Ganassi in several of his musical examples is fingered in a fairly conventional way. Two general points are worth noting; parallel thirds are quite often fingered with a change of position (Example 13); and three-part chords often make use of a *barré* fingering (Example 14). In an article on Ganassi's fingering techniques I included a summary of the various left-hand techniques advocated in *Lettione Seconda*.[14] For the convenience of the reader a slightly revised version of this resumé is given below:

i     *shifting position*
a     To move into a position a semitone or a tone higher, two consecutive notes may be played with the first finger: 1–1–2–4 or 1–1–3–4.
b     To move into a position a third higher, change after using the second or third finger: 0–1–2–1 or 0–1–3–1.
c     Avoid shifting into a higher position directly after using a fourth finger.
ii     *string crossings*
    Avoid rapid string crossings in fast passagework by using a higher position on a lower string.
iii     *playing above the frets*
    In very fast high passages more than a major sixth above the open strings, all four fingers may be used consecutively in a diatonic scale.
iv     *half position*
    Half position may be used if it simplifies the fingering of any given passage or if it makes better musical sense.
v     *extended positions*
    Extended positions (two consecutive whole-tone steps fingered 1–2–4) are especially useful when transposing music up a semitone or a tone (without retuning the viol) by means of a first-finger *barré*.
vi     *double-stopping*
    Consecutive thirds may be played by means of simple position changes:
    1–1      1–1      1–1      1–1
    2–2      2–3      3–3      3–2     (see Example 13).
vii     *three-part chords*
    For three-part chords a *barré* fingering may be used.

For Ganassi, all playing techniques, no matter how advanced, were simply a means to a musical end. Throughout both volumes of his tutor he constantly reiterates the view that the supreme goal of the viol player is not so much the acquisition of a fluent technique *per se*, but the ability to make use of technical facility in achieving an artistically satisfying musical performance. Nowhere is this belief stated more clearly than in the opening chapters of *Regola Rubertina*, where Ganassi stresses the importance of the visual element of performance. To achieve the perfect performance – one that commands the silence of an audience – the viol player must delight his viewers with the beauty of his deportment and the grace of his movements at least as much as he must impress his listeners with his technical skills and move them with the eloquence of his playing. A performance will be marred if either element is lacking. This belief explains Ganassi's insistence on correct posture and his abhorrence of anything ungraceful such as the humpbacked slouch or the grotesque attitudes of the *moresca* dancer. And Ganassi was certainly not alone in his concern with posture. In a letter on the art of singing (1562) Maffei urges singers not to make unnecessary movements with their hands and feet while singing; these are considered ugly ('brutti').[15] Yet the preoccupation with visual gracefulness could be taken to a ridiculous extreme, as becomes clear from an amusing little anecdote recounted by Doni in his *Dialogo della musica* (1544):

> M. Giovaniacopo Buzzino was playing the soprano *violone*, as he does so marvellously, when some nobody came up to him in the midst of his performance to say 'O Signore, move your fingers a bit more slowly; it looks so ugly to see you move your fingers so much on the neck of the instrument.' Buzzino, accommodating himself to this bit of insolence, began to play without diminutions, whereupon the poor dolt, hearing the melody so lacking in grace, shamefacedly asked him to start moving his fingers again.[16]

In the second chapter of *Regola Rubertina*, Ganassi explains further why the physical movements of the viol player are so important. Apart from the purely aesthetic pleasure to be gained from graceful playing, the movements of the viol player's body also help to express the emotions of the music. Just as an orator chooses those exclamations, gestures and tones which best suit the subject matter of his speech, so the viol player should regulate the movements of his body in accordance with the mood of the music. An orator would not dream of laughing during a sad tale; nor should a viol player use movements appropriate for a sad passage during a lively piece. It is worth emphasising again that when Ganassi writes of body movements, he expressly includes those parts of the body not directly involved in playing a viol such as the head and neck. This is not to say that he neglects the expressive possibilities of the more technical aspects of viol playing, bowing and fingering. Indeed, Ganassi is very conscious of the different tone qualities that result from different types of bowing. The bow, he writes, can be drawn loudly, softly or at an intermediate dynamic. For music that is sad, it should be drawn lightly, and to create a suitable effect for music that is especially 'sad and afflicted' ('mesta e afflitta') both the bowing arm and the left hand may be made to shake ('tremar'). While his precise meaning is not clear, Ganassi seems here to be referring to the effects now known as tremolando and vibrato, both, be it noted, to be used as a special plangent effect, not as an integral part of normal tone-production. Apart from the brief allusion to vibrato, Ganassi has little to say about the expressive uses of the left hand. Yet his musical examples demonstrate a readiness to make use of higher positions, not for technical reasons, but to exploit a different tone quality. One example will suffice from the first of the two chordal ricercars in *Lettione Seconda*. The sudden move to the

Ex. 15       The opening of the *Recercar Primo* with fingerings for bass viol (*Lettione Seconda*, 1543, Chapter 15)

higher position in bar 4 (Example 15) can only be for tonal reasons, as it could
be played perfectly well in first position.

The message from Ganassi's tutor is clear: a proficient technique by itself
was not enough for mid 16th-century audiences. Expressive and varied playing was all-important, and technical facility was of use only in so far as it contributed to this end. To Ganassi, a viol consort ploughing through piece after
piece in first position with no variation in dynamics, tone colour or style of
bowing would have sounded like a storyteller reciting an exciting adventure in
a deadpan monotone.

# 10

## Music for solo viol in 16th-century Italy

The development of advanced playing techniques by Italian virtuosi of the mid 16th century stimulated the growth of music for solo viol. In their search for an idiomatic mode of composition suited to the viol as a solo instrument, Italian musicians explored two contrasting styles: virtuoso division playing and chordal writing. The first of these exploited the viol's agility, clarity of articulation and wide range and, in its early stages at least, owed much to contemporary lute music. The second probably stemmed from a desire to emulate the more inspired efforts of Italian *lira* players.

The need to provide viol players with compositions suitable for exercising and extending their techniques was an important factor in the emergence of this solo repertory. The most direct response to this need was the technical exercise, a form of composition in which practical utility, not artistic merit, was the chief goal. The first published exercise of this type appears in *Regola Rubertina*. To help bass viol players who use the 'quarta regola' familiarise themselves with the position of the notes on the neck of the instrument, Ganassi prints an exercise which he entitles 'Modo del pratichar il manicho' (Plate 91). The first half of this lesson comprises three hexachords, each followed by a short series of scales outlining the intervals of a third, fourth, fifth and sixth. These preliminary hexachords are followed by a somewhat haphazard study in leaps ('salti') intended to make the violist more fluent in his playing ('piu abile al sonar'). A more extensive set of exercises appears at the end of a treatise published in Basle in 1589 entitled *Porta Musices*. The author, Samuel Mareschall, discusses singing, the modes and viol tunings (see Chapter 13). The last part of the work is devoted to a sequence of lessons for practising the intervals most frequently encountered in 16th-century polyphony, starting with simple scales and working up to the perfect fifth (Example 16). Further exercises deal with rests and there are one or two quite tricky studies in cross-rhythms (Example 17).

The dividing line between purely technical exercises of this kind and the didactic solo ricercar was sometimes a fine one. In *Lettione Seconda* there are two pairs of ricercars which Ganassi undoubtedly intended as technical studies. The two ricercars 'a sola voce' are exercises in playing diminutions,

Ex. 16        Four exercises ('Übung für die Jugent') (*Porta Musices*, 1589, 26-27)

Ex. 17        Two exercises in rhythm (*Porta Musices*, 1589, 28-29)

which aim to test the agility of the bowing hand ('la agelita del manizo de l'archeto') and the fluency of the left hand in high positions up to the end of the fingerboard ('alla estremita del manico della Viola'). Both pieces consist, in the main, of running scale passages interspersed with cadential turns using the full three-octave compass of the viol (Example 18). The other pair of ricercars which appear at the end of Chapter 15 are studies in the chordal style. Ganassi restricts himself to two-part chords with the occasional three-part chord at cadences (Example 19). The two-part writing – counterpoint is too strong a term – is rudimentary, but, to be fair to Ganassi, he does not claim artistic merit for these pieces and indeed is at pains to comment on their practical application – as an aid to adjusting the frets and tuning the strings.

Musically more advanced than these studies in technique are the four ricercars in *Regola Rubertina*, which show Ganassi trying to solve the problem of how to integrate the two contrasting, yet equally idiomatic, styles of solo viol playing into a satisfactory musical whole. The first three pieces of the group each follow a similar pattern: a point of imitation is briefly tossed around; this quickly gives way to running scale passages; a series of chords provides a sonorous conclusion (Example 20). The result, a curious mixture of imitative

Ex. 18    *Recercar Secondo 'a sola voce' (Lettione Seconda,* 1543, Chapter 20)

Ex. 19    *Recercar Secondo (Lettione Seconda,* 1543, Chapter 15)

ricercar and rhapsodical prelude, is lightweight but not unattractive. The very
brevity of these pieces enables Ganassi to avoid one difficulty – how to adapt
the essentially imitative style of the ricercar to a solo melody instrument.
Ortiz, on the other hand, confronts this problem head-on in his *Trattado de
glosas*. Rejecting the chordal possibilities of the viol, he concentrates instead,
in his four ricercars for solo viol, on a much more densely imitative style
(Example 21). In the absence of any contrapuntal interest, however, the points
of imitation tend to become repetitive, and his only escape is into florid passagework. These solo pieces are on the whole the least successful compositions
in Ortiz's otherwise excellent compilation, and Ganassi's single attempt at a
more extended, discursive ricercar (the 'rechercar quarto') must likewise be
adjudged a failure, since he too is unable to control the number of repetitions
of any given point. Francesco Rognoni in *Selva di varii passaggi* (Milan, 1620)
makes precisely this point when discussing the *viola bastarda*, stating that it is
best to restrict the number of repetitions of a point of imitation to six or seven

Ex. 20    *Recerchar Secondo* (*Regola Rubertina*, 1542, Chapter 20)

Ex. 21    The opening measures of *Recercada tercera* for bass viol (*Trattado de glosas*, 1553, *Libro Segundo*)

to avoid tedium ('mà bisogna auertire, che le imitationi non habbino più di sei, ò sette riposte al più perche farebbe poi tedioso'). Yet leaving their musical merits aside, these early pieces for solo viol are true 'ricercars' in the strict sense of the term, ricercar meaning literally a 'seeking out' or 'discovery'. Using these pieces, the player is afforded the opportunity to 'run over' the instrument, loosening the fingers and checking the placing of the frets and the tuning of the strings, before embarking upon material of greater musical substance.

Apart from the four ricercars for solo viol, the whole of the second part of *Trattado de glosas* is devoted to the art of playing solo viol with keyboard accompaniment, a combination for which no other 16th-century writer published any music. There are, Ortiz writes, three ways in which a viol can play with a keyboard: free improvisation ('fantasia'); using a cantus firmus ('sobre canto llano'); using a polyphonic composition ('sobre compostura'). To perform a free improvisation the keyboard player should begin with 'well-ordered harmonies' ('consonancias bien ordenadas') and then the viol player should enter with 'graceful passagework' ('algunos pasos galanos'). When the viol plays an unornamented line, the keyboard player should respond, and in this way improvised counterpoint can be performed, the one instrument waiting for the other. Ortiz does not illustrate this type of improvisation, pointing out that each individual performs in his own style.

The second type of viol–keyboard duet makes use of a cantus firmus. To illustrate this style, Ortiz prints six ricercars, all of which are based on the 'La Spagna' melody, a time-honoured cantus firmus for *basse danse* improvisations. The tune appears in the bass clef, and the keyboard player is expected to improvise a harmonization and also some counterpoint to fit in with the viol. In the style of the written-out examples provided by Ortiz, this latter task would not be an easy one, since the viol 'improvises' over the 'La Spagna' melody in a fairly concentrated fashion, leaving little room for retorts by the keyboard player. These pieces are more successful than the solo ricercars; the cantus firmus provides a framework for the 'improvisation' and also acts as a foil to the syncopation of the solo instrument.

Ortiz includes further examples of this style at the end of his treatise, using not the 'La Spagna' cantus firmus but a selection of Italian 'tenors' such as the *passamezzo antico*, the *passamezzo moderno*, the *romanesca* and the *folia*. Four-part harmonizations for the keyboard player are given, although, as Ortiz himself notes, they would work perfectly well with just the bass line (presumably as duets for two bass viols). The ostinato bass patterns provide a much tighter structural framework than the 'La Spagna' cantus firmus, and Ortiz avoids the sterility of so many 16th-century sets of variations by ensuring that the 'improvising' viol is not in any way tied down by the rigid structure of its support. The solo viol moves with great freedom and rhythmic vitality from one figuration to another, and Ortiz is particularly adept at introducing a new idea in the viol part just before the repetition of the bass to conceal the join between the sections. Sometimes a new motif appears in the middle of a section and this can serve to highlight very effectively a chord in the middle of the pattern. Running passagework, which so often bedevils compositions of this type, is kept within strictly controlled limits, and yet is used with all the more telling effect to build up climaxes (Example 22). All in all, these ricercars form a delightful set of pieces and well deserve their popularity with present-day viol players.

Introducing his third way of playing a viol with a keyboard, Ortiz instructs his readers to take 'a madrigal, motet or any other work', arrange it in the usual manner for keyboard and then perform the piece up to three or more times with the viol adding each time a new embellishment. To illustrate the various methods of ornamentation open to the viol player, Ortiz supplies four complete versions of a madrigal (Arcadelt's 'O felici occhi miei') and four of a chanson (Sandrin's 'Doulce memoire'). The four methods are as follows:

  i    the bass line ornamented by a bass viol
  ii   the treble line ornamented by a treble viol
  iii  the bass line ornamented in a more virtuoso style by a bass viol
  iv   a completely new fifth voice added by a bass viol.

Ex. 22    The closing measures of *Recercada segunda* for bass viol and keyboard (*Trattado de glosas*, 1553, *Libro Segundo*)

To facilitate comparison, the opening measures of 'O felici occhi miei' are given in Example 23 with the four different embellishments. In these chanson and madrigal arrangements, for the first time, the developing solo viol idiom produces music of real artistic merit. The keyboard player performs a transcription of a piece of polyphony, and the viol player adds grace to what is already perfect, gilding the lily, 'delighting', as Ortiz himself puts it, 'the listeners with the different sound of the strings'. Ortiz shows himself to be an arranger of considerable skill. He treats his solo viol flexibly; it moves freely between the literal rendition of the original vocal line, ornamental passage-work usually of a fairly restrained character, and independent motivic development, this last 'adding a new dimension to the arrangement'.[1] Ortiz departs furthest from the original composition in his fourth method in which the viol adds a completely independent part. Needless to say, some skill in composition is necessary to bring this off effectively, but Ortiz is equal to the task. In demonstrating practically how to arrange vocal music for viol and keyboard, Ortiz opens up the considerable riches of 16th-century polyphony to the solo viol player. Any piece of four- or five-part polyphony, sacred or secular, can be arranged for viol and keyboard following his guidelines. Indeed, given the shortage of 16th-century music for solo viol, it is rather surprising that there have been so few attempts to enlarge the repertory with pastiches of his style.

Ex. 23    The opening measures of the madrigal 'O felici occhi miei' with four embellishments for: (i) bass viol (ii) treble viol (iii) bass viol (iv) bass viol (*Trattado de glosas*, 1553, *Libro Segundo*)

(Ex. 23 contd.)

The embellishment of vocal part music by a solo viol was not confined to the medium of the accompanied solo; it is also recorded in ensemble performances. A description of the *intermedii* performed during the wedding of Francesco de' Medici to Joanna of Austria in 1565 notes that one of the songs was accompanied by a band of instruments amongst which were two viols adding ornamental parts: 'sotto basso di viola aggiunto sopra le parti'; 'soprano di viola aggiunto anch'egli'.[2] As Brown points out, these added parts 'can only have been lines embellished so elaborately that they sounded like new ones, or else genuinely new obbligati, improvised in the manner described by Diego Ortiz'.[3]

Towards the end of the 16th century, the somewhat restrained style of embellishing vocal part-music adopted by Ortiz gave way to a much more elaborate virtuoso manner. A new term was coined for any viol playing the ornate soloistic divisions now in fashion – the 'viola bastarda'.[4] The instrument is twice named in the reports of the *intermedii* performed for the wedding of Ferdinand I and Christine of Lorraine in 1589: the second *intermedio* included a 'viola bastarda' and the fourth a 'basso di viola bastarda'.[5] Praetorius (1618) suggests that the term 'bastarda' derives, not from any physical feature of the instrument, but from an aspect of its musical style; in ornamenting part-music the *viola bastarda* is not tied to any one voice of the original composition, but migrates from one line to another over a very wide range, becoming, as it were, a 'bastard' of all the voices, embellishing now the soprano, now the tenor or alto, now the bass. Praetorius gives a series of *viola bastarda* tunings: $d'$ $a$ $e$ $c$ $G$ $D$; $d'$ $a$ $e$ $A$ $E$ $A'$; $d'$ $a$ $d$ $A$ $D$ $A'$; $d'$ $g$ $d$ $G$ $D$ $A'$; $d'$ $a$ $e$ $c$ $G$ $C$. The low A' is no mere formality; it is actually required in some *viola bastarda* music of the early 17th century. Concerning the size of the instrument, Praetorius comments that its body is a little longer and deeper than that of a 'tenor' viol. (In modern terminology Praetorius's 'tenor' viol is, of course, a bass viol.) The vogue for this large bass viol and its virtuoso repertory persisted well into the 17th century. Music for the instrument was published in the following works:

| | | |
|---|---|---|
| 1584 | Girolamo dalla Casa | *Il vero modo di diminuir* (Venice) |
| 1591 | Giovanni Bassano | *Motetti, madrigali et canzoni francese* (Venice)[6] |
| 1592 | Richardo Rogniono | *Passaggi per potersi essercitare nel diminuire terminatamente con ogni sorte d'istrumenti* (Venice) |
| 1620 | Francesco Rognoni | *Selva di varii passaggi* (Milan) |
| 1626 | Vincenzo Bonizzi | *Alcune opere di diversi auttori, a diversi voci, passagiate principalmente per la viola bastarda, ma anche per ogni sorte di stromenti, e di voci* (Venice)[7] |

A number of virtuoso *viola bastarda* players flourished around the turn of the century, of whom the best known was Orazio Bassani (Orazio della Viola). A few of his celebrated embellishments of madrigals have survived in manuscript sources; British Library Add. ms. 30491 contains two: 'Susanna di Oratio: per le Viola bastarda', and 'Cara la vita mia, per Viola bastarda passaggiate da Oratio della Viola'.[8] The *viola bastarda* style is perhaps best summed up by Praetorius: 'a good player can set himself to play madrigals, or whatever else he likes, on this instrument: with great effort, he can produce the harmony and counterpoint of all the parts, playing now up in the cantus, now down in the bass, now in the middle on tenor and alto, and decorating the whole piece with divisions – thus nearly all the parts can be distinctly heard at entries and cadences.'[9] A short extract from Bonizzi's embellishment of Sandrin's 'Doulce memoire' illustrates the very florid character of *viola bastarda* writing, the wide compass required of the instrument (over three octaves) and the manner in which the solo ornamentation moves freely through the various voices of the polyphonic original (Example 24).[10]

Another repertory of music played by solo viol players of the mid 16th century was the accompanied song. For this, Italian composers made full use

Ex. 24    An extract from the embellishment of the chanson 'Doulce memoire' by Vincenzo Bonizzi
          (1626) for *viola bastarda*

Ex. 25    The opening measures of the madrigal 'Io vorei Dio d'amore' for tenor with bass viol accompaniment (*Lettione Seconda*, 1543, Chapter 16)

of the chordal possibilities of the viol, taking as their model the *lira da braccio*, the instrument favoured by *improvvisatori*. Ganassi is our only significant source of information about this practice, for, in addition to the two chordal exercises in *Lettione Seconda*, he prints a madrigal for voice and solo viol, 'Io vorei Dio d'amore'. Introducing the piece, he adopts a somewhat defensive tone and comments on the physical limitations of the viol in this kind of arrangement. Since the viol is restricted to chords formed from adjacent strings, the arranger must compromise; some notes perforce will have to be omitted, others included unnecessarily. Ganassi specifically states that 'Io vorei Dio d'amore' is an imitation of the style of playing associated with the *lira da braccio* and the similarities are obvious. There is one important difference, however. Whereas *lira* players are known to have declaimed to the bass line, improvising the harmony above,[11] the deeper-pitched bass viol plays the lower parts with the vocal line on top. Ganassi manages his accompaniment quite skilfully, preserving points of imitation where possible, yet keeping the texture simple (Example 25). No other mid 16th-century viol accompaniments have survived, but independent confirmation of the practice comes from a report of one of the *intermedii* performed at the wedding of Cosimo I and Eleanor of Toledo in 1539. After the third act Silenus sings the song 'O begli anni del oro' while accompanying himself on a 'viol playing all the parts' ('violone sonando tutte le parti').[12]

In the latter part of the 16th century the continuing need for a low-pitched bowed instrument to perform chordal accompaniments led to the development of the *lirone*. The appearance of this specialist chord-playing instrument is perhaps indicative of the dissatisfaction felt by some (including Ganassi) with the viol in this rôle. As its name suggests, the *lirone* was conceived as a bass version of the *lira da braccio*. With its pair of drone strings, its nine to fourteen melody strings and its tuning of ascending fifths and descending fourths (see Ceretto, 1601: *G g c c' g d' a e' b f♯' c♯'*) the instrument was probably rather unmanageable, and yet it enjoyed a certain vogue. In the Florentine *intermedio* orchestra it may have been used as a form of continuo instrument.[13] Its first recorded appearance was in the *intermedii* performed for the wedding of Francesco de' Medici to Joanna of Austria.[14] Earlier occurrences of the term are almost certainly references to the viol, the words 'lire' and 'viole' and 'lironi' and 'violoni' being to some extent interchangeable in the first part of the 16th century.

The two styles of solo viol playing developed in mid 16th-century Italy enjoyed lasting popularity, largely as a result of their transmission to England and their subsequent adoption by 17th-century English composers. Mid 16th-century Italian instrumental treatises such as Ganassi's *Regola Rubertina* may have achieved a limited circulation in northern Europe. Mersenne was able to refer to a copy of the 'regle Rubertine' when compiling his *Harmonie Universelle* in 1636. And in England Ganassi's works were not unknown. *A Catalogue of Ancient and Modern Musick Books* (London, 17 December 1691) lists 'A Book that treats about Musick, by Silvester Ganussi'. Yet the direct influence of such works was probably minimal. Of much greater significance were the many Anglo-Italian contacts between composers and musicians around the turn of the century. It was thus the more highly refined solo styles of the early 17th century, associated with the *viola bastarda* and the *lirone*, that were to provide the main stimulus for the development of the distinctively English schools of solo viol writing and their instruments, the division viol and the lyra viol.

# 11

## The viol consort and its music in 16th-century Italy

Important though the development of a solo idiom was for the future of the instrument, the viol remained throughout the renaissance period quintessentially a consort instrument. Whether played alone, in concert with other instruments or as an accompaniment for voices, the viol consort had the distinction of being one of the most widely acceptable forms of music-making in Italian society, attractive to amateur and professional alike. It occupied an important position in many of the major spheres of Italian public life – courtly, civic and theatrical – and was in addition highly regarded as an instrument of private recreation. The rôle of the viol consort in 16th-century Italy thus deserves an examination, even though Italian composers, unlike their 17th-century English counterparts, did not progress very far in developing an idiomatic consort repertory.

The first clear statement of the viol consort's suitability for amateur musicians of good breeding comes in a well-known passage from the second book of Castiglione's *Il Libro del Cortegiano*. At one point in the discussion, Signor Gaspar Pallavicino asks what kinds of music should be performed by the courtier, and in reply Federico Fregoso lists the following: singing; singing to the accompaniment of the 'viola'; reciting to the accompaniment of the 'viola'; all keyboard instruments. 'No less delightful', he continues, 'is the music of four bowed viols, which is very sweet and artful' ('E nò meno diletta la musica delle quattro viole de arco, la qual' è soavissima & artificiosa'). As to when the courtier should engage in the pastime of music-making, the best time is when he finds himself among friends, without urgent business, and especially when ladies are present. In rating the music of the viol consort so highly, Fregoso was not simply stating a personal opinion. Other high-ranking noblemen of his day were taking up the viol, among whom may be numbered Alfonso d'Este and Piero Gonzaga (see Chapter 5). No doubt there were many others. As the century progressed, the viol consort took its place beside the vocal ensemble in private musical entertainments sponsored by affluent households. In a letter to the Marchese Malvicino of Piacenza appended to the *Dialogo della musica* (1544) Doni reports that 'the music made by viols at S. Guido dalla Porta's house is marvellous'. He continues: 'There is here a gentlewoman Polisena Pecorina . . . at her house I heard a concert of viols ['violoni'] and voices at which she played and sang with others.'[1] Private concerts at the home of Lodovico Felicini who died in 1536 were apparently even more elaborate. It is recorded that he delighted in the sound of musical instruments: 'liuti, violle, dolsemelle, ciavasembali, manacorde, organi, violunni, pifari, cornitti e multi altri istromenti e canturi'.[2]

Detailed evidence of the important place of the viol consort in amateur music-making may be gleaned from Turrini's study of the Verona Accademia Filarmonica.[3] From the year of its foundation (1543) the academy was in possession of several chests of viols. An inventory drawn up in 1543 lists: 'Una Cassa cum sette violoni' ('a chest with seven viols'); 'Due Casse depente cum cinque violonj' ('two painted chests with five viols').[4] Another inventory of this period lists a further chest of six viols.[5] By 1569 the academy owned no fewer than 5 sets of viols, one with seven instruments, two with six and two with five.[6] The supply of instruments and equipment was partly the responsibility of the professional musician employed by the academy. On 15 November 1548 Nasco, the current professional, was paid for 'ten viol bows' ('diese archeti da violla') brought from Venice.[7] Some instruments, however, were bequeathed to the academy by private individuals; a set of six viols, for example, was left by Zuane Severino. Day-to-day maintenance of the viols would also have been the responsibility of the professional player. A document concerning the duties of Francesco Portinaro, employed by the short-lived Accademia degli Elevati (1557–1560) in Padua, spells this out quite clearly: 'the superintendent is obliged to be present on all days when there is a meeting to sing and play and to keep the viols in order' ('Il Capelan sij obligato tutti gli giorni delle sessioni esser presente per cantar et sonar et a tenir le Viole in aconzo').[8]

Other items in the inventories of the Verona academy make very interesting reading. In 1543 was listed 'Uno libro da insegnar la regula deli violonj' ('an instruction book in the rule of the viols').[9] The identity of this volume is revealed in 1545: 'Regula rubertina per il sonar de viola coperto de Carton' ('the Rubertine Rule for playing the viol, covered with board').[10] It was for just such a public that Ganassi surely produced his tutor, and it is interesting to note how soon after its publication the academy were in possession of a copy. There are several references in the inventories of the academy to a round table for use 'in playing viols' ('per sonar con le viole').[11] This, in all probability, was the octagonal table (or one like it) depicted in Domenico Brusasorzi's painting of a musical academy in the Museo Civico, Verona – Brusasorzi was himself a member of the Verona Accademia Filarmonica. Around this table are grouped viol players reading from a set of oblong partbooks. Additional pieces of equipment are recorded in 1562: 'Tre tenaglie una de fero, et due de legno per acordar le viole' ('three grips, one of iron and two of wood, for tuning the viols').[12] These interesting items may have been intended to assist inexperienced players in coping with stiff pegs. In 1569 they are listed as 'keys for tuning the viols' ('Chiave per le viole d'acorda').[13] Viol strings were kept in one of two boxes ('due scatole, una per le corde della Viole').[14] With their chests of viols, their box of spare strings, their tuning keys, their specially designed table and their copy of *Regola Rubertina*, the academy evidently took viol playing very seriously, and, as lists of the academy's musical library show, they kept a substantial collection of part music, instrumental and vocal, upon which to draw. For practical tuition, members of the academy could no doubt turn to their professional musician or, in his absence, to the invaluable Ganassi.

Professional musicians, no less than cultivated amateurs, made much use of the consort of viols. Some individuals even possessed their own set of viols. When on 9 October 1518 the lutenist Giovanni Angelo Testagrossa wrote to Federigo Gonzaga from Casale Monferrato offering his services as a music teacher, he was able to list among his instruments 'five very good viols' ('cinque violoni bonissimi').[15] As in most European countries, wealthy courts often employed a professional consort on a regular basis. The Vatican, for example, seems to have maintained a consort of viols. In a letter of 26 July 1513 Alessandro Gabbioneta reports that after visiting His Holiness, there was 'a concert of viols given by Zoanne Maria the Jew which lasted a long time' ('et poi la musica di violoni che fece Zoanne Maria Judeo, la qual durò molto').[16] Then in a letter dated 23 May 1524 the Bolognese theorist Spataro mentions a performance of Willaert's celebrated 'duo', 'Quid non ebrietas'. The papal singers, he reports, attempted unsuccessfully to perform the piece. Next the 'violoni' tried and succeeded in reaching the end, 'ma non troppo bene'.[17] Two years later a concert in the Vatican given by Francesco da Milano consisted of 'music for two lutes and a viol' ('musica con dui liuti et uno violone').[18] For important banquets the professional Ferrarese viol players, along with many of their colleagues, were expected to provide incidental music.[19] During the thirteenth course of a banquet given by Ippolito d'Este II on 20 May 1529 five viols played. And during the fourth course of a banquet given by Ercole d'Este II on 24 January 1529 a composition by Alfonso della Viola was performed on 'cinque viuole da arco con uno rubecchino' with 'a viol called The Ogress as a bass' ('una viuola chiamata la orchessa per contrabasso') and many other instruments.[20] Performances by professional viol players are also recorded outdoors. In 1538 a procession was observed to include a cart full of men playing 'liuti, violoni, arpe e cornamuse'.[21]

In addition to their routine duties, the professional viol consort could also expect glamorous engagements at the spectacular *intermedio* performances mounted for special events such as marriages. The viol consort quickly established itself as an integral part of the musical force employed on these occasions. In 1506, in a letter to Isabella d'Este, Bernardino Prospero reported that the first *intermedio* at an entertainment had consisted of, among other instruments, 'lire grande sonate da octo persone' ('large liras [i.e. viols] played by eight people').[22] In 1513 a performance of Cardinal Bibbiena's *La Calandria* in Urbino concluded with 'the hidden music of four viols, and then four voices with viols who sang a stanza with a beautiful melody' ('una musica nascosa di quattro viole, e poi quattro voci con viole che cantorno una stanza con un bello aere di musica').[23]

Much information on the rôle of the viol consort in the Florentine *intermedio* orchestra throughout the 16th century is given by Brown in *Sixteenth-Century Instrumentation*. It seems that the basic Florentine consort consisted of four instruments, augmented on occasion by others. Usually the four-part viol consort performed as part of a larger grouping, combining or alternating with consorts of contrasting instruments, commonly trombones and transverse flutes. As in the concluding item of the Urbino performance of *La Calandria*, viols sometimes accompanied voices alone. In 1518, for example, sopranos sang to the sound of four 'violoni', and in 1568 a similar scoring – four sopranos with four bass viols ('bassi di violoni') – was apparently suggested by Duke Francesco de' Medici himself. As well as performing relatively simple consort parts, professional viol players hired for Florentine *intermedii* were also expected to play in the two virtuoso solo styles described in Chapter 10. On stage, viols were sometimes disguised as props. Winternitz cites an order made before the 1589 *intermedio* requesting that 'four violoni be covered with taffeta painted green, and scales, and gilded to look like serpents.'[24]

In both professional and amateur circles four seems to have been the most usual number of players in a viol consort,[25] but the internal constitution of the mid 16th-century Italian viol consort differed from that of later periods. The standard four-part grouping today, which derives from the 17th-century English tradition, is a treble, two tenors and a bass with a second treble for five-part music. In the mid 16th century, however, the consort usually consisted of the two larger sizes alone, sometimes indeed of basses only. The evidence is twofold: iconographic and documentary. Taking first mid 16th-century Italian pictures of viol consorts of three or more (whether playing alone or with other instruments and voices), a clear pattern begins to emerge:

i    The title-page woodcut of *Regola Rubertina* (1542) shows three viol players accompanying a singer – a large tenor and two basses (Plate 93).

ii   In Nicolò dell'Abate's painting of a domestic consort in the Galleria Estense, Modena two men play tenor and bass viols; a third plays another (largely obscured) viol which, to judge by the position of the neck, is a bass; in addition there are two lutes (Plate 94).

iii  Aurelio Luini's painting of an angelic viol consort in San Maurizio (Milan) depicts three basses and a small tenor (Plate 95).

iv  A painting of an angelic viol consort attributed to Giacomo Francia similarly shows a quartet consisting of three basses and a tenor (Plate 96).

v   Domenico Brusasorzi's portrait of a musician in the Museo Civico, Verona shows in the background a group of musicians seated round a table playing viols. The detail is not very clear, but there appear to be three or four large viols. (The painting is reproduced in Turrini, 1941.)

The mid 16th-century Italian viol consort thus typically consisted of bass viols headed by a single tenor. This emphasis on bass instruments is confirmed by reports of the make-up of some of the viol consorts in Florentine *intermedii*. In 1568 a consort consisting of four 'bassi di violoni' was required and similarly in 1586 four 'bassi di viuole'. Moreover, as Brown points out, it is likely that some four-part viol consorts simply termed 'viole' or 'violoni' were also made up of bass instruments because they double trombone parts. The overall range of a consort of four basses (in first position) would be two octaves and a fourth: somewhat restrictive, but perfectly practical for many compositions. The addition of a single tenor would greatly enhance the consort's potential. The overall range of such a consort would be about three octaves, adequate for much 16th-century polyphony. If a wider overall range or a higher top part were required, there were many possible options: the adoption of a system of transposition, rewriting the lowest notes of the bass as suggested by Ganassi; the use of a voice, flute or recorder on the highest line; or the use of a small treble viol. In fact, as the century progresses, the small treble viol begins to appear more frequently. Small viols are mentioned in the later Florentine *intermedii*. In 1586, 'bassi, tenori e soprani di viuole' are required, and in 1589 a 'sopranino di viola' was played with great skill by Alessandro Striggio.[26] However, the appearance of the high *d* consort tuning system in both Lanfranco (1533) and Ganassi (1542) indicates that the treble instrument was in use earlier in the century, though not perhaps widely so. (As we shall see in Chapter 12, in the late 16th century there was a growing tendency to make viols in a wide range of sizes, large double-basses as well as small trebles.)

The range of music played by 16th-century Italian viol consorts, professional and amateur alike, must have been considerable, and yet, paradoxically, the medium of the viol consort is hardly ever mentioned on title-pages of the period, let alone composed for in a truly idiomatic manner. The failure of Italian composers to write music specifically for the viol consort may simply have been a tacit acknowledgement of the quality and quantity of other music available. With so much fine polyphonic music, vocal and instrumental, suitable for performance by groups of viol players and readily available in sets of partbooks, the need for a specifically idiomatic repertory was perhaps not great. Thus, while Italian composers began to develop instrumental forms such as the ricercar and to evolve a distinctively instrumental dialect of the universal polyphonic language, there was no serious attempt to exploit the individual resources of the viol or the unique sonorities of the viol consort as the English later did.

Among the earliest instrumental compositions played by Italian viol consorts were the textless duos of the early 16th century. Two paintings of the period by Costa (Plate 53) and 'Il Garofalo' (Plate 57) depict viol duets, and there is also Sanuto's report in 1506 of a delightful performance by 'due viole grande da archetto'.[27] The first published collection of duos was Eustachio Romano's *Musica Duorum* (Rome, 1521).[28] Although viols are not mentioned on his title-page, the compositions are well suited to performance by a viol duet. In style the pieces belong to the tradition of the two-part mass movements of Josquin and his contemporaries often copied out without text for instrumental performance. The most notable sign of the newly-emerging idiom of instrumental polyphony is the frequent use of quite wide leaps. The suitability of *bicinia* for the viol duo is explicitly recognised by Agostino Licino in the dedication of his *Il secondo libro di duo cromatici* (Venice, 1546). Licino writes that he has composed the duets for his patron's sons Lodovico and Leone to help them 'learn to play bowed string instruments such as the *viole*, the *violoni* and other similar instruments' ('ad imparar a sonare gli stromenti da arco, come sono viole violoni & altri stromenti simili'). As Licino implies, the duo is an excellent medium for instructing young singers and players of all types of instrument, and this knowledge ensured a continuing flow of publications in several European countries. Composers of importance, Lassus and Morley, contributed to the genre. No other publication explicitly mentions viols; all are suitable for them. Even today, 16th-century *bicinia* have not been surpassed as pleasant practice pieces for beginners on the viol.

The publication in Venice in 1540 of *Musica Nova* introduced to the Italian public a new and important source of recreational music for viol consort, the ensemble ricercar.[29] Although, as usual, the title–page avoids requesting a specific ensemble instrumentation – 'Musica Nova accomodata per cantar et sonar sopra organi, et altri strumenti' – the ricercars in this volume are well suited to performance on a consort of viols. They are constructed from a series of points of imitation, thoroughly worked out in a continuous flow of polyphony. Slim has aptly noted their 'quiet lyricism', and yet, effective though they are, there is an air of the monochrome about them, and they lack something of the drama that the best of the Jacobean composers were later able to impart to the English madrigalian fantasia. In the years following the appearance of *Musica Nova*, there was a steady flow of publications devoted to the imitative ensemble ricercar. Especially active were a group of Venetian composers headed by Willaert. That these publications were intended in part for viol players is apparent not so much from any noticeably idiomatic writing for viol consort and certainly not from any specific comments on the title-pages, but from the fact that some of the more significant composers are known to have been viol players. Giuliano Tiburtino, who with Willaert was a contributor to *Fantasie, et recerchari a tre voci* (Venice, 1549), is commended by Ganassi as an excellent viol player, and Jacques Buus, who published two sets of ricercars in Venice (1547 and 1549) is reported as a player of the 'violone il soprano'.[30] After the middle of the century, the steady trickle of instrumental ensemble publications turned into a flood. Huge numbers of ricercars, fantasias and canzonas were produced for an apparently insatiable public. But the viol is hardly ever mentioned. Sebastián Raval's *Il primo libro di ricercari a quatro voci* (Palermo, 1596) is exceptionally specific in asking for 'liuti, cimbali, et viole d'arco'. Far more common is the all-embracing, financially prudent wording of Giovanni Bassano's *Fantasie a tre voci per cantar e sonar con ogni sorte d'istrumenti* (Venice, 1585). The repertory thus remained an all-purpose one, suitable for performance on instruments or voices, and this precluded any serious attempt to develop an idiomatic mode of composition for the viol consort. In fact, of the multitude of 16th-century ensemble publications, those with the closest links with the viol consort are probably the mid 16th-century publications of Willaert and his circle.

As well as textless instrumental prints, 16th-century viol consorts had at their disposal a vast amount of vocal polyphony, sacred and secular, and almost certainly this formed the basic core of their repertory. Once again, firm evidence is provided by the records of the Accademia Filarmonica of Verona. In the 1543 inventory are listed 'five books of motets for the viols' ('Libri 5 de motteti per li violoni').[31] Even more interesting are comments made by Giovanni Nasco in two letters to the academy. On 22 March 1552 Nasco writes from Treviso about various of his compositions including a madrigal 'for low voices, arranged for trombones, that will, I believe, go well on your large flutes, if not, then at least on the viols' ('a voce Mutate fece per li trombone qual mi penso sara buona per le vostre flauti grosse se no almeno per le viole grande').[32] Then in 1553 Nasco writes again about a five-part madrigal that he is sending, which he believes 'will be successful on the viols' ('che riuscirà con le viole').[33] These comments clearly indicate that vocal part music (of which the academy possessed a large collection) was, if chosen with care, considered suitable for performance on instruments, especially viols, flutes and trombones – the very consorts most frequently encountered in the Florentine *intermedii*. It goes without saying that printed collections of madrigals and chansons rarely mention viols as a possible mode of performance. However, the forward to De Monte's *Il Quintodecimo Libro de Madrigali a Cinque Vocis* (1592) does refer to the performance of madrigals on viols.[34] It is also interesting to note that viols were chosen by Vincenzo Galilei for an early experiment in the recitative style. According to Pietro de' Bardi, the lament of Count Ugolino from Dante's *Inferno* was sung 'in istile rappresentativo' over a consort of viols ('sopra un corpo di viole').[35] Even settings of the mass were performed on occasion with viol accompaniment. In a letter to Ercole d'Este dated 29 April 1532, Ercole Gonzaga recalled a seven-part mass by Maistre Jhan, which was performed with viols ('colle viole').[36]

For guidance on how to play vocal part music stylishly, the viol consort could turn to the first part of Ortiz's *Trattado de glosas* (Rome, 1553) which deals with the music of the consort ('concierto de vihuelas'). Ortiz offers his book as an exemplar of how to ornament. It is the player's responsibility, however, to perform with grace, and on this subject Ortiz proffers a few pertinent com-

ments. The viol player should aim to play sweetly ('tocar dulcemente') and
include from time to time some quiet trills or running passagework ('algunos
quiebros amortiguados y algunos passos'). The bowing hand should avoid
making sharp accents or 'blows' ('golpes'), rather it should draw the bow
quietly. The left hand is responsible for the harmony, especially when there
are two or three semiminims of which only the first is accented, the others
passing without being played by the bowing hand – a clear reference to the
slurring of fast notes (see Chapter 9). These brief remarks form a valuable
supplement to Ganassi's more extensive discussion on the aesthetics of viol
playing. A difference of emphasis is apparent. Ganassi aims above all else for
variety of timbre and mood, the forceful qualities of the extrovert setting off
the quieter tones of the introvert. Ortiz speaks only the language of calm
restraint; words such as 'dulcemente' (sweetly) and 'amortiguados' (muffled or
deadened) predominate in his brief description; heavy accents are
depreciated. One could imagine that the virtuoso display of a Ganassi would
offend the severer tastes of an Ortiz. The detailed instructions in *Trattado de
glosas* about how to ornament have been very adequately described elsewhere.[37] Suffice it to say that the same quality of restraint, the same anxiety to
keep well within the bounds of good taste, is apparent throughout this section
of the book. Ortiz has little to say about the selection of music, preferring to
leave the choice to the players. But in discussing solo embellishments, he does
imply that any piece of vocal polyphony may be arranged for viol and keyboard – 'take a madrigal, a motet or any other work you wish to play' – and
this, as the records of the Verona Accademia Filarmonica show, was also valid
for consort arrangements.

It is no accident that the major original Italian treatises on viol playing
(those by Ganassi and Ortiz) date from the mid 16th century, for this period
saw the tradition of the viol consort at its most vigorous in Italy. Thereafter,
the early stages of the decline gradually became apparent. The consort still
had a place in Italian musical textbooks: Zacconi (1592), Ceretto (1601) and
Banchieri (1609) all refer to it.[38] Ceretto, indeed, writes with some enthusiasm
about the consort, commenting that the sound of four or five viols played well
together produces 'a perfect and sweet harmony' ('una perfetta, & soave
armonia'). But these musical encyclopaedias contain little original comment.
Their authors are generally content with a few rather superficial observations
on matters such as tunings, basic fingering (the position of the fingers on the
frets), basic bowing (the direction of the bow stroke) or the relative merits of
the viol and violin families. No new specialist tutors were published. Inventories, of course, still frequently record chests of viols, many of which must have
been purchased during the mid century. A list of the instruments owned by
the music-loving Count Mario Bevilacqua compiled on 6 August 1593
includes twelve viols ('Due coppie di viole, cioè 12').[39] These instruments were
bequeathed to the Verona Accademia Filarmonica to add to its already size-

able collection. In the early 17th century the viol consort still had a place, though one of diminishing importance, in large ensembles employed for polychoral works. In the preface to his *Prima parte dei salmi concertati* (Venice, 1609) Giacobbi recommends viols as a possible alternative to sackbuts in the 'choro grave'. (The use of viol consorts in polychoral works will be discussed further in Chapter 12.) But as a congenial vehicle for amateur music-making, the viol consort was now falling out of favour. By 1628 Giustiniani could give as one reason why people no longer entertained themselves with consorts of viols or recorders (apart from the fact that he considered such activities conducive to sleep!) the difficulty of bringing together enough players to form a consort.[40] Henceforth, it was to be the northern countries of Europe, especially England, where the viol consort had been established since the 1530s, that the traditions of amateur ensemble music-making with viols were to be upheld.[41]

## 12

# The viol consort in late 16th-century Germany

An assessment of the viol consort and its music in Italy would be incomplete without a brief examination of the German tradition. Evidence is plentiful that in the second half of the 16th century the viol consort played a comparable rôle in the musical life of German courts, especially those in the Catholic South – Munich, Innsbruck, Graz and others – which were close, geographically and culturally, to the Italian sphere of influence.

Detailed information about the music played by German viol consorts, as in Italy, is to be found in published descriptions of the celebrations devised for state weddings. Of these, the most significant was undoubtedly the marriage of Duke William of Bavaria to Renée of Lorraine in 1568. The musical entertainments, lavish even by Florentine standards, were observed by an Italian, Massimo Troiano. He later published his impressions in *Dialoghi di Massimo Troiano* (Venice, 1569).[1] According to Troiano, the large ensemble of instruments employed during the festivities sometimes included an eight-part viol consort. On one occasion a 40-part piece, possibly Striggio's motet 'Ecce beatam lucem', was sung with the following instruments: eight 'tromboni'; eight 'viole da arco'; eight 'flauti grossi'; an 'instrumento da penna' and a 'liutto grosso'. Choirs of viols, sackbuts and flutes or recorders were exactly the instrumental groupings so often favoured by the organisers of the Florentine *intermedii* for their 'orchestrations' of madrigals and motets. Individual viols, again as in Florence, were also used in mixed groups of instruments. During the wedding banquet itself, a 'Viola di Gamba' (presumably playing the bass line) featured in a colourful ensemble consisting of the following: 'uno strumento da penna, un Trombone, un flauto, un Lauto, una Cornamusa, un Cornetto muto, una Viola di Gamba, e un Fiffaro'.

In one respect, however, the use of string instruments in the Munich orchestra differed markedly from that of the typical Florentine ensemble: a consort of 'Viole da brazzo' (violins) performed side by side with the viol consort. At a banquet a few days after the wedding, eight viols ('otto viole da gamba'), eight violins ('otto viole da braccio') and a mixed eight-part wind ensemble joined forces in a 24-part polychoral piece. Nor was the consort of violins restricted to large ensembles. During the fish course of one banquet,

the performance of a six-part motet by Rore was entrusted to the 'viole da
brazzo' alone. The equal status accorded the viol and violin ensembles in the
Munich orchestra is unusual for the time, and it suggests that Jambe de Fer's
rather contemptuous opinion of the violin as an instrument best suited to
dance music (1556)[2] was already becoming outdated. Instruments fit merely
for dance music would hardly have been chosen to perform a sophisticated
piece of six-part polyphony in one of the most magnificent musical spectacles
of the age. Towards the end of the century, of course, increasing use was made
of the violin ensemble in both German and Italian performances of polyphonic music, either to contrast with viols, or to replace them completely. By
the time Praetorius was engaged in the compilation of the third volume of his
monumental work *Syntagma Musicum* (1619) both string groups could expect to
receive (and did receive) equality of treatment in the orchestration of large-
scale polychoral works.[3]

An event of the magnitude of the 1568 Bavarian wedding and the forces
employed for the occasion could hardly be described as typical. Yet the evidence of musical instrument inventories of the period shows that most German courts, like their Italian counterparts, maintained substantial collections
of viols and violins for use on major state occasions, and for regular use in the
more mundane tasks of 16th-century instrumentalists such as the provision of
dance music. The following selection of extracts includes some interesting
details on the different sizes of viols and violins in German consorts. (The terminology used in these inventories is not always clear. While terms such as
'violen' or 'grosz geigen' usually refer to viols, and 'cleine geigen' or 'geigen da
prazo' to violins, the unmodified 'geigen' could mean either.)

1566    Inventory of instruments belonging to Raymund Fugger:[4]
seven 'gross geygen' made in Burghausen
eight 'geigen' made in Burghausen
one set of Italian 'geig' in a white case made in Brescia
1573    Inventory of instruments belonging to the Kassel Hofkapelle:[5]
four 'violen'
1575    Inventory of instruments belonging to the Nuremberg town band:[6]
'7 Violen, i grossen bass, i kleinen bass, 3 tenor, und 2 discant' (seven viols, one large
bass, one small bass, three tenors and two trebles)
1577    Inventory of instruments belonging to the Graz Hofkapelle:[7]
'Ain copia geigen . . . ain basz, drei tenor und ain discant' (a chest of viols . . . one
bass, three tenors and a treble)
'Ain alte copia geigen, darunder ain basz, swen tenor und swen discant' (an old chest
of viols with one bass, two tenors and two trebles)
'Mer ain alte copie geigen da prazo' (another old chest of violins)
'Mer ain grosze baszgeigen' (another large bass viol)
1582    Inventory of instruments belonging to the Baden-Baden Hofkapelle:[8]
'ein Italiänisch Stimwerckh von Geigen, darinn ein discant, drey tenor und ein bass'
(an Italian chest of 'Geigen' with one treble, three tenors and a bass)
'ein phyola de gamba' (one viola da gamba)

'eine grosse Braune phyola de gamba' (one large brown viola da gamba)
several lyre da gamba

1582    Inventory of instruments belonging to the Brandenburg Hofkapelle:[9]
'5 Newe Geygen als ein Bass, 2 Tenor, ein Altt unnd ein Discantt' (five new 'Geygen',
a bass, two tenors, an alto and a treble)

1589    Inventory of instruments belonging to the Stuttgart Hofkapelle:[10]
39 string instruments
(The terminology is unusually varied and difficult to interpret. The following terms
are found: 'Geigen'; 'kleine Geigen'; 'kleine Violen'; 'grosse Violengeige'; 'klein hand-
geiglin'; 'Violen'; 'handgeigen'.)
Of special interest is a reference to a 'double-bass made by Hans Vogel of Nuremberg'
('I doppelter bass, durch Hans Vogel zu Nürnberg gemacht'). A large viol by this
maker has survived (see Plate 87).

1590    Inventory of instruments belonging to the Graz Hofkapelle (additional items bought
or found since the 1577 inventory):[11]
'Drei newe baszgeigen' (three new bass 'geigen')
'Ain grosze basz, ain klaine basz, drei tenor und ain discantgeigen' (a large bass, a
small bass, three tenors and a treble 'geigen')

1596    Inventory of instruments belonging to Archduke Ferdinand in Ambras Castle,
Innsbruck:[12]
'viole de gambe oder die grosz geigen . . . 2 pasz, 4 tenor, 2 discant und ain clainer discant' (viols, two basses, four tenors, two trebles and a small treble)
'viole de praz oder cleine geigen' (violins)
'viole . . . ain grossen pasz, ain clain pasz, 3 tenor, ain discant' (viols, a large bass, a
small bass, three tenors and a treble)
'viole de gamba, ain copie . . . 2 pasz, 2 tenor und 2 discant' (a chest of viols, two
basses, two tenors and two trebles)

1613    Inventory of instruments belonging to the Kassel Hofkapelle:[13]
'Ein Steinwerck Jtalienischer Viole di gamba von schwartz Jbenholtz, darunder, Ein
bass, drey Tenor, swey Soprani undt ein violino di brazzio' (a chest of Italian black
ebony viole da gamba, a bass, three tenors, two trebles and a 'violino di brazzio')
'Ein Steinwerck Englischer Viole di gamba darunder Ein bass, drey Tenor undt zwey
Soprani' (a chest of English viole da gamba, a bass, three tenors and two trebles)
'Ein Steinwerck gelbe Viole di gamba So fritz von Nürnbergk gemacht, darunder Ein
bass, drey Tenor, undt zwey Soprani' (a chest of yellow viole da gamba made by Fritz
of Nuremberg, a bass, three tenors and two trebles)

It is clear that major German establishments were in possession of at least one
set of string instruments by the end of the 16th century. The larger collections
were no doubt accumulated gradually over the years. With the significant
advances in string instrument construction of the mid 16th century, older
instruments probably became obsolete quite quickly. When this happened,
new sets of viols and violins were bought, often from Italy or (later) England.
The collection of 39 string instruments owned by the Stuttgart Hofkapelle was
only exceeded in the 16th century by the 41 'vyoles' and 13 'vyolens' reputedly
kept at Nonesuch in England in 1596.[14] If enough players could be hired,
major collections such as these could provide the spectacle of an 'orchestra' of
viols. A remarkable ensemble of 30 viols with a solitary violin is reported to
have performed in an orchestra of 64 instruments at a concert in honour of

some Venetian noblemen who visited Florence in 1579 with the father of Bianca Cappello.[15]

The most interesting feature of the German inventories is their practice of listing the sizes of individual instruments in each set of viols. (Italians were, on the whole, less thorough in this respect.) Six size names are recorded, though no more than four occur in any one set: large bass; small bass; tenor; alto; discant; small discant. If the terminology used in these inventories is that of Praetorius, then most late 16th-century German consorts were of the low $a$–$d$–$a$ tuned variety – tenor, bass and large bass in modern terminology. One possible report of a low-pitched German consort comes from Troiano's *Dialoghi*. During the fifth course of one of the Bavarian wedding banquets in 1568 a piece was performed for three choirs, one of which consisted of 'six large viols playing a fourth lower than the usual' ('con sei viole di gamba grosse, quali vanno quarta piu basso del li altri ordinarii'). An Italian observer, used to the high $d$–$g$–$d$ consort tuning, might well have considered an $a$–$d$–$a$ consort a fourth lower than normal viols.

As was suggested in the previous chapter – and as is certainly reflected in the German inventories – there was a tendency in the late-16th century to make viols in a wide range of sizes, trebles for the high $d$–$g$–$d$ consort, and, at the other extreme of range, deep basses, one size larger even than the $a$-tuned bass of the low consort. The appearance of the double-bass instrument (presumably the 'gross bass geigen' of the German inventories) is of particular note. There are scattered references to very large viols in the first part of the 16th century – a viola 'per contrabasso' is reported to have performed at Ferrara in 1529[16] – but it is only after about the 1550s that a true double-bass appears regularly in German and Italian paintings. A huge double-bass string instrument, oval-shaped with pointed ends and with three to five strings, is quite frequently depicted in German sources.[17] Grown men are shown reaching up to finger the top of the neck. Other large viols were made with pointed corners like those of the violin. For information about the tuning of these large German basses Praetorius's *Syntagma Musicum* is invaluable.[18] The largest instrument of all, the 'gar grosse Viol de Gamba' had $G$ as its top string and was tuned in fourths like the modern double-bass: $G\,D\,A'\,E'\,D'$. Such a tuning would have suited some of the massive oval-shaped instruments mentioned above. For other (presumably smaller) double-basses three alternatives are given: $c\,G\,D\,A'\,E'$; $d\,A\,E\,C\,G'$ $D'$; $f\,c\,G\,D\,A'\,E'$. The second of these is the tuning given by Banchieri for the 'violone in contrabasso'. Praetorius makes some interesting comments about the use of the double-bass viols in consort. A possible grouping was the following: a small bass playing the top line; large basses playing the alto and tenor lines; a double-bass playing the bass line – in effect the high $d$–$g$–$d$ consort an octave lower. Praetorius had apparently intended this great consort to double five choral parts in his 'Lauda Hierusalem Dominum', but the massive ensemble produced too much 'throbbing and beating' and so he decided upon an alternative disposition with normal viols on the upper parts, but the double-bass instrument retained for the bass line. Several German inventories describe viol consorts with both a 'klein bass' and a 'gross bass'. The 'gross bass' could well have been used as an alternative to the usual small bass, exploiting the richer sonorities of a 16' bass line without having the whole consort at an unmanageably low pitch.

Of all deep bass instruments in the late 16th century, the double-bass viol was possibly the most versatile and widely used. In both Germany and Italy the instrument frequently appears in large mixed ensembles, providing a firm and sustained bass line. Hans Mielich's well-known depiction of the Munich court ensemble is a typical example: a completely heterogeneous assortment of wind and string instruments are shown grouped round a harpsichord with a large (violin-shaped) double-bass viol providing a 16' bass line. The large ensemble of instruments specified in the printed score of Monteverdi's *Orfeo* (1607) includes two double-bass viols. Of particular note is the use of a single double-bass viol ('un contra basso de Viola da Gamba') in Act III. The final stanza of Orfeo's great aria 'Possente spirto' is accompanied by three 'viole da braccio' with a double-bass, playing very softly ('pian piano') – a scoring that exactly confirms Praetorius's suggestion for the use of deep bass string instruments. Even wind ensembles apparently relied on double-bass viols. In 1608 Thomas Coryat reported that in Venice 'sometimes sixteene played together upon their instruments, ten Sagbuts, foure Cornets, and two Violdegambaes of an extraordinary greatnesse' – an early instance of a time-honoured practice.[19]

Summing up this brief survey of the viol in late 16th-century Germany, it would be fair to say that in almost every respect German sources confirm Italian practice: the important place of the viol consort in the large-scale festive ensemble, the use of viols in 'orchestrations' of motets or madrigals, the development of the large double-bass viol, the growing prominence of ensembles of violins in polyphony – all are very well documented in Italy. After the first decades of the 17th century, the traditions of viol consort playing suffered a marked decline in southern Germany – again, the parallel with Italy is clear – but in the North the influence of travelling English viol players and the popularity of English consort music (especially consort dances) ensured the survival of the instrument.

# 13

## The viol in France and the Low Countries

The penultimate stage of the viol's migration northwards saw the instrument beginning to penetrate the Low Countries and France, the domains of the Habsburg and Valois dynasties. The pattern of the viol's earlier progress across the Mediterranean into Italy and then northwards across the Alps was repeated; the instrument made an early appearance in the households of the ruling families and its acceptance by these aristocratic arbiters of taste ensured its subsequent popular success. Just how early the first viols may have appeared in the French royal court is shown by a letter from Cesare Borgia to Ercole d'Este cited by Bridgman.[1] In 1498, Cesare, about to embark upon a diplomatic mission to France, wrote to Ferrara asking Ercole to send him players of bowed 'viole' so that he could take them with him to France, where, he claimed, they were highly regarded. Direct contacts of this kind between one ruling family and another probably led to the early, unrecorded appearance of viols in royal households long before the growth of a documented indigenous tradition of viol playing.

The first Habsburg monarch to employ viol players from the Low Countries may have been Philip the Handsome (d.1506) but the evidence for this, though suggestive, is far from conclusive. A document dated 1504 records a payment to Philip's three *musette* players, Bertrand Brouart, Guillaume Terro and Mathieu de Wildre.[2] Two of these players were subsequently employed as players of bowed string instruments. In 1505 Guillaume Terro is recorded as a 'joueur de vyole du roy',[3] while over a decade later Mathieu de Wildre reappears in the service of Henry VIII as Matthew de Weldre, player upon 'lutes and veoldes' (see Chapter 14). Needless to say, the use of the unmodified term 'vyole' as early as 1505 cannot be regarded as firm documentation of the viol.

Much more convincing is the evidence that Philip's son Charles was taught the viol while at the court of his aunt Margaret of Austria, Regent of the Netherlands. In 1512 Henry Bredemers, music tutor to the young prince and his sister, received the following payment: 'A maistre Henry Bredemers, etc., dix neuf livres . . . pour avoir fait mectre à point, gardé et entretenu les grandes violes, pour le desduit et passetemps de mondit s$^r$ et de madite dame'.[4] The use of the term 'grandes violes', the exact equivalent of the common early

16th-century Italian for viols, 'viole grande', definitely suggests the presence of a viol consort in the Habsburg household for the instruction of the royal children. The names of Margaret of Austria's own viol players are not recorded. The accounts merely list payments to a single 'joueur de vyole' or to an undisclosed number of 'tambourins et joueurs de viole'.[5] On one occasion she was entertained by a visiting German consort. On 1 May 1524 'quatre Allemans joueurs de vyoles et maryonettes' were paid for performing during dinner.[6] In his later life, perhaps as a direct result of his early training on the viol, Charles V maintained a viol consort in his own household. Unusually for the time, but certainly reflecting the extent of his territorial dominions, his viol consort was of mixed nationality. In 1547 his 'cytharaedi' included Franciscus Canis, Franciscus Massy and two German brothers from Nuremberg, Johannes and Thomas Herman. In 1556 the 'tañedores de vihuelas de arcos' included Gaspar Payen and François Cornette as well as the two aforementioned Germans.[7] Important servants of the imperial court also owned viols. In 1539 a list of instruments belonging to Pedro de Santa Cruz, chamberlain to the Empress, included the following: 'Una vihuela grande con un lazo' ('a large viol with a bow'); 'otra vihuela mediana con dos lazos' ('another viol of medium size with two bows'); 'otra vihuela mas pequeña que las susodichas' ('another viol smaller than the aforementioned').[8]

By the mid 16th century at least one member of the Habsburg family was in possession of a collection of viols to rival that of Henry VIII. Mary of Hungary, sister of Charles V and Regent of the Netherlands from 1531 to 1555, left a remarkable collection of instruments. The inventory drawn up by Roger Pathie in 1559 lists 20 *vihuelas de arco*. The following extracts are from Vander Straeten's transcription:[9]

Siete vihuelas de harco grandes y pequenas, con sus arquillos, que estavan en otro cofre de madera blanca ('seven viols large and small with their bows in another wooden chest of pale wood')

Siete vihuelas de arco, con siete arquillos grandes, hechas in Alemania ('seven viols, with seven large bows, made in Germany')

Seis vihuelas de arco, hechas en Alemania, con doz[e] arquillos, los seis dellos con los cabos de plata ('six viols, made in Germany, with twelve bows, six of them with silver ends')

In addition to these, 'a chest of vihuelas that came from England' ('un cofre de vihuelas que vinjeron de Ynglaterra') belonging to Mary of Hungary was taken to Spain in 1559 by one of her servants Estevan de Notero.[10] These English 'vihuelas' (almost certainly viols) could have been a gift from her nephew Philip II following his nuptial visit to England in 1554.

During the second half of the 16th century the Habsburg collection of viols continued to expand. An inventory of Philip II's instruments drawn up in 1602 lists 23 viols including five that had once belonged to Mary of Hungary. The following extracts are again from Vander Straeten:[11]

Un cofre grande . . . con siete bihuelas de arco, grandes, dentro con sus arquillos, estas viguelas servian de enseñar los niños cantorcillos ('a large chest with seven large viols and their bows – these viols were used to teach the children of the choir')

Un cofre . . . cinco bihuelas de arco cada una muy grande, y las quatro pequeñas de madera de Alemania, e fueron de la Reyna Maria ('a chest . . . with five viols, each one very large, the four smallest made from German wood; they belonged to the Queen Mary')

Una arca de madera . . . con seis bihuelas de arco, la trasera y lados de hevano, y las tapas de madera de Alemania, con sus arquillos y cuerdas ('a wooden chest . . . with six viols with backs and sides of ebony and bellies of German wood, with their bows and strings')

Cinco vihuelas de arco de madera blanca, con unos quadros samblados de taraçea de mano de Domenico ('five viols of pale wood with inlaid decorations in the hand of Domenico')

Only the most illustrious of patrons could have afforded five viols with inlaid decorations. The skill with which the back of a viol could be decorated with marquetry is illustrated by the back of Gaspar Tieffenbrucker's celebrated 'Plan de Paris' viol. Such artefacts were surely intended for visual display as much as for musical performance.[12]

The presence of a four-part viol consort in the household of the French King Francis I is attested by a performance given during the Cambrai conference of 1529. On 10 August Margaret of Austria was visited at her residence by 'quatre joueurs de vyole du roi de France', one of several goodwill visits by the French royal musicians.[13]

As elsewhere in Europe, the growth of a viol-playing tradition in the households of the ruling families stimulated interest in the new instrument throughout their territories, and so the viol spread quickly throughout northern Europe. The growth of popular interest here occurred rather later than it had done in the viol's southern homelands, probably not much before the 1530s, and it was not until the mid century that a French treatise specifically devoted to the viol was published. (There was a similar time-lag between the initial vogue for the viol and the appearance of commercial publications for it in both Italy and Germany – reflecting, perhaps, the financial prudence of publishers.) One unmistakable sign of the growing importance of the viol in northern Europe during the 1520s and 1530s was the employment of French and Flemish viol players abroad, notably in England and Scotland (see Chapter 14).

From the 1540s onwards the viol consort, usually consisting of four players, was frequently heard at important festivities and in theatrical performances. The following selection of notices will give some idea of the wide geographical spread of the viol by this period and also the range of engagements that a professional consort might expect:

1546    Barthelemé de la Crous opened a school for 'viols, lutes and other instruments' in Marseilles.[14]

1548    The entry of Henry II and Catherine de' Medici into Lyons was celebrated by a per-
        formance of Cardinal Bibbiena's *La Calandria*. The *intermedio* following the first act
        was accompanied by 'violoni da gamba' together with 'flauti d'Allamagna'. [15]

1549    In August Mary of Hungary arranged a festival at Binche to celebrate the visit of
        Charles V and his son Philip. At one point, a cortège of gods, goddesses and nymphs
        was accompanied by four 'vihuelas de arco'. [16]

1558    Among the musicians performing at the marriage of the future Francis II to Mary
        Stuart in Paris were a number of 'violes' and 'violons'. [17]

1559    The company of Roland Guinet is reported to have played 'moralités, farces, jeu de
        viole et de musique' for ten days in Amiens. [18]

1560    Amiens town council gave permission for another company to perform 'moralitez,
        histoires, farces et violles'. [19]

1561    During the visit of the Duke of Longueville to Berne in 1561 music was provided by
        the viols of Lausanne ('Man hat ouch Sytenspyl mit den vyolen von Losanna'). [20]

1578    The 'violes et violons de Poitiers' provided incidental music for a tragedy, a comedy
        and a farce given by the children of Saint-Maxient. [21]

1599    The company run by Adrien Talmy performed 'plusieurs histoires, tragedies et come-
        dies avecq Musicque et voix, violes et regales'. [22]

The fairly regular appearance of the viol consort in theatrical performances
from the middle of the 16th century onwards echoes developments in England,
where the use of viols in the early Elizabethan interlude gave rise to the consort song (see Chapter 14).

The spread of viol playing beyond professional circles to amateur musicians
led to the publication in French of instruction books on the viol, Claude Gervaise's *Premier Livre de Violle* (Paris, *c*1546) and Philibert Jambe de Fer's *Epitome
musical* (Lyons, 1556). These two works together with Samuel Mareschall's
*Porta Musices* (Basle, 1589) and a few retrospective comments in Marin Mersenne's *Harmonie Universelle* (Paris, 1636) and in Jean Rousseau's *Traité de la Viole*
(Paris, 1687) document the development of a distinctively French tradition of
viol playing in the 16th century. [23]

The earliest French viol tutor, Claude Gervaise's *Premier Livre de Violle*, is
regrettably lost. Its existence is known from an entry in Sebastian Brossard's
*Catalogue des livres de Musique theorique et Pratique, Vocalle et Instrumentale* (1724)
which reads: 'Premier Livre de Violle contenant dix chansons avec l'introduction d'accorder et apliquer les doigts selon la manière qu'on a accoutumé de
jouer, le tout de la composition de Claude Gervaise. 14 Feb. 1554'. The work
was thus clearly designed for amateurs – an introduction to the basic rudi-
ments of viol playing, tuning and fingering, with a selection of French chansons transcribed for viols, something akin to Gerle's *Musica Teusch* (1532) in
scope. Brossard adds further useful comments. He notes that: 'Toutes ces
chansons sont d'abord en tabulature par a, b, c, d etc pour la violle, et en suite
le sujet est tres bien notté en Musique et nottes ordinaires, 32 feuillets ou 64
pages.' The use of letters suggests that Gervaise was adapting French lute tablature to the viol, just as Gerle and Ganassi made use of the systems most
familiar to their respective readerships.

It has been suggested that the *Premier Livre de Violle* was the first in a series of six volumes, all either composed or edited by Claude Gervaise and published by Attaingnant. Volumes two to six of this series have survived, but volume one is missing and thus could have been the lost viol tutor. In this context, Brossard's statement that the *Premier Livre de Violle* had 64 pages is significant. The second volume of the series (published in 1547) has a signature 'I–Q' which suggests that the hypothetical first volume had a signature 'A–H', that is 64 pages, exactly the number of pages of the *Premier Livre de Violle*. If the lost viol tutor was indeed part of this series, then its first edition must have been published in or before 1547. The subsequent volumes of the series of *Danceries* do not specifically mention viols. Nonetheless, the music is clearly suited to a viol consort. A note in a contemporary hand in a contratenor partbook of the *Sixième Livre de Danceries* suggests that the music may also have been considered suitable for violins: 'Qui est fait bonne pour les violons'.[24] At about the same period Moderne published *Musique de Joye*: 'appropriée tant a la voix humaine, que pour apprendre a sonner Espinetes, Violons, & fleustes'.[25]

Jambe de Fer's *Epitome musical* of 1556 includes a brief but fascinating chapter on the viol in France. His treatise makes the first unambiguous reference to the amateur, 'upper-class' status of the viol. In answer to the question 'Why do we call some instruments viols and others violins?', Jambe de Fer writes: 'we call viols those with which gentlemen, merchants and other men of virtue pass their time' ('on appelle violes celles des quelles les gentilhommes marchands et autre gens de vertu passent leur temps'). The violin, by contrast, occupied a much lower position in the social hierarchy of instruments, there being, in Jambe de Fer's words, 'few people who play it except those that make their living from it'. This division between the amateur status of the viol and the professional status of the violin was something of an over-simplification – there were many professional violists in the 16th century. Yet throughout its history the viol retained a fairly close association with the amateur musician.

More than any other theorist of the 16th century, Jambe de Fer was aware of the regional differences between viol playing in France and Italy and sought to point these out wherever possible. (His comments on the different playing positions in use in Italy and France have already been noted in Chapter 9.) On the subject of tuning, he notes that whereas in Italy the viol is tuned like a lute with fourths and a central major third, in France the viol has only five strings tuned in fourths throughout. This French manner of tuning is confirmed by Mareschall in his *Porta Musices* of 1589:

| Jambe de Fer | | | | | Mareschall | | | | |
|---|---|---|---|---|---|---|---|---|---|
| c" | g' | d' | a | e | d" | a' | e' | b | f♯ |
| g' | d' | a | e | B | g' | d' | a | e | B |
| c' | g | d | A | E | c' | g | d | A | E |

Music keys with *b* naturals is, according to Jambe de Fer, more pleasant on viols tuned thus than music with *b* flats. Correct choice of key to suit a particular tuning was, as I have shown, also a concern of Ganassi and his Italian contemporaries. To tune a consort, Jambe de Fer takes the bass player first and advises him to tune the instrument in fourths beginning with the second string *g*, the keynote of the French consort tuning. This unusual procedure gives us a hint about the origins of the tuning. If the notional pitch levels of the French viol consort had once been *g–d–g* (the equivalent of the German low *a–d–a* consort tuning), an extra string a fourth above the others might well have been added, as elsewhere in Europe, to cope with the high range of superius parts. Jambe de Fer himself remarks that the 'dessus' viol is aptly named because it is constantly using its top string. Concerning the overall compass of the viol, Jambe de Fer observes that on each string there are three tones ('tons'), the open string, the first or second fret, and the third or fourth fret. The fifth fret is the equivalent of the next open string, which produces a clearer sound than the stopped note, though when playing diminutions it is sometimes more convenient to use the fifth fret. (This recalls Ganassi's concern to avoid ungainly string crossings during fast passagework by using a higher position.) On the top string four, five or six tones can be played, giving the instrument an overall compass of seventeen or eighteen tones. The 'dessus' viol in Jambe de Fer's tuning would thus be able to reach the notes $f''$, $g''$ and $a''$. By raising his treble viol a tone, Mareschall enables these notes to be reached more easily.

The repertory of music performed by French viol consorts probably consisted largely of vocal music and dances. The suitability of the four-part Parisian chanson for viol consort is demonstrated by contemporary intabulations of chansons both in the *Premier Livre de Violle* (*c*1546) and in Gerle's *Musica und Tabulatur* (1546). A viol consort able to read from mensural notation would have been able to choose any of the wide range of partbooks being produced by the presses of Attaingnant and other printers by the mid 16th century. It was not the custom at this period to limit potential sales of a print by mentioning specific instruments on the title-page – rarely is there anything more specific than a phrase such as 'convenable a tous instruments musicaulz' – but any music produced in this format could have been played on viols, even mass settings, motets or psalms. In one exceptional case, a volume of Gombert's four-part motets published in Venice (*c*1539), the title-page of a volume of sacred pieces does mention string instruments: the motets are suitable for 'lyris maioribus, ac tibiis imparibus', presumably 'viols' and wind instruments.

No contemporary source describes the physical appearance of the mid 16th-century French viol, and iconographic evidence is sparse before the end of the century. There are at least two surviving viols by Gaspar Tieffenbrucker, who worked as an instrument maker in Lyons from 1533 until *c*1571, but neither one is in its original state. The beautiful 'Plan de Paris' viol, so called because of the depiction of the city of Paris on its back, was drastically modified by a later craftsman, who turned it into a seven-string bass viol. The Tieffenbrucker viol

97    *Escole de Musique*: an outdoor viol quartet
(1584, anonymous drawing: Bibliothèque Nationale, Paris, Département des Estampes)

in the Gemeentemuseum, The Hague, possibly retains more of its original form (Plate 100). Its outline, steeply sloping shoulders, sharp upper bouts and smoothly rounded lower belly, is certainly unusual but not entirely unknown in the 16th century. Interesting information about early French viols is given by a much later writer, Jean Rousseau, in his *Traité de la Viole* (Paris, 1687). In his dissertation on the early history of the viol Rousseau writes: 'The first viols played in France had five strings, were very large and were used for accompaniment; the bridge was very low and was positioned below the soundholes; the bottom of the fingerboard nearly touched the belly; the strings were very thick and were tuned in fourths throughout' ('Les premieres Violes dont on a joüé en France estoient à cinq chordes & fort grandes, leur usage estoit d'accompagner: le chevalet estoit fort bas & placé au dessus des oüyes, le bas de la touche touchait à la table, les chordes estoient fort grosses, & son accord estoit tout par Quartes'). Rousseau also noted that these early French viols resembled the 'basse de violon' and that their necks were round and large and sloped too far forward. He accredits the French with being the first to slim the neck down and angle it backwards, and he remarks that even the much-prized old English viols always needed a new neck put on.

Writing over a century after the period in question, Rousseau's comments must be treated with caution, and yet they can be confirmed in many respects. His remarks about the necks of early French viols correspond with what is known about the 16th-century Italian viol. The influence of the violin on the

98    A five-string French viol
(woodcut from P. Jambe de Fer: *Epitome Musical*, Lyons, 1556; reprinted in M. Mersenne:
· *Harmonie Universelle*, Paris, 1636)

viol's outline is very well documented in 16th-century French sources. Indeed,
there are some grounds for believing that a majority of French viols of the
period adopted this outline. The woodcut of a viol printed by Jambe de Fer
(1556) and reprinted by Mersenne (1636) illustrates an instrument of this type
(Plate 98). A set of drawings of musical instruments made by Jacques Cellier
in about 1585 (Bibliothèque Nationale, ms. Fr. 9152, fol. 175) includes another
viol with corners slightly pointed, though less 'turned out' than those of the
violin in the set (Plate 99).[26] A caption below explains that the viol differs from
the violin only in that it is tuned in fourths and that its belly is much larger,

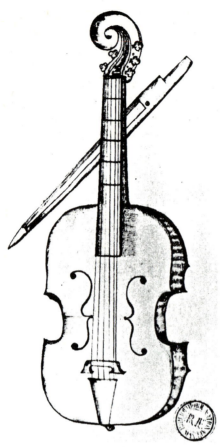

99   A five-string French viol
(*c*1585, drawing by Jacques Cellier: Bibliothèque
Nationale, Paris, ms. fr. 9152, fol. 175)

100   Viol by Gaspar Tieffenbrucker (altered?)
(16th century: Gemeentemuseum, The Hague)

being played near the foot ('La Violle differe seullement du violon en ce qu'elle
s'accorde a la quarte et qu'elle est plus enflee beaucoup que le violon par le
ventre se iouant sus le pied'). Many other examples could be cited.[27] The very
large size of some mid 16th-century French viols is confirmed by the inventories of several Parisians: in 1556 Yves Mesnager, maker of instruments, left a
'bassecontre de violle'; in 1557 Nicolas Robillard, player of instruments, left a
'double basse contre de viole'; and in 1587 Claude Denis, maker of instruments, left a 'double basse contre de viole de Cambray'.[28] How large a French
'double-bass' viol could be in the 16th century is illustrated by a drawing of a
viol quartet performing outdoors during a visit by Queen Louise of Lorraine
in 1584. The bass member of the consort is playing a huge instrument almost
as tall as himself (Plate 97).

Our picture of viol playing in 16th-century France remains rather hazy because the chances of survival have been less than kind to the French renaissance viol and to the Gervaise tutor. It is evident, however, that a French school of viol playing had developed and that in some respects it differed markedly from the dominant Italian tradition. Only in the early 17th century, after the influx of English viol players with their music and instruments, did this regional line of development shed some of its most distinctive characteristics (such as the tuning in fourths) and return closer to the central tradition.

# 14

## The viol in 16th-century England

'Beere *and* viols da gamba *came into* England *both in one yeare* in *Henry* the Sevenths time.' Thus wrote Peacham in *A Pleasant Dispute between Coach and Sedan* (1636).[1] His proposition that the viol first arrived in England during the reign of Henry VII, though unorthodox, is by no means improbable. As was suggested in the previous chapter, the initial contact of the Habsburg and Valois courts with the new viol may have occurred many years before the general advance of the instrument northwards, as a result of direct contacts between ruling families and their personal musicians. One dramatic and totally unforeseen encounter between musicians from northern Europe and the early Tudor court occurred in 1506 when, during the course of his second journey to Spain, Philip the Handsome – together with his entire entourage, including his musical establishment – was shipwrecked off the English coast.[2] Philip's party was subsequently entertained at Windsor by Henry VII. Accompanying Philip on this disastrous voyage were three household musicians, Bertrand Brouart, Guillaume Terro and Mathis de Wildre, usually listed as musette players, but also apparently string players.[3] (Terro received a payment as 'joueur de vyole du roy' in 1505.)[4] Perhaps as a direct result of their experience in England, two of these musicians were later employed by the Tudor court; in 1509 Bartram Brewer (i.e. Bertrand Brouart) was a minstrel of the chamber, and in 1517 'Matthew de Weldre' made a brief appearance in the royal accounts as the King's minstrel and player of lutes and 'veoldes'.[5] Humble musicians such as these were probably responsible for the introduction of the viol into England, perhaps as early as the 1506 shipwreck. Needless to say, at this period Philip the Handsome is unlikely to have employed specialist viol players, but his chamber musicians such as Brouart and de Wildre may well have played viols with a range of other *bas* instruments.

There is one intriguing piece of evidence to suggest that the ancestor of the true viol, the *vihuela de arco*, may have made a brief appearance at the early 16th-century Tudor court. The inventory of Henry VIII's great collection of instruments drawn up shortly after his death in 1547 includes the following item: 'four gitterons with iiij cases – they are called Spanish vialles'.[6] It is almost certain that these 'Spanish vialles' were bowed instruments of some sort

– by 1547 the term 'vial' had become a fairly standard one for the bowed viol – and the use of the word 'Spanish' suggests that they may have been *vihuelas de arco*. A plausible explanation for the appearance so far north of instruments which originated in the Kingdom of Aragon, and were largely confined to the Mediterranean area during their brief existence, may be found in the presence of Henry VIII's first wife, Catherine of Aragon, who had been at court ever since her marriage to Prince Arthur in 1501.

It is difficult to establish precisely the position of the viol during the early years of the reign of Henry VIII. On 6 January 1515 the Revels Accounts note that there was a pageant, the music for which was provided by six minstrels with strange sounds 'as sag[buts], shawms, viols etc.', but there is nothing to indicate whether these players were in regular employment or not.[7] The first viol player to appear in the accounts as one of the King's own viol players was the aforementioned 'Matthew de Weldre'. Henry's employment of musicians from the north of Europe reflects the close cultural ties between the French and English courts at this period, ties that were reinforced by the celebrated meeting at the Field of the Cloth of Gold. The lavish celebrations that graced this 'summit' provided many opportunities for the English party to familiarise themselves with instruments popular in France. On one occasion an Italian observer noted that, having finished their repast, King Francis and Queen Catherine came into the hall for the dance which commenced to the sound of the tabour, pipe and viol.[8] While it would be unwise to be dogmatic about the precise identification of this viol – terms such as 'vial', 'viola' and 'vielle' could still at this period refer to the medieval fiddle – reports of this kind do at least illustrate how Henry might have come into contact with north European viol players.

In the 1520s references to viol players at the English court become more frequent. The accounts for an entertainment given by Wolsey on 4 March 1522 include a payment for 'boards for the standdyng of the mynstrells with vyalls and other instrements'.[9] Then from 1526 two viol players with Flemish names, Hans Hossenet and Hans Highorne, begin to appear regularly in lists of royal musicians. This pair of 'vialls' commenced at a wage of 33s. 4d. a month each, a sum that was apparently never increased as Hossenet was still receiving this amount in 1551.[10] On one occasion the number of viol players was increased to three. A warrant issued on 26 November 1531 instructed the Keeper of the Great Wardrobe to deliver to 'our vyalx mynstrelles' (Peter Savage, Hans Hossenet and Hans Highorne) a quantity of material for their liveries; each of them was to receive four yards of black cloth for their gowns 'with as moch black bogy as woll suffice to fur every of the said gowns' with an additional eight yards of black material for their jackets and three yards of black velvet for their doublets 'with as much canvas and white fustian as wol suffice to line every of the said doublets'. Peter Savage, one of the recipients of this livery, was possibly the first viol player of English origin to enter the ranks of the King's 'vialls', but his tenure of the position appears to have been relatively brief.[11] The royal viol players, like other musicians, accompanied the King on visits to his subjects. On the occasion of Henry VIII's visit to Wulfhall in 1539 the Earl of Hertford rewarded the 'violls' with 20s.

The largest single expansion of the 'vialls' took place on 1 May 1540 when six players from Italy were hired at a wage of 1s. a day: Ambrose, Alexander and Romano from Milan, Vincent and Albert from Venice and John Maria from Cremona. This new group retained its own identity, quite distinct from that of the two long-serving Flemings. In accounts of the period they were often listed separately as the King's 'old vialls' and the King's 'newe vialls'.[12] They were also paid different rates; the old viols remained on 33s. 4d. a month, but in December 1547 the new players overtook them after receiving an increase of 8d. a day to bring their daily wage to 20d.[13] Replacements for the new viols were brought in from Italy; two new members had joined the band by 1 May 1545, Mark Anthony Galyardello from Brescia and George de Come from Cremona.[14] The two old viols, however, were replaced by Englishmen.[15]

The arrival of the King's 'newe vialls' was something of a landmark in the history of the viol in England. It augmented the number of royal viol players to eight, and it signalled the start of a period of growth in the popularity of the consort of viols in England. By 1547, the year of Henry's death, the royal household had acquired a considerable number of viols; the inventory of that year lists 25 in all: 'xix Vialles great and small with iii cases of woodde covered with blacke leather to the same' and 'a chest collored redde with vi Vialles having the Kinges Armes'.[16] The royal viols were probably selected for Henry by his own players. In later years they continued to supply the court with new cases of viols. In 1550, for example, Mark Anthony Galyardello received remuneration for 'a case of vialles',[17] and in 1563 Francesco de Venetia 'one of our vyolons' was paid £15 'for a sett of vyalls by him sold to us'.[18] This reference to Francesco as a player of the 'vyolon' is not an isolated one. As early as 1545 Mark Anthony Galyardello and George de Come were paid as 'vial-lonns',[19] and after 1550 the new consort are quite frequently listed as 'vyolons' or 'vyolans' which suggests that the King's new 'vialls' may have been able to play the violin as well.[20] The viol consort from Italy retained a virtual monopoly of string-playing positions in the royal band throughout the 16th century, thereby preventing native-born violists from establishing an effective presence. Nonetheless, a number of English musicians in the Chapel Royal took up the instrument in the 1540s, and two of them later entered the ranks of the royal string players in the only way open to them – as replacements for the two ageing Flemings, the 'old vialls'. The list of singing-men and children in the Chapel Royal in 1547 includes the two Englishmen in question, Thomas Kent and Thomas Browne.[21] In 1549 Thomas Kent was admitted to the viols in place of 'great Hans' [Highorne], and in 1554 Thomas Browne replaced

Hans Hossenet.[22] Judging by the length of his service – he remained at court as a viol player until 1582 – Thomas Browne was very likely a child when he first learnt to play the viol in the Chapel Royal, sometime in the mid 1540s.

The impact made by the viol consort from Italy was a lasting one. Even in the early 17th century the tradition still persisted that Italians had been responsible not only for the introduction of the viol into England but also for its original invention. In *The Guide into Tongues* (London, 1617) Minsheu defined the viol as an instrument 'said to have been invented by the Venetians and brought to England at the time of King Henry VIII' ('fertur iuventum Venetijs fuisse & huc allatum in Angliam tempore Regis Henrici octavi'). This, of course, was an accurate reflection of the general state of knowledge about the viol in the 16th century; it was regarded as an Italian or Venetian instrument, and its Spanish antecedents were forgotten.

North of the border the formation of a royal viol consort was initiated in 1535 when the accounts of the Lord High Treasurer of Scotland record a payment of £20 to an Englishman, Richard Hume, to 'mak violis to the Kingis grace'.[23] In 1538 four viol players entered the service of the Scottish court and were provided with smart red and yellow liveries.[24] The following year a violist called Jakkis [Jaques] Collumbell made an appearance. From the first he seems to have been accorded a higher status than his three colleagues and wore a slightly more expensive livery. While Jakkis was allowed 20s. for 'ane reid scarlat bonet', the 'uthir thre that playis upoun the veolis' had to be content with 17s. each for their red bonnets.[25] The accounts for 1538 even include a payment for one term's boarding for his son at Stirling, an unusual gift for a paid servant.[26] The high esteem with which he was evidently regarded suggests that Collumbell was a violist of no mean ability, brought to Scotland in order to lead and train the newly-formed viol consort and thus establish a viol-playing tradition.

Like the earliest viol players at the Tudor court, Jakkis Collumbell was almost certainly of north European origin. By the early 1540s, however, native Scotsmen were beginning to take up the viol. The accounts of the Lord High Treasurer for 1541 record a payment for the liveries of 'Schir Johnne Fechyis children that plays on the viols'.[27] Sir John Fethy was a canon of the Scottish Chapel Royal and was probably responsible for the musical education of the children there. Among the more unusual duties of Scottish viol players at this period were their appearances at 'aires' or courts of justice. In 1552 the 'veolaris' were paid £10 for their expenses at the aire of Aberdeen,[28] and the following year they performed at the aires of Perth and Coupar.[29] Except for Jakkis Collumbell, foreign viol players do not seem to have been employed at the Scottish court. In 1558 the 'veolaris' are named individually; they all appear to have been native-born musicians, Jakkis Dow, Johnne Feildie, Johnne Dow, Johnne Ra, Morris Dow, Williame Hog, Alexander Feildie.[30] Evidence that some of these were children comes from 1561 when a payment is recorded to

'Johnne Feildie and his barnis [bairns] violaris'.[31] In 1562 two new players appear, Johnie Fyn and Patrik Cochrame, the latter apparently a viol player of Irish extraction.[32] In Scotland, as elsewhere in Europe, playing the viol was a family affair, and the royal consorts of the early 1560s were dominated by the Dows and the Feildies.[33] After the flight of Mary Queen of Scots in 1567 an English consort took over, the Hudson family, comprising Thomas the elder, Robert, William, James and Thomas the younger.[34] This consort was described on one occasion as the five 'pagis that playis on the violis' and on another as the 'Inglis violaris'.[35] In October 1579 a consort of viols and voices (quite possibly including the Hudson family) played during the entry of James into Edinburgh. The 'violeris and sangsteris' received a payment of £3 for their efforts, and an observer of their performance noted that 'the musicians song the xx Psalme, and others played upon the viols'.[36]

The growth of a viol-playing tradition at both the English and Scottish courts during the 1530s was accompanied by the appearance of viols in private households. Eminent servants of the crown, anxious to keep up with the latest tastes of their sovereign, began to buy viols of their own. One of the first to do so was the Earl of Essex.[37] On 23 February 1534 his account books record the following: 'To Richard the Minstrels coste to London for the vyalls', and his costs homewards by water, 4s. 2d. The Duke of Rutland was not far behind. His accounts contain some interesting details concerning the purchase and upkeep of viols:[38]

1537    Item payd, the xxvij daye of July, for iiij vyalles bought at London, liii *s*. iiij *d*.
1540    To a man to helpe to bryng the wyalls betwixt Croxton and Beliver, ij *d*.
1541    Item paide, the xj[th] day of July, to Richard Pyke for strynges for the virgenalles and vialles that he bought in London, x *s*.
1542    Item payd, the same day [March 11], to Pycke for ij dossen off lewte strenges callyed menekyns, at xx *d* the dossen, and x dossyn off bressell strenges for the wyalles at iij *d* the dossen, v *s*. x *d*.

From these entries we learn that the cost of a single viol in 1537 was 13s.4d. and that a professional musician – Richard Pyke subsequently entered the royal band – was responsible for the purchase of the Duke's viols. By 1538 the Marquis of Exeter owned a substantial number of viols; an inventory of his goods compiled in that year lists nine.[39] One of his servants, moreover, was commended as an able viol player; Thomas Harrys, the report noted, 'luteth and singeth well and playeth cunningly upon the viols and divers other instruments'.[40] Thomas Seymour, Earl of Hertford, was also in possession of a consort of viols by the end of 1538; in December he transported his 'sett of violles' from Wulfhall to London and the following year augmented it by purchasing two more viols from the King's organ maker.[41] It is evident from these references that the late 1530s saw quite an upsurge of interest in viol playing in the private households of a number of the King's most influential subjects. The arrival of the King's 'newe vialls' in 1540 naturally stimulated further interest.

These newly-formed private viol consorts drew their players from several sources. Some were ordinary household servants who took up the viol on the instructions of their employer. In 1540, for example, Thomas Barnaby indicated in a letter that he had received a request from Wallop to have his servant taught to play on the viols.[42] On the other hand, a few of the largest households could probably afford to employ their own professional musicians. Some of these may have been trained locally. At the end of their period of apprenticeship, musicians could expect from their master a sum of money together with the instruments upon which they had been taught. The Bristol Apprentices Register records the instruments given to three young apprentices trained by Thomas Rancock and his wife Dorothy. In 1548 William Drowry received a 'vyall', in 1549 John Rowe a 'vyall, a rebuke, a still shalme and a lowd shalme'; and in the same year William Wells received a 'vyall' and a 'rebuke'.[43] If suitable musicians could not be found locally, then foreigners might be recruited. In December 1545 Sir William Paget decided to hire a band of musicians from Europe and asked Thomas Chamberlain, Governor of the English merchants at Antwerp, to act as his agent. On 16 December Chamberlain replied to Paget that he had thus far heard 'divers upon violles only' but that he was continuing to audition candidates.[44] Two days later he wrote again to say that he had found five musicians who could play upon five or six sorts of instruments; four of them were young and would, he considered, remain in Paget's service, but the fifth, to whom the instruments belonged, had been persuaded to go only with difficulty.[45] The original group of Italians who could only play viols were rejected out of hand as 'no musicians'. Finally on 27 December Chamberlain wrote to ask whether Paget liked his musicians, a letter for which no reply survives.[46]

By the mid 16th century quite a few wealthy households were in possession of a set of viols. The following is a list of references to viols in private households in the third quarter of the 16th century taken from Woodfill[47] and other sources:

*c*1550    Thomas Howard, Duke of Norfolk, is reported to have had in his possession at Kenninghall several 'sets of viols'.[48]

1550    The accounts of Sir William Petre for the month of June include payments for a 'small vyall' (13s. 4d.) and other items such as a canvas bag to put the viol in (4d.) and viol strings (12d.). In 1556 one Thomas Jeffe was paid 14d. for 'violle stringes'.[49]

1552    Sir Thomas Chaloner, the son of a London mercer, paid John Rose 'for an other vyall to be made xxixth October of the finest sort xl*s*'. This statement implies that Rose had supplied Sir Thomas with at least one viol previously.

1558    An inventory of the goods of Richard Brereton, younger son of Sir William Brereton of Kent, includes 'iij old broken vyalles' valued at only 4s.[50]

1564/5    The accounts of the Earl of Northumberland include a payment for viol strings.

1566/7    Sir Henry Sidney paid £10. 10s. for a 'Sette of Vialles' and a further 16s. for strings.

1573    Sir Thomas Kytson purchased two dozen 'cattelins' for his viols. According to his Christmas accounts for 1574, one of his servants, Robert the Musician, was responsible for the 'base vyalles'.[51]

1575    Among the decorations erected for the visit of Queen Elizabeth to Kenilworth, the Earl of Leicester's residence, an eyewitness noted a number of musical instruments which included 'luts, violls, shallms, cornets, flutes, recorders and harpes'.[52] In 1580 an inventory of goods at Leicester House included among the musical instruments 'Two settes of vyalles in 2 chestes'.[53] In 1583 another inventory included two chests, one containing six 'vialles' and the other five 'violens'.

To put this list in perspective, it should be pointed out that there are many hundreds of references to the private ownership of lutes and virginals at this period. But this discrepancy is not really surprising, for in the third quarter of the 16th century viols were still played chiefly by servants or professional musicians, and the expense of hiring or maintaining enough players to form a consort, to say nothing of the costs involved in the purchase, delivery and upkeep of a set of viols, was probably still beyond the means of all but the wealthy. A lute or a pair of virginals, however, could be obtained relatively cheaply, as is shown by the frequent appearance of these instruments in the wills of gentlemen, merchants and farmers of quite modest means. There are, it is true, some signs that the viol was becoming more widely disseminated in the middle years of the reign of Elizabeth. In 1573, for example, Roger Rede of Hornchurch, a smith, bequeathed to his servant Stephen Prentice 'the viol that he brought to me and my treble'.[54] And in 1583 John Peers of Mountnessing bequeathed to his daughter his six viols.[55] But viol playing could hardly yet be described as a genuinely popular activity in private households. Not until the advent of the 17th century was this the case.

Very little of the music performed by the privately employed viol consorts of the mid 16th century appears to have survived. One set of partbooks, however, (British Library, Royal App. ms. 74–76) are believed to have been used by the household musicians of the Earl of Arundel, Henry Fitzalan. The instrumental items were probably copied into the partbooks during the 1560s when the family was living at Nonesuch. The repertory is exactly what one would expect to find in a manuscript used by household musicians: most of the pieces are dances – pavans, galliards, almans and branles. A few of their titles, notably *Smythes* pavan and galliard and *Milord Markes* galliard, suggest an English connection, though, as Doe points out, the style of the collection as a whole resembles that of contemporary continental dance music.[56] Needless to say, dances of this type were not written specifically for viols, but could have been performed on a wide variety of instruments. This solitary set of partbooks contains all that remains of English ensemble dance music of the mid 16th century, the music probably played by professional viol consorts in private employment – it is a meagre legacy indeed.

Towards the end of the reign of Henry VIII there occurred a development of considerable importance for the future of the viol and its music in England – the realisation that the instrument was admirably suited for teaching chil-

dren to play. As noted previously, there is evidence to suggest that by the mid
1540s at the latest children of the Chapel Royal were beginning to take up the
viol. At about the same period the viol was introduced into London choir-
schools such as St Paul's and Westminster, where it quickly became popular.
Certainly by the mid 16th century, playing the viol had come to be regarded as
a very important element in the education of choirboys, at least of those attending the aforementioned institutions. Having mastered the instrument,
the young choirboy viol players contributed much to its success. As a result of
their performances, the viol was introduced to a wider audience than would
have encountered the instrument if it had remained in the confines of the
court and a few of the largest private households. To judge by contemporary
reports, demand for the services of the children viol consorts reached a peak in
London in the early 1560s:

c1545    An early reference to choirboy viol players occurs in an interlude *Wyt and Science* by
        John Redford, organist of St Paul's, in which a viol consort enters twice to perform
        incidental music: 'Here the cum in with vyols'; and again 'Heere cumth in fowre wyth
        violes and syng, Remembre me, and at the last quere all make cursye and so goe forth
        syngyng.'[57]

1549    The accounts of the Merchant Taylors list a payment of 10s for having the children of
        'Poulles' playing upon 'vials' and singing at their annual dinner. The St Paul's chil-
        dren returned in 1551 and 1554, presumably still playing viols, and on the latter occa-
        sion they were joined by the musicians of Lord Pembroke.[58]

1553    Holinshed records that during the celebrations attending the coronation of Mary
        Tudor there was 'a pageant made against the dean of Paules gate, where the
        quéeristers of Paules plaied on vials and soong'.[59]

1555    Machyn reports the appearance of viols (perhaps played by the children of Westmin-
        ster) at a May Day celebration: 'The sam day was a goodly May-gam at Westmynster
        as has ben synes, with gyantes, mores-pykes, gunes and drumes, duwylles, and iij
        mores-dansses, and bagpypes and wyolles.'[60]

1559    In Machyn's Diary there is the following indistinct and incomplete passage: 'and the
        morrow a grett dener . . . chylderyn of the hospetalle, and a-for and after . . .
        unyalles, and there was a goodly compene of. . .'. it is just possible that the word
        'unyalles' should be read as 'v*yalles' and that the passage refers to another perform-
        ance by children viol players.[61]

1560    On 10 February the children of St Paul's were paid 6s.8d. for playing on the marriage
        day of Thomasine Petre, daughter of Sir William Petre, and two men 'that carried the
        chests wherein their playing garments were and instruments' received 12d. One of
        these chests was very likely the 'cheste of vyalyns and vialls' left to the Almonry of St
        Paul's in 1582 by the long-serving master of the children, Sebastian Westcote.[62]

1560    On 17 June the Goldsmiths employed the children of St Paul's to provide incidental
        music for their election feast: 'And all y^e dynner tyme y^e syngyng chyldren of Paules
        played upon their vialles & songe verye pleasaunt songes to y^e delectacion & reioy-
        synge of y^e whole companie.'[63]

1561    On 16 June Machyn records the appearance of viols at the Grocers' election feast:
        'The xvi day of June was the masters the Grossers fest; ther dynyd my Lord mare, Ser
        Roger Chamley . . . and mony worshepull men and mony lades and gentyllwomen;
        and grett chere; boyth the whettes and clarkes syngyng, and a nombur of vyolles play-
        hyng, and syngyng.'[64]

1561    Two weeks later the children of St Paul's again entertained the Goldsmiths at their election dinner: 'All y$^e$ dynner tyme y$^e$ syngyng children of paules played upon their vyalls and songe very pleasaunt songes to y$^e$ great delectacion & reioysyng of y$^e$ whole companie.'[65]

1562    According to Machyn, the children of Westminster played viols at the Clarkes dinner: 'The sam day of May was the Clarkes of London ther communion at the Gyldhalle chapell . . . and after to ther halle to dener, and after . . . chylderyn of Westmynster with whyalles and regalles.'[66]

At the height of their popularity in the 1550s and early 1560s the musical children must have led a varied and interesting life, performing at May Day celebrations, coronation festivities, public pageants, weddings, and above all at the annual election feasts of important City companies. Their main task at these ceremonial dinners was to provide incidental music during or after the meal, and reports of their performances suggest that the audience was usually treated to a mixture of singing and viol playing. This combination certainly proved a great success with the Goldsmiths whose chronicler noted the 'great delectacion and reioysyng' of the whole company at the choirboys' performance.

Something of the impact of the viol-playing children on the musical life of London at this period may be discerned in the reaction of the London waits who felt obliged to take up the viol themselves. In 1561 at the height of the vogue for the viol-playing children the waits petitioned the Court of Aldermen for £12 'to bye certain Instrumentes called a sette of vialles'.[67] The report of their application which is headed 'London vialles' notes that the waits were ordered to return the following week with the viols that they were intending to purchase. Their request was subsequently granted and the sum of £12 delivered to them 'to pay of the vyalles that they have by order of this court providyd and bought to the cyties use and for newe cases that are also to be provyded for the same'. With their new set of viols the London waits could now compete for work on equal terms with the popular St Paul's consort.

The skills of the viol-playing choirboys may also have impressed visitors from the Continent, the most significant of whom was Philip II of Spain in 1554. An inventory of Philip's instruments drawn up in 1602 includes the following item: 'un cofre grande . . . con siete bihuelas de arco grandes, dentro con sus arquillos, estas viguelas servian de enseñar los niños cantorcillos' ('a large chest with seven large viols and their bows, these viols were used to teach the children of the choir').[68] It is certainly possible that the tradition of teaching young Spanish choirboys the art of viol playing was stimulated by Spanish contact with English musical life of the mid 1550s. One of Philip's own musicians on this visit was Melchior Cançer 'tañedor de bihuela de arco' ('player of the bowed vihuela').[69] He, at least, would have taken an interest in the choirboy viol players, as he was employed not only as a player of the *vihuela de arco* but also as minstrel to the royal children ('menestreil a las Serenissimas Ynfantas').

By the mid 1560s this fashion for musical entertainments given by choirboys singing and playing on viols had passed its zenith. The Goldsmiths who had on at least two occasions employed the St Paul's children to perform at their St Dunstan's day election feast were obliged in 1564 to look elsewhere. A description of their 1564 dinner concludes with the observation that 'in stead of the children of poules we had this tyme currauntes noyse and his children who performed all thinges by them requisyte to be done in like manner and sorte as the children of poules were wonte to do'.[70] Evidently the past performances of the St Paul's children were being used as the pattern for their successors which suggests that Currance's children played viols. Currance's 'noyse' also replaced the St Paul's children at weddings of the Petre family. Whereas it was the children of St Paul's who put on an entertainment for the marriage of Thomasine Petre in 1560, for the weddings of Catherine Petre in 1561 and John Petre in 1570 Currance's band was engaged.[71]

Why were the viol-playing children so popular in the City of London at this period and why did their activities there decline somewhat in the mid 1560s? The answer to these questions may lie in the uncertain political and religious climate of the mid 16th century. During the reign of Henry VIII choirboys under the direction of their masters were quite often engaged to perform interludes at court. That viols were sometimes included in such performances, even at this early date, is evident from Redford's *Wyt and Science* in which a group of viol players twice enter to provide music. The death of Henry, however, was followed by a marked reversal in the fortunes of the children's companies; relatively few choirboy dramas received a royal hearing during the short reigns of Edward and Mary since, to use Lennam's words, 'neither of these sovereigns was particularly impressed by the appeal of the children's companies'.[72] Indeed, Mary, perceiving their potential for exacerbating political instability and religious heresy, was hostile to the playing of interludes from the first and a month after her accession issued an edict prohibiting the printing and performance of all interludes except those that had been given 'her graces speciall licence in writynge'. The reduction in demand for their services at court presumably resulted in a drop in income for the choirboy companies. For financial reasons, then, the children may have been obliged to seek additional employment elsewhere, and it was to the City of London, a traditional source of income for musicians of all kinds, that they turned their attention. Making use of their talents as musicians, they began to develop a reputation as performers of incidental music and by the early 1560s had established an important niche for themselves in the musical life of the capital, posing enough of a threat to the official waits to cause them to take up the viol. By now, however, Elizabeth was on the throne, and the children's companies were once again in great demand for their performances of plays and interludes. It was probably this swift return to royal favour that led the children to relinquish some of their engagements in the City. In some instances the children were replaced by the waits with their newly acquired case of 'vialles', but other engagements were taken over by lesser groups such as Currance's 'noyse'.

After the full resumption of their theatrical careers the children continued to make good use of their viol-playing skills to help in the provision of incidental music and songs for their plays. Viol playing thus remained an important element in the musical life of the choir-schools in the second half of the 16th century even after this vogue for musical presentations by children viol consorts in the City had passed its peak. There is a good deal of documentary evidence of this. In 1599, for example, Edmund Hooper, master of the choristers at Westminster, received a payment for viol strings,[73] and in his will dated 3 April 1582 Sebastian Westcote, almoner of St Paul's and master of the children, bequeathed to the almonry a 'cheste of vyalyns and vialls to exercise and learne the children and choristers there'.[74] By this time the children of St Paul's had apparently extended their range of accomplishments to include violin as well as viol playing, probably in response to prevailing fashion at court. At the end of the 16th century the song school at Newark also possessed a set of violins; an inventory of 1595 mentions five 'violine' books and five 'violins' with a chest.[75] Evidence of viol playing in choir-schools outside London is admittedly rather sparse. At Ely, however, teaching the viol was recorded as a duty of the master of the choristers in 1567,[76] and a payment 'per chordis violar' is said to appear in the accounts of Lincoln Cathedral in 1594.[77]

Though it is beyond the chronological scope of this study, it is worth pointing out that the traditions of viol playing in the choir-schools were maintained in the 17th century. Edwards cites a passage in the *Custom Book* of St Omer, an English Jesuit college in France, which lists four types of instrumental music; first is the music of viols alone ('musica mere ex violis') in which young people should be carefully instructed.[78] And the viol players of St Paul's were still in demand for royal occasions. Thomas Dekker's *The Magnificent Entertainment* which describes the festivities devised for King James on the day of his triumphant procession through the city of London (15 March 1603), reports the activities of the children viol players of St Paul's during 'the device at Soperlane end'.[79] His majesty was delighted with music 'sent from the voyces of nine Boyes (all of them Queristers of *Paules*) who in that place presenting the nine *Muses* sang the dittie following [a consort song] to their Viols and other Instruments'. From a subsequent passage it appears that the viols were played on stage unlike the other instruments: 'Wee might (that day) have called it, *The Musicke roome*, by reason of the chaunge of tunes, that danced around it; for in one place were heard a noyse of cornets, in a second, a consort, the third (which sate in sight) a set of Viols, to which the *Muses* sang.'

What kind of music was played by the choirboy viol consorts of the mid 16th century? A good case can be made in support of the view that textless polyphonic music of the period, by far the largest part of which consists of 'In nomine' settings, was associated in some way with their activities, either as public performers or as private students of music. The arguments in favour of this supposition may be summarised as follows:

i   The vogue for viol-playing children coincides almost exactly with the appearance of 'In nomines' and other textless pieces. Most authorities would agree with Doe[80] that this repertory dates in the main from the third quarter of the 16th century, from the reigns of Edward VI (1547-1553), Mary Tudor (1553-1558) and the first decade or so of the Elizabethan era. A more precise dating, however, is proposed by Neighbour,[81] who argues that the 'In nomine' settings of the major composers were unlikely to have been produced sporadically over a period of time, but instead occupied 'a relatively brief period of intense activity, from the late fifties for White and Parsons, or early sixties for Byrd and Ferrabosco, until the mid-sixties'. The early 1560s were precisely the years during which the viol-playing children of London were at their most active in giving public performances.

ii   The major composers of textless polyphony were in fact church musicians associated with those very institutions for which there is documentary evidence of a choirboy viol-playing tradition in the mid 16th century, namely the Chapel Royal (and presumably St George's Chapel Windsor), St Paul's, Westminster and, outside London, Ely: Parsons at the Chapel Royal; William Mundy at Westminster, St Paul's and the Chapel Royal; White at Ely and Westminster; Tye at Ely and perhaps the Chapel Royal. The young William Byrd is also thought to have been in London at this period. Of the less significant figures, William Whytebrook and both Henry and Thomas Mudd may have had links with St Paul's.[82]

iii   There is a distinct element of the didactic in much textless polyphony of the mid 16th century suggesting, in Neighbour's words, that it had 'strong links with the professional musicians' schoolroom'.[83] Quite a few 'In nomines' appear to have been written as exercises to enlarge the composer's technique or to extend the sight-reading abilities of singers and players. Examples of this might include Tye's *Trust* with its five minims to a measure,[84] Mundy's second 'In nomine' (*a*5) with its elaborate cross-rhythms, and Picforth's unique 'In nomine' (*a*5) in which each voice has its own note value – the top part minims, the second part dotted minims, the third part semibreves, the fourth part (which has the cantus firmus) breves, and the fifth part dotted semibreves.[85] This last composition, apart from demonstrating its composer's technical ingenuity, could have made a very useful exercise for teaching individuals in a consort to sustain their own rhythm. Assuming that textless pieces of this type were not conceived as purely theoretical exercises in compositional technique, their performers would most likely have been the children of the choir-schools to which the composers were attached.

iv   The earliest extant manuscripts of mid 16th-century textless polyphony date from the 1570s and 1580s, several decades after the music was actually composed. By this time the repertory was being used for singing at least as much as for playing. One of the most important sources (British Library, Add. ms. 31390), copied *c*1578, is entitled 'A booke of In nomines & other solfainge songes of v: vi: vij: and viij parts for voyces or Instrumentes', and in other manuscripts there are textless pieces entitled 'a singinge songe' or 'a solfying songe'.[86] The practice of singing textless music to solmization syllables or to the 'bare note' is fairly well documented in the late 16th century. On occasion sol-faing singers were accompanied on instruments like the group of Nymphs in Peele's *The Arraygnement of Paris* who 'singe or solfa with voyces and instruments awhile'.[87] The appearance of textless sol-faing songs in manuscripts compiled many years after the repertory was actually being composed does not, of course, prove that this was the intended method of performance from the first. But if the practice was current in the mid century, it would certainly have suited the children consorts. Contemporary accounts are almost unanimous that singing as well as viol playing formed the basis of their musical entertainments.

A picture begins to emerge of a small, quite tightly-knit group of composers, centred around three important London choir-schools, the Chapel Royal, St Paul's and Westminster (possibly with an outpost at Ely). The fashion for composing textless polyphony may have developed in these institutions as a direct response to the needs of the children, whose singing and viol playing were currently in such demand in the City of London. Whether textless polyphony was used solely as a means of instruction for the young singers and violists, or whether it formed part of their public repertory is hard to determine with any degree of certainty, but it has to be admitted that wordless singing and instrumental music would have been ideally suited to the temper of that uneasy period when the slightest hint of political unorthodoxy or religious heresy, especially if uttered in public, could have the direst personal consequences.

In his recent edition of *Elizabethan Consort Music* Doe[88] notes that mid 16th-century textless polyphony is 'a good deal more heterogeneous than may at first appear': compositions with didactic overtones mingle with showy display pieces. This accords well with the idea that the repertory was associated with the choirboys; at this period they would probably have needed both instructional material and pieces for public performance. Though viols would certainly have been the preferred manner of performance by the boys themselves, wind instruments, as Doe suggests,[89] may also have been used. The London waits are known to have joined forces with the St Paul's consort on several occasions. One problem has always puzzled scholars – the overwhelming preponderance in the repertory of 'In nomine' settings. It is possible that these pieces were formally associated with the choirboy entertainments given at the annual feasts of City companies during the 1550s and 1560s. Their performances naturally included songs for the diversion of the assembled company, as reports of the Goldsmiths feasts show, but at some stage in the proceedings, perhaps after a formal Latin grace, a final benediction, or during a ceremonial procession, it may have been the custom for the choirboys to provide instrumental music of a more solemn character. At such moments, an instrumental composition based on the popular cantus firmus from the 'Benedictus' of Taverner's *Gloria Tibi Trinitas* mass could have been justified on the grounds that the text of the original passage, 'In nomine domini' ('In the name of the Lord'), accorded well with the solemnity of the occasion.

Another repertory of music almost certainly associated with the activities of the children viol players of the mid 16th century was the consort song, a new form in which the instrumentation was specified more exactly – a solo voice with an accompanying consort of three or four instruments, usually viols. The earliest examples of the genre to have survived, settings of simple strophic texts, probably date back to the 1550s,[90] and thus could have been performed in the musical entertainments of the choirboys. An anthology of poetry selected before 1566 by Richard Edwardes, Master of the Chapel Royal children, includes a number of early consort song texts. It was published posthumously in 1576 as *The Paradise of Dainty Devices*, and Henry Disle, the publisher, commented in his note to the readers that the contents were 'aptly made to be set to any song in 5 partes, or song to instrument', a palpable reference to the consort song. Of the musical settings that have survived from this anthology, the majority are in a simple chordal style, but two by Strogers, a composer of textless polyphony, are in a more elaborate, contrapuntal idiom.

Whatever the origins of the form, there can be no doubt that by the early 1560s at the latest the consort song had become a regular feature of the dramatic productions of the revitalised choirboy companies. Especially popular at this period were through-composed laments or 'death-songs', possibly inspired by tragedies, in which effective use was made of repeated sighing exclamations of a somewhat theatrical nature. A further development of the 1560s was the transformation of the simple strophic consort song into the refrain song in which a boy soloist (or soloists), accompanied by instruments, would sing the verses, with a vocal chorus interpolating a brief refrain after each verse. This is clearly the method of performance envisaged for the song at the end of the interlude *Tom Tyler and his wife* (c1565), for which the following rubric appears: 'Here they all go in, and one cometh out, and singeth this song following all alone with instruments, and all the rest within sing between every staffe, the first two lines.'[91] The manuscript of one interlude of the period John Jeffere's *The Buggbears* (c1565) actually includes the vocal parts of two consort songs of this type.[92] The fourth song 'Lend me, you lovers' is headed 'Giles Perperel for Iphigenia', Perperel presumably being the boy playing Iphigenia. The second vocal part only sings the refrain 'And therefore, away care'. The instrumental accompaniment for the verse and other vocal parts for the refrain (if any) have not survived. For the final song 'Sith all our grief is turned to bliss' three vocal parts survive, all sung by boys as is shown both by their vocal register and by the line: 'We boys are glad our pain is past'. Again the instrumental accompaniment (presumably viols) has been lost.[93] The intended method of performance is signalled quite clearly by the insertion of the word 'quere' (i.e. choir) below the refrain 'Sith all our grief'. The three boy soloists (on stage) thus sing the verses with an instrumental accompaniment, while everyone else joins in for the refrain. Another type of consort song especially apt for theatrical use was the dialogue song, in which two characters sing alternate verses (either with or without a chorus). In *The Plaie of Pacient Grissell* (c1560)[94] by John Phillipp, Gaultier introduces a dialogue song thus:

Come let us depart with all celeritie,
Sound up your Instrumentes, bee ioyfull Nobillitie?
And in token of Victorie, some Song I will singe,
Which to perform Ladie, I must have your helpinge.

The important place of the consort song in mid 16th-century choirboy productions raises the question of how the viol consort was integrated into the performance. For this, study of Redford's *Wyt and Science* is helpful.[95] Although this early interlude does not specifically describe a consort song, it does call for a four-part viol consort to accompany voices in an unspecified manner. To judge by the stage directions, it was the specific intention of the playwright to allow four actors to double as viol players. For example, the marginal direction 'al go out save honest recre [ation]' precedes Honest Recreation's instruction to the offstage musicians 'Go to, my men, Play!' This enables a group of actors to make their exit and pick up their instruments in time to accompany the ensuing galliard. The viol players remain offstage during the subsequent exchanges between Ignorance and Idleness and then re-enter as Fame, Favour, Riches and Worship upon the instruction 'here the cum in with vyols' to accompany the song 'Exeedynge Mesure' which Worship introduces with the words 'then let us not stay here muet and mum, but tast we thes instrumentes tyll she cum'. Similarly, at the end of the play after the unaccompanied song 'Wellcum myne owne' the following rubric appears: '& when the song is doone, reson sendyth instruccion, study and dyligence, & confidens out'. Again, this is to enable the four actors to leave the stage, pick up their viols and return for the concluding song which is announced with the instruction 'heere cumth in fowre wyth violes & syng'. The implication of this statement is that the viol players accompanied their own singing on stage. Whether as a rule viols were played in full view of the audience probably depended on the number of actor–musicians available. Viols, however, were so closely associated with choirboys at this period that performances on stage would probably have been considered quite acceptable. (As noted above, Dekker in *The Magnificent Entertainment* of 1603 refers to a set of viols played by choirboys 'which sate in sight', while other groups of non-acting musicians were apparently concealed.)

The continuing importance of the consort song in English music of the latter part of the 16th century was due in no small measure to its adoption by William Byrd whose magnificent contribution to the genre forms the most enduring legacy of music for viols to have survived from the Elizabethan era. A few of Byrd's consort songs may have been commissioned for theatrical performances,[96] but most of them were written for his patrons and colleagues at court and for friends in recusant households, a clear indication that by then the genre was no longer confined to the immediate environment of the choirboy entertainments.

In addition to the secular consort song repertory of the mid 16th century, there are a number of settings of sacred texts, notably metrical psalms. These may have been performed by choirboys on ceremonial occasions, as, for example, at the entry of the young King James into Edinburgh when it was reported that 'the musicians song the xx Psalme and others played upon the viols'.[97] Several of the earliest examples actually combine the common melody of the hymn or psalm with the 'In nomine' cantus firmus, a feature that suggests a link with the textless repertory. The practice of performing metrical psalms or portions of scripture as solo songs with instrumental accompaniment became very popular indeed and thus merited mention in published collections. In Tye's *The Actes of the Apostles* (1553) the lute is cited as a possible instrument of accompaniment, and Day's harmonized version of the Sternhold and Hopkins Psalter (1563) is entitled 'the whole psalmes in foure partes, which may be song to al musicall instrumentes'.

An important offshoot of the mid 16th-century sacred consort song was the consort anthem in which a solo voice or voices with an accompanying consort of viols was used with greater freedom.[98] There were in fact two quite distinct types of accompanied anthem, the one (now known as the verse anthem) in which the organ was the instrument of accompaniment, the other (now known as the consort anthem) in which a consort of viols was used. Which of the two types came first is by no means certain. One recent writer has argued that the consort anthem probably predates the verse anthem on the grounds that when an anthem survives in two different versions, the primary source in most instances transmits the consort version for viols.[99] Concerning the performance of consort anthems, choir-schools like St Paul's and Westminster with their traditions of viol playing would certainly have been in a position to include them in church services, yet the failure of even one liturgical manuscript to transmit the consort version of an anthem suggests that the organ was the preferred method of accompaniment in public worship. Consort anthems, like many consort songs, were thus probably written for small-scale private performances at court or in some of the larger households.

Although it was the choirboy companies who made most use of the viol in theatrical presentations, the instrument also had a part to play in the provision of incidental music for adult companies. Both viols and violins are known to have participated in the musical accompaniments to the dumb shows performed between the acts of some dramas. One of the dumb shows during *A Tragedie of Gorboduc*, enacted by the Gentlemen of the Inner Temple on 28 January 1562, included 'violenze';[100] and George Gascoigne's *Jocasta*, presented at Gray's Inn in 1566, opened with a dumb show accompanied by 'a dolefull & straunge noyse of Violles, Cythren, Bandurien and such lyke'.[101] The viol consort could also provide incidental music at important moments during the drama itself. In *The Rare Triumphes of Love and Fortune* (London, 1589) the Triumph of Venus is accompanied by the direction 'strike up a noise of viols', while Fortune triumphs to the much more dramatic sound of 'trumpettes, drummes, cornets and Gunnes'.

For some productions the music may have been provided by a consort of musicians hired especially for the occasion. Yet there is evidence to suggest that adult actors, like their choirboy counterparts, were sometimes trained musicians able to sing their own songs and provide their own incidental music. As early as 1543 there is documentary evidence of a musician, quite possibly a viol player, entering the theatre. John Maria of Cremona was one of the original members of the King's 'newe vialls' from Italy who entered the royal service on 1 May 1540. He apparently left the band at the end of June 1542, which is the date of his last recorded monthly payment. On 7 June the following year, a musician of the same name reappears in the records of the legal proceedings of the Mayor and Aldermen's Court, in connection with an application for a license to act: 'Item. John marya being a Synger borne & a player of Antyques [grotesque pageants] ys lycensed to play freyle w'in thys Cytye All suche feates of Antyquytye As he can.'[102] This singer–actor may possibly be identified with John Maria of Cremona, who thus may have the distinction of being the first recorded adult actor-viol player. Certainly by the end of the 16th century there are many indications that actors in adult companies were taking up the viol. An inventory of the goods of the Lord Admirall's men taken on 10 March 1598 includes 'iij trumpettes and a drum, and a trebel viall, a basse viall, a bandore, a sytteren',[103] and in 1605 the actor Augustine Phillips bequeathed a bass viol to his apprentice.[104] Moreover, some plays of the period require a viol player on stage. At one point in Jonson's *Every Man out of his Humour* (1599) Fastidious 'takes down the violl, and playes'. One of the actors at the first performance of this play was none other than Augustine Phillips who could have used his own viol.[105]

Towards the end of the 16th century companies of actors would increasingly have been able to turn to city waits if they required extra musicians. The waits of London were probably the first to purchase a consort of viols; they petitioned the Court of Aldermen for a 'sette of vialles' in 1561 probably, as noted above, in order to compete with the children viol players who were currently so popular in the City of London. Other cities followed. According to Woodfill, the Norwich waits could play both viols and violins by 1585 and the Chester waits 'violens' by 1590.[106] The versatility of the Norwich waits was noted by Will Kemp in 1599: 'besides their excellency in wind instruments, their rare cunning on the Vyoll and Violin: theyr voices be admirable, everie one of them able to serve in any Cathedrall Church in Christendoome for Quiristers.'[107] The Chamberlain's accounts of the town of Aldeburgh record payments to an individual wait, 'blind Harry', in 1579: as well as money for a shawm and a case, he received 12s. 8d. for a 'vyall' and 3s. 6d. for a case.[108] The more notable bands of waits were sometimes asked to accompany sailors on their voyages abroad, an exciting if arduous task. In 1589 Sir Francis Drake requested the Mayor of Norwich to allow the city waits to travel with him on his forthcoming Portuguese venture. The Mayor agreed, and the waits were provided with new cloaks and instruments.[109] The viol was thus introduced to some unexpectedly remote and exotic locations quite early on in its history. In 1577 John Winter and Francis Drake embarked upon a voyage to the South Seas via the Magellan Straits. Edward Cliffe, whose report of the venture appears in Hakluyt's *Voyages*, noted that Winter put ashore on the coast of South America near the Cape of Good Hope to establish relations with the natives by presenting them with gifts: 'Then the countrey people came and tooke them [the gifts] and afterward approached neerer to our men, shewing themselves very pleasant, insomuch that M. Winter daunced with them. They were exceedingly delighted with the sound of the trumpet and vialles.'[110]

Very little is known about English viol makers of the 16th century, the crafts-men who by the end of the reign of Queen Elizabeth must have been supply-ing a wide range of professional violists, to say nothing of the growing body of amateur players, with their instruments. There are occasional payments in account books to the makers themselves, such as the Englishman Richard Hume who in 1535 was paid £20 by the Scottish court to 'mak violis to the Kingis grace'.[111] But in most cases – infuriatingly enough for the researcher – the person named is the professional musician responsible for procuring the instruments rather than their original maker. Some information, however, has survived about the greatest English viol makers of the 16th century, John Rose and his brilliant son, several of whose instruments have survived the ravages of time.[112]

John Rose, the elder, first appears in 1552 in the private account books of Sir Thomas Chaloner in which there are three payments for mending lutes and a further payment of 40s. 'for an other vyall to be made xxixth October of the finest sort'. By 1561 he had built himself a small lodging in Bridewell Hospital. An extended entry in the Bridewell Court Books dated 8 August granting him a lease on the property is most informative: 'the said John Rose together with Jone his wife are of right virtuous and honest conversation and the said Rose hathe a most notable gift given of God in the making of instruments even soche a gift as his fame is sped thorough a great part of Christendom and his name as moche and now both for virtue and conning commended in Italy than in this his natural contery'. To have achieved such a reputation, Rose must have been making viols for some time.[113]

That John Rose had a son who also made viols is shown by the well-known entry in Stow's *Annales*: 'In the fourth Year of Queen Elizabeth John Rose, dwelling in Bridewell, devised and made an instrument with wyer strings, commonly called the bandora and left a son, far excelling himself in making Bandoras, Voyall de Gamboes and other instruments.' Excellent though his father's reputation was, John Rose, the younger, was apparently an even more skilled instrument maker. Evidently of a somewhat mercurial disposition, the younger Rose tended to fall foul of authority. On 16 November 1568 he

101    Portrait of Sir Henry Unton: detail of a domestic viol consort
(*c*1596: National Portrait Gallery, London)

received a sharp reprimand from the Mayor and Aldermen's Court for
putting on puppet shows: 'Iohn Rose of brydwell was this daye streightly
charged & comaunded by the courte here utterly to desyste and leve of that
kinde of pastyme that he there useth to make w[th] puppettes and such other
lyke thinges whereby great numbers of people do thither resorte.'[114] It seems
likely that the younger Rose's career as an instrument maker dates from this
abrupt termination of his activities as a popular puppeteer.[115] Then towards
the end of his life he was periodically in arrears with his rent. On 21 October
1602 he was ordered to pay three weeks outstanding rent and in 1607 he again
fell behind with his payments. Several viols by John Rose survive, but with
one possible exception (the bass in the Victoria and Albert Museum) they all
date from the very end of the 16th or the early 17th century.[116] The earliest
recorded Rose viol may be the instrument advertised in *The Post Man* on 10
September 1719: 'A fine Consort Viol, made by John Rose in the Year 1592, is to
be disposed of. Inquire at the Wheat Sheaf in Bell Alley.' Of the numerous
viols that must have been made by English craftsmen of the mid 16th century,
none appear to have survived.

Iconographic evidence, for once, is not helpful. There are very few representations of viols in England before the end of the 16th century. One possible
source of information is the celebrated group portrait of the family of Thomas

102   Viol by John Rose
(1598: Ashmolean Museum, Oxford)

103   English viol
(early 17th century, attributed to John Rose:
Ashmolean Museum, Oxford)

More by Hans Holbein (*c*1527). This survives in two versions, an original
drawing by Holbein himself, and later copies of the painting, notably one by
Lockey in Nostell Priory ('Richardus Locky Fec. ano 1530').[117] Two different
instruments are depicted. In the drawing is a string instrument (sketched only
in outline) hanging on the wall behind the family: in the Lockey painting a
bowed string instrument (together with a lute) is displayed to the far left. The
size of the latter instrument – far too large to be played *a braccio* – strongly suggests that it is a viol. The physical structure of both instruments confirms the
evidence of Henry VIII's household accounts that in the 1520s and 1530s it was
north European rather than Italian string players who introduced the viol into
England. The instrument sketched by Holbein himself is reminiscent of the
German *gross Geigen* in shape, not perhaps very surprising in view of this
artist's nationality: the shoulders are pointed; there are two inward facing c-
holes in the upper part of the belly; and there is a large central rose. The
Lockey viol exhibits none of the most characteristic features of the 16th-
century Italian schools of viol making – the deep ribs and the bend in the

upper part of the back. It is much closer in design to some Flemish instruments of the period, like the one depicted in a 16th-century Flemish 'Allegory of Inspiration'.[118] It is certain that later in the century Italian viols did enter the country – much of the early 17th-century English viol design developed by John Rose was derived from Italian models – but evidence is lacking.[119]

Even though, except for John Rose and his son, their names are not known and their instruments have not survived, the prices charged by English viol makers of the 16th century can be estimated from the following prices and evaluations taken from references already cited in this chapter:

| | | |
|---|---|---|
| 1535 | £20 | 'to mak violis to the Kingis grace'[120] |
| 1537 | 53s. 4d. | 'for iiij vyalles bought at London' (i.e. 13s. 4d. each)[121] |
| 1550 | 13s. 4d. | for a 'small vyall'[122] |
| 1552 | 40s. | 'for an other vyall to be made [by John Rose] of the finest sort'[123] |
| 1561 | £12 | 'to bye certain Instrumentes called a sette of vialles'. (six at £2 a piece or five at £2. 8s.?)[124] |
| 1563 | £15 | 'for a sett of vyalls by him [Francesco de Venetia] sold to us' (six at £2. 10s. each or five at £3?)[125] |
| 1566/7 | £10. 10s. | for a 'sette of Vialles' (five at two guineas each?)[126] |
| 1579 | 12s. 8d. | for a 'vyall'[127] |
| 1595 | 10s. | for a 'viole'[128] |

At the top end of the market John Rose could charge 40s. for a viol of the finest sort. In line with this valuation, sets of five or six good viols purchased in London in the mid 16th century were commanding a fee of somewhere between ten guineas and £15, that is, between £2 and £3 an instrument, a marked increase over the 13s. 4d. paid by the Duke of Rutland in 1537 for each of his four viols. This reflects not only fiscal inflation but also the growing popularity of the consort of viols in the mid century. Outside the capital, however, provincial musicians probably played much cheaper instruments. Viols like those valued at 12s. 8d. or 10s. – roughly one quarter of the best London price – would have been within the means of those with less affluent patrons. Interestingly enough, in *The Rates of the Custome House* (London, 1582) 'viols the peece' are valued at only 6s.8d. Even allowing for wholesale prices, this is a very low valuation.

In drawing this survey of the viol in 16th-century England to a close, it may be useful to emphasise once again the fundamental importance of the choir-boy viol players and their masters, both in the evolution of a repertory of music idiomatically conceived for viols and in the wide dissemination of the instrument. The legacy of ensemble music for viols by 16th-century church musicians, masters of choristers, gentlemen of the royal chapels and even mere singing-men was a rich and lasting one; it included forms such as the 'In nomine', the consort song and the consort anthem. Even in the early 17th century this tradition was still bearing fruit in the music of Byrd and Gibbons. But what now remains of the music associated with the activities of viol players in predominantly secular employments, the city waits, the actors, the household musicians and even the much-vaunted royal band? – a meagre quantity of dance music. Only with the advent of the Jacobean viol fantasy at the turn of the century did secular musicians begin to contribute music for viol consort of lasting value. [129]

The choirboy viol-playing tradition was also probably the single most influential factor in the spread of the instrument throughout English society. Admittedly it was adult professional players at court and in private employment who were responsible for the initial introduction of the viol in the 1530s, but their influence seems not to have extended much beyond the establishment of a limited level of professional activity. On the other hand, the training of several generations of young choristers in the art of viol playing during the second half of the 16th century was of vital importance in helping to prepare the ground for the sudden upsurge of interest in the instrument among amateurs in the early 17th century. Having completed their training in the choir-schools, successive generations of young singers and viol players dispersed to various types of employment; the best of them remained in the choir-schools as adult singers, thereby ensuring continuity of tradition; others were provided with a university education to fit them for a new career; others still sought employment in private households, the largest of which maintained their own chapels. Though it is hard to prove, this steady influx of ex-choristers into the universities, Inns of Court and private establishments probably contributed greatly to the adoption of the viol by genuinely amateur players. There is certainly evidence of viol playing both at the University of Cambridge and at the Inns of Court in the 1590s. In 1594 an entertainment given by the gentlemen of Gray's Inn included music for viols and voices,[130] and in 1595 the accounts of Trinity College included a payment for 'a sett of newe vialls' (£8) and one for 'viall strings and mending the Colledge Instruments' (12s.).[131] There is also evidence that children in private households were beginning to take up the viol in the 1590s. The celebrated portrait of Sir Henry Unton (c1596) depicts a domestic consort of five viol players making music around a table (Plate 101); two of the participants are young children playing small viols appropriate to their stature. At the age of eight the young William Cavendish was taught the treble viol; his father's accounts for 1599 record payments for 'a treble viol for Master William' (£1. 5s. 0d.), 'a box to put Master William's viol in' (20d.) and 'strings for the said viol' (2s.).[132] Edwards cites further instances of youthful viol players around the turn of the century.[133] The long-established traditions of teaching the viol to the children of the choir-schools were thus beginning to bear fruit in private households, and the result was a new generation of amateur viol players who were to provide an appreciative audience for the Jacobean viol fantasy which in the early 17th century began to displace the madrigal as the favoured form of domestic ensemble music-making. In the words of Dodd, 'all the best people, with voices grown hoarse from a generation of madrigal-singing, were taking up their bows'.[134] The start of its Jacobean 'Age of Plenty' is an appropriate point to conclude the early history of the viol.

# Conclusion

It has been the purpose of this study to follow the rise of the viol from its late-medieval origins through to its years of renaissance prosperity. Viewing the story as a whole, it becomes clear that the middle decades of the 16th century were the zenith of the early viol. By this time the instrument had achieved a position of unquestioned eminence in European musical life. Yet as the century declined, so the fortunes of the viol appeared to wane. The first round of the long running contest between viol and violin was played out, and the violin appeared for a time to be gaining the upper hand. In Italy composers turned increasingly to the violin with its brighter, louder timbre for large-scale ceremonial works. In France the violin was beginning to exert a profound influence on the form of the viol. Even in England, the last decades of the 16th century saw newer forms such as the madrigal and the 'broken' consort beginning to attract the imagination of composers and public alike. With the remarkable upsurge of interest in the viol consort in early Jacobean England, however, the balance was redressed. Now, with a turning of the tide, there was a movement south. It was now English viol players travelling south who revitalised the traditions of viol playing on the Continent, and English viol makers whose instruments, more than ever before, were admired and respected.

If, with the declining years of the 16th century, the trend against the viol had not been reversed and the instrument had faded away into relative obscurity as it did in Italy, our modern perception of the instrument would have to be drastically altered. The whole course of its early history from its emergence in the Moorish enclaves of Valencia to its success at the hands of the London choirboys is marked by diversity rather than uniformity. When examining evidence of the 'renaissance viol', we are confronted by a bewildering array of different body shapes, sizes and constructional techniques, a plethora of variant tunings and numerous different playing techniques. With hindsight, of course, it is possible to trace the lines of development that exerted a lasting influence on the viol of the 17th and 18th centuries but, in doing so, it is easy to forget that to the 16th century other, now long forgotten forms, may have appeared equally significant at the time.

228

With the recent upsurge of interest in reproducing the instruments of some of the finest 16th-century viol makers – Francesco Linarol, the Cicilianos and John Rose – we can now perform and listen to renaissance music on viols of the period. The study of early viols and their construction is admittedly in its infancy, but already it has become clear that viols of the 16th century had their own distinctive tone qualities well worth reproducing in modern performance. With or without copies of renaissance instruments, however, viol players can still explore the music of the renaissance. Indeed, consorts who focus their attention solely upon the 17th-century English repertory – rich though that is – are guilty of neglecting the superb legacy of 16th-century vocal polyphony: not, it is true, composed specifically for viols, but certainly played on viols and, with its predominantly polyphonic language, admirably suited to the viol consort. Transcriptions of chansons, madrigals, motets and even mass movements are perfectly 'authentic' performed either in their original unadorned state, or, perhaps using Ortiz as a guide, with a small amount of stylish embellishment. Furthermore, with a little imagination and again using the admirable Ortiz as a precept, there are unlimited possibilities for the solo viol player – even the hard-done-by tenor viol soloist – in arrangements of 16th-century vocal music for viol and keyboard. Composers of renaissance polyphony from Josquin onwards are part of the viol player's legitimate heritage and deserve to be treated as such.

# Notes

## Introduction

1 This invaluable treatise was published in two volumes: *Regola Rubertina* (Venice, 1542) and *Lettione Seconda* (Venice, 1543). A facsimile of both volumes has been published by Forni (Bologna, 1970). A German translation and full commentary has been published by W. Eggers: *Die 'Regola Rubertina' des Silvestro Ganassi, Venedig 1542/43: Eine Gambenschule des 16. Jahrhunderts* (Kassel, 1974). An English translation of the first volume by R. Bodig appears in *JVdGSA*, vol. 18 (1981).

2 A translation of the relevant passage is given by E. Winternitz in *Musical Instruments and their Symbolism in Western Art* (London, 1967) 199: 'Notice how the violone is made with six strings. I often wondered which was more ancient, the lute or the violone, when I wanted to describe its origin. Having discussed the question with various people, I recalled having seen among the antiquities of Rome, in a history with many marble figures, one figure who had in his hands a bowed viola similar to those mentioned above. There I immediately recognized that the violone was more ancient than the lute, on the evidence of the story of Orpheus, who is not mentioned as using the lute, but rather the instrument with strings and bow that is the lira, which with its strings and its bow is like the violone. But as to its name, it was lira or lirone, although most people call it violone. But it is more correct to call it lirone, and, in the plural, lironi, rather than violone or violoni: our evidence is based on Orpheus and his lyre . . . '

3 Winternitz (1967) 198

4 J. Rousseau: *Traité de la viole, qui contient une dissertation curieuse sur son origine* (Paris, 1687). An English translation by N. Dolmetsch has been appearing in *The Consort* from vol. 33 (1977).

5 W. Bachmann: *Die Anfänge des Streichinstrumentenspiels* (Leipzig, 1964; Eng. trans. 1969) 8

6 Two of these are reproduced by K. Schlesinger in *The Instruments of the Modern Orchestra and Early Records of the Precursors of the Violin Family*: vol. 2: *The Precursors of the Violin Family, Records, Researches and Studies* (London, 1910) 231.

7 Schlesinger (1910) 484

8 E. S. J. van der Straeten: *The History of the Violin* (London, 1933) 27

9 Canon F. W. Galpin: *Old English Instruments of Music* (London, 1910; 4th rev. edn. 1965) 64–65

10 N. Bessaraboff: *Ancient European Musical Instruments* (Boston, 1941) 267

11 G. R. Hayes: *Musical Instruments and their Music 1500–1750*, (2 vols., London, 1928 & 1930): vol. 2: *The Viols and other Bowed Instruments*, 56

12 D. Munrow: *Instruments of the Middle Ages and Renaissance* (London, 1976) 85

13 M. Remnant: 'The Use of Frets on Rebecs and Medieval Fiddles', *GSJ*, vol. 21 (1968) 146–151

14  A. Baines: *European and American Musical Instruments* (London, 1966) 17

15  Bachmann (1969) 11 writes of the 'limited value of philology – both the etymological interpretation of words and comparative linguistics – as a tool' for investigating the subject of his research.

16  Munrow (1976) 85

17  S. Marcuse: *A Survey of Musical Instruments* (London, 1975) 496

18  R. T. Dart: 'The Viols' in A. Baines, ed.: *Musical Instruments Through the Ages* (London, 1961) 184–190

19  Review of Baines (1961) by R. Conant in *JAMS*, vol. 16 (1963) 397

20  D. D. Boyden: *Catalogue of the Hill Collection of Musical Instruments in the Ashmolean Museum, Oxford* (London, 1969) 3

21  Schlesinger (1910) 481

22  Galpin (1965) 66

23  M. Morrow: '16th Century Ensemble Viol Music', *EM*, vol. 2, no. 3 (1974) 160–163

24  Marcuse (1975) 501

25  C. Sachs: *The History of Musical Instruments* (New York, 1940) 347-348

26  H. Panum: *Middelalderens strengeinstrumenter* (Copenhagen, 1915-1931); Eng. trans.: *The Stringed Instruments of the Middle Ages* (London, 1939)

27  Baines (1966) 17

28  D. D. Boyden: *The History of Violin Playing from its Origins to 1761 and its Relationship to the Violin and Violin Music* (London, 1965) 14

29  An early date of c1475 is often claimed for the 'Vohar' viol in the Dolmetsch Collection. This claim, however, seems to have been based on a dating given to Arnold Dolmetsch by someone in the British Museum for the *parchment linings* inside the instrument. This, of course, does not prove that the instrument itself dates from that period; its maker could as easily have used old parchment as new. I am grateful to Mr. Ian Harwood for information on this point.

30  The following remarks are intended only as an outline of the approach I have adopted in this study. For more extensive comment on general questions associated with the study of musical iconography, see H. M. Brown & J. Lascelle: *Musical Iconography: A Manual for Cataloguing Musical Subjects in Western Art before 1800* (Cambridge, Mass., 1972).

31  H. M. Brown: 'Iconography and the Study of Particular Repertories of Music', *RIdIM Newsletter*, vol. 2, no. 2 (1977) 27–29

32  H. M. Brown: 'Iconography of Music', *The New Grove* (London, 1980)

33  Boyden (1965) 16

34  B. Castiglione: *Il Libro del Cortegiano* (Venice, 1528)

## 1. The medieval viol

1  W. Bachmann: *Die Anfänge des Streichinstrumentenspiels* (Leipzig, 1964; Eng. trans. 1969) Plate 1

2  Bachmann (1969) Plate 2

3  For illustrations of some of these instruments, see *The New Grove* (London, 1980): articles on North Africa; Turkey; Afghanistan; India; China; Vietnam; Indonesia.

4  Bachmann (1969) Plate 51

5  M. Remnant: 'Rebec, Fiddle and Crowd in England', *PRMA*, vol. 95 (1968-1969) 24

6  Bachmann (1969) Plate 59

7  M. Remnant: *Musical Instruments of the West* (London, 1978) 49

8  Bachmann (1969) 119

9  I. D. Woodfield: 'The Origins of the Viol' (diss., University of London, King's College, 1977) Plates 4 & 5

10 Woodfield (1977) Plate 6

11 D. Munrow: *Instruments of the Middle Ages and Renaissance* (London, 1976) 85

### 2. The Moorish *rabāb* in Aragon

1 The *rabāb* is still played today in North Africa, in Morocco, Algeria and Tunisia. Photographs of 20th-century instruments and players are reproduced in Salah el Mahdi: *La Musique Arabe* (Paris, 1972) 15, 27, 60 & 72.

2 W. Bachmann: *Die Anfänge des Streichinstrumentenspiels* (Leipzig, 1964; Eng. trans. 1969) Plate 21

3 *Roman de la Rose*, lines 20995-21002, cited in L. Wright: 'The Medieval Gittern and Citole: A Case of Mistaken Identity', *GSJ*, vol. 30 (1977)

4 *Oeuvres de Guillaume de Machaut*, ed. E. Hoepffner, vol. 2, Société des Anciens Textes Français (Paris, 1911): *Remède de Fortune*, line 3962

5 Wright (1977). The appendix to this article contains a very useful selection of references.

6 *The Complete Works of Geoffrey Chaucer*, ed. W. W. Skeat (Oxford, 1894): *The Milleres Tale*, line 3331 ('and playen songes on a small rubible'). See also *The Cokes Tale*, line 4396 ('Al conne he playe on giterne or ribible').

7 *Lydgate's Reson and Sensuallyte*, ed. E. Seiper, Early English Text Society, Extra Series, vol. 84 (London, 1901) line 5581

8 M. Remnant: 'Rebec, Fiddle and Crowd in England', *PRMA*, vol. 95 (1968-1969) 15

9 Reese translates the passage as follows: 'The shame-faced Binchois I have seen / Silent before their rebec-tones / And frowning Dufay in spleen / Since no such melody he owns.' Quoted in *Music in the Renaissance* (London, 1954) 51

10 D. Poulton: 'The Lute in Christian Spain', *LSJ*, vol. 19 (1977) 37-38

11 J. Read: *The Moors in Spain and Portugal* (London, 1974) 220-231

12 C. R. Post: *A History of Spanish Painting* (14 vols., Cambridge, Mass., 1930-1966) vol. 3, 164-168

13 Post, vol. 3 (1930) 212

14 I. D. Woodfield: 'The Origins of the Viol' (diss., University of London, 1977) Plate 39

15 Woodfield (1977) Plate 40

16 See, for example, B. Berenson: *Italian Pictures of the Renaissance: Florentine School* (2 vols., London, 1963) vol. 1, Plates 331, 333 & 335; and R. van Marle: *The Italian Schools of Painting* (19 vols., The Hague, 1923-1939) vol. 8, Figure 229.

17 J. Lamaña: 'Los instrumentos musicales en los últimos tiempos de la dinastía de la Casa de Barcelona', *AM*, vol. 24 (1969) 59-61

18 J. Ruiz: *Libro de Buen Amor*, ed. R. S. Willis (Princeton, 1972) stanza 1230

19 J. B. Trend: *The Music of Spanish History to 1600* (London, 1926) 253

20 P. Thornton: *The Voice of Atlas* (London, 1936) 80-81

21 For an edition of Jerome's *Tractatus de Musica* (the section on the *rubeba* and *vielle*) see C. Page: 'Jerome of Moravia on the *Rubeba* and *Vielle*', *GSJ*, vol. 32 (1979) 77-98

22 Thornton (1936) 80-81

23 Post (1930) 214

24 Page (1979) 88-89

25 London, 1659

26 For an edition of the treatise, see K. Weinmann: *Johannes Tinctoris (1445-1511) und sein unbekannter Traktat 'De inventione et usu musicae'* (Regensburg, 1917). An English translation of the sections dealing with musical instruments is given by A. Baines: 'Fifteenth-century Instruments in Tinctoris's *De Inventione et Usu Musicae*', *GSJ*, vol. 3 (1950) 19-26.

27 Wright (1977) argues convincingly that the instrument known to Tinctoris and countless others as the *gittern* was in fact the small lute-like instrument hitherto designated in 20th-

century organology as the *mandora*, while the waisted, plucked instrument now known as the *gittern* would have been recognised by medieval musicians as the *citole*. His argument certainly makes sense of the passage in Tinctoris in which an instrument 'invented by the Catalans, which some call the *guiterra* and others the *ghiterne*' is described as being shaped like a small lute.

28  Bachmann (1969) 55

29  J. Ribera: *La Música de las Cantigas* (Madrid, 1922; Eng. trans. Stanford, 1929) 114

30  J. M. Kennedy: *A Critical Edition of Yong's Translation of George of Montemayor's Diana and Gil Polo's Enamoured Diana* (Oxford, 1968)

31  Jorge de Montemayor: *Los siete libros de la Diana*, Clássicos Castellanos 127 (Madrid, 1946) 9-10

32  Ibid. 230-231

33  Ibid. 30

34  *The Adventures of Don Quixote by Miguel de Cervantes Saavedra*, trans. by J. M. Cohen, Penguin Classics (London, 1950)

35  A. Salazar: 'Música, Instrumentos y Danzas en las Obras de Cervantes', *Nueva Revista de Filogía Hispánica*, vol. 2 (1948) 34

36  Gaspar Gil Polo: *Diana Enamorada*, Clássicos Castellanos 135 (Madrid, 1953) 122

37  A. Livermore: 'The Spanish Dramatists and their Use of Music', *ML*, vol. 25 (1944) 142

38  C. Engel: *A Descriptive Catalogue of the Musical Instruments in the South Kensington Museum* (London, 1870) 9

39  D. Munrow: *Instruments of the Middle Ages and Renaissance* (London, 1976) 27. Two of the *rabābs* depicted in the *Cantigas de Santa María* also have slight waists to the lower half of the belly.

40  C. Sachs: *The History of Musical Instruments* (New York, 1940) 255

41  Thornton (1936) 80-81

42  H. G. Farmer: *Historical Facts of the Arabian Musical Influence* (London, 1930) 347

43  H. Gerle: *Musica Teusch* (Nuremberg, 1532)

44  S. di Ganassi: *Regola Rubertina* (Venice, 1542); *Lettione Seconda* (Venice, 1543)

### 3. The vihuela de mano

1  R. T. Dart: 'The Viols' in A. Baines, ed.: *Musical Instruments Through the Ages* (London, 1961) 184-185

2  Of several recent works on the *vihuela* and the guitar, the most reliable is J. Tyler's *The Early Guitar: A History and Handbook* (London, 1980).

3  D. Munrow: *Instruments of the Middle Ages and Renaissance* (London, 1976) 84

4  Florence, Biblioteca Riccardiana, ms. 492, fol. 75. I am grateful to Christopher Page for drawing my attention to this miniature.

5  There are a number of earlier examples of waisted instruments, possibly plucked fiddles, in the hands of the Elders of the Apocalypse (for example, at Santiago de Compostela), but these may simply be instruments held for display rather than serious performance.

6  For an edition of the treatise, see K. Weinmann: *Johannes Tinctoris (1445–1511) und sein unbekannter Traktat 'De inventione et usu musicae'* (Regensburg, 1917). An English translation of the sections dealing with musical instruments is given by A. Baines: 'Fifteenth-century Instruments in Tinctoris's *De Inventione et Usu Musicae*', *GSJ*, vol. 3 (1950) 19-26.

7  D. Poulton: 'The Lute in Christian Spain', *LSJ*, vol. 19 (1977) 34-49

8  Tinctoris may here have been referring to the greater depth and bulk of the lute with its vaulted ribs.

9  It might be useful to list additional examples of the cornered *vihuela* from the province of Aragon. Of considerable iconographic interest is a mid 15th-century Aragonese retable of the Visitation owned by the Hispanic Society of America; no fewer than five of its six

panels are graced by angelic musicians, five harpists and two *vihuela* players. One of the musical duos appears in a painting-within-a-painting, a panel illustrating the Celebration of Mass in which the celebrant stands before a small triptych which itself has a musical subject (Plate 22). A slightly later Aragonese retable of St Anne, St Michael and the Virgin in the Metropolitan Museum of Art depicts a tiny *vihuela* player perched on a turret above one of the arms of a typically elaborate Gothic throne (Plate 23). There are two further panels in Spain, the first a late 15th-century Aragonese Madonna and Child with angel musicians in the Episcopal Palace at Jaca (Plate 32), the second an early 16th-century Catalan panel of St Vincent in the Diocesan Museum at Lerida in which two tiny grotesque figures appear, squatting on the back of the saint's throne and playing exceptionally long-necked *vihuelas* (Plate 24).

10 Galpin in his *Old English Instruments of Music* (London, 1910) wrongly ascribed the invention of corners to the Italians: 'In the 15th century the Italians had altered the flowing outline of the viol by the addition of corners or angles, somewhat similar to those of the violin but not so pronounced.'

11 The length of this period of transition is made very clear by L. C. Witten II in his article 'Apollo, Orpheus, and David: A Study of the Crucial Century in the Development of Bowed Strings in North Italy 1480–1580 as Seen in Graphic Evidence and Some Surviving Instruments', *JAMIS*, vol. 1 (1975) 5–55.

12 I. D. Woodfield: 'The Origins of the Viol' (diss., University of London, King's College, 1977) Plate 56

13 Osuna, 1549 & 1555

14 For a description of this instrument, see M. Prynne: 'A Surviving Vihuela de Mano', *GSJ*, vol. 16 (1963) 22–27. See also P. Abondance: 'La vihuela du musée Jacquemart-André: restauration d'un document unique', *RdeM*, vol. 66 (1980).

15 Woodfield (1977) Plate 73

16 The late 15th-century Kingdom of Aragon does not spring to mind as one of the great and influential centres of renaissance string instrument manufacture, like Brescia or Venice, and yet the achievements of this relative backwater were phenomenal. Not only may Aragonese makers of this period be credited with the initial development of two of the most successful European string instruments, the guitar (from the *vihuela de mano*) and the viol (from the *vihuela de arco*), but they may also have been responsible for one of the decisive steps in the evolution of the violin outline – the development of 'cornered' medieval fiddles.

### 4. The Valencian viol: its structure, playing techniques and music

1 The various schools of Valencian painting are fully discussed in two volumes of C. R. Post's monumental study *A History of Spanish Painting* (14 vols., Cambridge, Mass., 1930–1966): vol. 6: *The Valencian School in the Late Middle Ages and Early Renaissance* (1935); vol. 11: *The Valencian School in the Early Renaissance* (1953).

2 Post, vol. 7: *The Catalan School in the Late Middle Ages* (1938) 672–678

3 London, 1659

4 One such fiddle appears in a panel of St Agatha now kept in the Museo de la Historia de la Ciudad, Barcelona. See I. D. Woodfield: 'The Origins of the Viol' (diss., University of London, 1977) Plate 41.

5 An early 15th-century Catalan panel of the Madonna and Child with angel musicians illustrates this custom well; the bellies of the three string instruments are all decorated with little square motifs in black and white like miniature chessboards. See Woodfield (1977) Plate 68.

6 M. Prynne: 'A Surviving Vihuela de Mano', *GSJ*, vol. 16 (1963) 22–27. See also P. Abon-

dance: 'La vihuela du musée Jacquemart-André: restauration d'un document unique', *RdeM*, vol. 66 (1980) 57-69

7  I. Harwood & M. Edmunds: 'Reconstructing 16th-century Venetian Viols', *EM*, vol. 6, no. 4 (1978) 519-525

8  R. T. Dart: 'The Viols' in A. Baines ed.: *Musical Instruments Through the Ages* (London, 1961) 184-190

9  *Celestine; or the tragick-comedie of Calisto and Melibea by Fernando de Rojas; translated by James Mabbe*, ed. G. M. Lacalle (London, 1972)

10  D. D. Boyden: *The History of Violin Playing from its Origins to 1761 and its Relationship to the Violin and Violin Music* (London, 1965) 16

11  See, for example, two illustrations in Salah el Mahdi's *La Musique Arabe* (Paris, 1972) 15 & 72, the latter showing a violin played 'a gamba'.

12  An early 15th-century Majorcan painting in the Musée d'Art Ancien, Brussels, appears to illustrate another cross-fertilisation – an unusual species of fiddle, held downwards and bowed underhand: see Woodfield (1977) Plate 14.

13  For an edition of the treatise, see K. Weinmann: *Johannes Tinctoris (1445–1511) und sein unbekannter Traktat 'De inventione et usu musicae'* (Regensburg, 1917). An English translation of the sections dealing with musical instruments is given by A. Baines: 'Fifteenth-century Instruments in Tinctoris's *De Inventione et Usu Musicae*', *GSJ*, vol. 3 (1950) 19-26.

14  See, for example, Woodfield (1977) Plates 71 & 72.

#### 5. The introduction of the viol into Italy

1  An exception is a Valencian Madonna and Child in the Art Museum of the Romanian Republic at Bucharest. See G. Oprescu: *Great Masters of Painting in the Museum of Roumania*, 3rd edn. (Bucharest, 1963) Plate 67.

2  M. Mallett: *The Borgias* (London, 1969) 76

3  Mallett (1969) 89

4  Mallett (1969) 207

5  I am grateful to William Prizer for sending me the full text of this important reference: 'Heri anche il prefato Duca de Barri gli condusse Madama & tuta la turba e poi se presono a fare sonare quelli sonadorj spagnoli che mandò el Reverendissimo Monsignore Ascanio da Roma, qualj soano viole grande quasi come mj, & invero il sonare suo è più presto dolce che de multa arte... Vigelani vj martij 1493, E de vostra Illustrissima, servitor devotus, Bernardinus Prosperus.'

6  E. E. Lowinsky: 'Ascanio Sforza's Life: A Key to Josquin's Biography and an Aid to the Chronology of his Works' in E. E. Lowinsky, ed.: *Josquin des Pres* (London, 1976)

7  *I Diarii di Marino Sanuto* (58 vols., Venice, 1879-1903) vol. 6, col. 175

8  Mallett (1969) 129

9  Mallett (1969) 196

10  G. Vasari: *Le vite de' più eccelenti pittori scultori ed architettori*, ed. G. C. Sansoni (9 vols., Florence, 1878-1885) vol. 4, 494-498. Vasari commented on Timoteo Viti's own musical abilities; he could apparently perform well on every kind of musical instrument, notably the *lira*, to which he sang improvisations with grace.

11  B. Castiglione: *Il libro del cortegiano* (Venice, 1528)

12  The importance of Ferrara as a musical centre is discussed by L. Lockwood in the following articles: 'Pietrobono and the Instrumental Tradition at Ferrara', *RIM*, vol. 10 (1975) 115-133; 'Music at Ferrara in the Period of Ercole I d'Este', *Studi Musicali*, vol. 1 (1972) 101-131.

13  Another plucked *vihuela de mano* appears in a painting attributed to the Ferrarese artist Ercole di Roberti. See F. V. Grunfeld: *The Art and Times of the Guitar* (New York, 1969) 32.

14  *I Diarii di Marino Sanuto*, vol. 4 (1880) col. 230. A Ferrarese inventory of 1511 includes the following: 'Viole da gamba, numero sei, con sei archetti'. See W. F. Prizer: 'Isabella d'Este and Lorenzo da Pavia', *EMH*, vol. 2 (1982) 110.

15  Mallett (1969) Plate 7

16  M. Remnant: *Musical Instruments of the West* (London, 1978) Plate 42

17  N. Bridgman: *La Vie Musicale au Quattrocento* (Paris, 1964) 216

18  Prizer (1982)

19  J. Tyler: 'The Renaissance Guitar 1500-1650', *EM*, vol. 3, no. 4 (1975) 342

20  The use of this phrase suggests that these viols may have been *lira*-shaped like the viols depicted in 1497 by Costa (Plate 53).

21  The text of this letter is given by W. F. Prizer: 'Lutenists at the Court of Mantua in the Late Fifteenth and Early Sixteenth Centuries', *JLSA*, vol. 13 (1980) 32.

22  Elsewhere in *De inventione et usu musicae*, Tinctoris states quite unambiguously that the *vihuela* ('viola sine arculo') was played in both Italy and Spain. See K. Weinmann: *Johannes Tinctoris (1445-1511) und sein unbekannter Traktat 'De inventione et usu musicae'* (Regensburg, 1917) 45.

23  *I Diarii di Marino Sanuto*, vol. 6 (1881) col. 175

24  V. Galilei: *Dialogo della musica antica, et della moderna* (Florence, 1581) 147: 'La Viola da Gamba & de braccio, tengo per fermo che ne siano stati autori gli Italiani, & forse quelli del regno di Napoli.'

25  In its unmodified form 'viola' could refer to the lute, the *vihuela de mano*, the viol, the violin, the *lira da braccio* and perhaps even the rebec.

26  Conclusive evidence on this point comes from a Ferrarese inventory of 1511, cited by Prizer (1982) 110, in which 'Quattro violonj alla napolitana' are listed under the general heading 'lauti', while the 'viole da gamba' appear under 'viole'.

27  *I Diarii di Marino Sanuto*, vol. 6 (1881) col. 175

28  Bridgman (1964) 216

29  *Opere di Teofilo Folengo*, La Letteratura Italiana: Storia e Testi, vol. 26, 1 (Milan): *Orlandino*, Quarto Capitolo, 20.

30  Bridgman (1964) 216

31  A. Doni: *Dialogo della musica* (Venice, 1544)

32  See H. M. Brown: *Sixteenth-Century Instrumentation: The Music for the Florentine Intermedii* (*AIM*, 1973) 103

33  S. Marcuse: *A Survey of Musical Instruments* (London, 1975)

34  In the words of Louise Litterick: 'any secular music other than that composed on texts in the native language was predominantly and perhaps even exclusively the domain of instrumentalists'. See 'Performing Franco-Netherlandish Secular Music of the Late 15th Century', *EM*, vol. 8 (1980) 474–485.

35  B. Disertori, in 'Un incunabolo di assolo per il violone', *RMI*, vol. 46 (1942) 455-471, discusses one such piece, 'Fortuna desperata', in the manuscript Cappella Giulia XIII 27, fol. 64. The setting by 'Felice' (a4) has an additional, very lively part in the bass register which, Disertori argues, may have been intended for viola da gamba. He makes a comparison between this setting and the later mid-century ricercars for bass viol and keyboard by Ortiz.

36  An interesting line of further research would be to attempt to trace the influence of long-vanished Spanish instruments, such as the *vihuela de arco*, in the New World. If the bowed *vihuela* did survive in something close to its original form for any length of time, it could only have been in the new Spanish colonies in Central and South America.

## 6. The viol in early 16th-century Germany

1　A. Aber: *Die Pflege der Musik* (Leipzig, 1921) 107

2　S. Marcuse: *A Survey of Musical Instruments* (London, 1975) 501

3　J. von Schlosser: *Die Sammlung alter Musikinstrumente* (Vienna, 1920) 20

4　Virdung's *Musica getutscht* was an influential work. French, Latin and Flemish translations were published in the 16th century: *Livre plaisant et tres utile pour apprendre a faire & ordonner toutes tablatures* (1529); *Musurgia seu praxis musicae* (1536); *Dit is een zeer schoon Boecxken, om te leeren maken alderhande tabulaturen* (1554 & 1568). A facsimile edition was published by R. Eitner in *Publikationen älterer praktischer und theoretischer Musikwerke*, vol. 11 (Leipzig, 1882). Another facsimile edition by L. Schrade, *Sebastian Virdung: Musica getutscht 1511*, was published in 1931.

5　E. M. Ripin: 'A Re-evaluation of Virdung's *Musica getutscht*', *JAMS*, vol. 29 (1976) 189–223

6　Sir J. Hawkins: *A General History of the Science and Practice of Music* (London, 1776) Chapter 71

7　P. Ganz: *The Paintings of Hans Holbein the Younger* (London, 1950) Plate 193

8　See, for example, B. Geiser: *Studien zur Frühgeschichte der Violine, Publikationen der schweizerischen musikforschenden Gesellschaft*, series 2, vol. 25 (Berne & Stuttgart, 1974) Plates 54–57. An instrument which looks very like a German *gross Geigen* appears in a wall painting by Il Garofalo in the Sala del Tesoro of the Palazzo di Ludovico il Moro at Ferrara. See M. Remnant: *Musical Instruments of the West* (London, 1978) Plate 16.

9　A part-facsimile edition of *Musica instrumentalis deudsch* has been published by R. Eitner in *Publikationen älterer praktischer und theoretischer Musikwerke*, vol. 20 (Leipzig, 1896).

10　There has been much debate about the 'reverse' bowing method depicted here, with the bowing hand held across the front of the instrument in order to bow from the opposite side. A few isolated occurrences might be dismissed as artistic aberrations, but it happens just often enough to raise the suspicion that some players did bow in this extraordinarily perverse manner.

11　Another example of a German viol with pointed shoulders is Albrecht Altdorfer's 'Geigenspieler' which may be seen in G. Kinsky: *Geschichte der Musik in Bildern* (Leipzig, 1929; Eng. trans. 1930) 80.

12　One German viol type that has yet to be investigated is the huge contrabass, oval-shaped viol with pointed ends (See Chapter 12). An early example (1518) is illustrated in the 'Double Bass' article in *The New Grove* (London, 1980). Other examples appear in Kinsky (1930) 81.

13　A revised edition was published in 1546 under the title *Musica und Tabulatur*.

14　See A. Silbiger: 'The First Viol Tutor: Hans Gerle's *Musica Teusch*', *JVdGSA*, vol. 6 (1969) 34–38

15　H. Gerle: *Musica und Tabulatur* (1546) fols. B – B2

16　A different fingering system was advocated by Ganassi (see Chapter 9).

17　Gerle (1546) fols. B4ᵛ–C

18　Ibid. fol. Cᵛ

19　M. Agricola: *Musica instrumentalis deudsch* (1545) fol. 40

20　Munich University Library 4° Cod. ms. 718 is a book of notes on mathematics and music made by the student Jorg Weltzell in 1523 and 1524, possibly while he was at Ingolstadt University. For a description of the manuscript and an inventory of its musical contents see C. Gottwald: *Die Musikhandschriften der Universitätsbibliothek München* (Wiesbaden, 1968) 55–62. See also M. Morrow: '16th Century Ensemble Viol Music', *EM*, vol. 2, no. 3 (1974) 160–163.

21　The tuning charts (including some for *a*- and *g*-tuned lutes) are on fol. 93ᵛ, fol. 97 and fols. 98ᵛ–99ᵛ.

22 The parts for this piece are copied on fol. III, fol. 114$^v$, fol. 125$^v$ and fol. 148$^v$.

23 Gerle (1546) fol. H4$^v$ and fol. J3

24 Agricola (1545) fols. 38$^v$–39

25 In Chapter 12 of *Regola Rubertina* (Venice, 1542) Ganassi describes how Gombert would rearrange the bass part when he was forced to transpose music down to avoid straining the upper voices (see Chapter 8).

26 Morrow (1974) 160–163

27 H. M. Brown, in 'Notes (and Transposing Notes) on the Viol in the Early Sixteenth Century' in I. Fenlon, ed.: *Music in medieval and early modern Europe: patronage, sources and texts*, (Cambridge, 1981), tested Gerle's tuning system against a volume of vocal music of the period chosen at random. He found that 36 of the 49 compositions fitted five-string viols in the low *a–d–a* tuning.

28 In this context it is interesting to report that, in a letter to the Verona Accademia Filarmonica, Nasco wrote of a madrigal 'a voce mutate' (for low voices, i.e. without soprano parts) which, he believed, would go well on the academy's large flutes or viols. Even after the general expansion upwards of the vocal range, the low *a–d–a* viol consort could still perform (without transposition) pieces composed 'a voce mutate' for ATTB or ATTBB combinations (see Chapter 11).

29 Agricola (1545) fol. 36$^v$

30 Ibid. fol. 37$^v$

31 A. Schlick: *Tabulaturen etlicher lobegesang und lidlein uff die orgeln und lauten* (Mainz, 1512)

32 At the head of each section Weltzell made a note of the size of viol on which the subsequent parts were to be played and also the year in which they were copied. It is interesting to note that the first parts to be copied were those for the tenor viol beginning on fol. 126 and labelled 'Tenor auff der Geygen Im 1523 Iar'. The parts for the other viols were copied later, mostly in 1524.

33 H. Gerle: *Musica Teusch* (1532) and *Musica und Tabulatur* (1546) fol. B

34 Gerle (1546) fols. J4$^v$–K

35 D. Ortiz: *Trattado de glosas* (Rome, 1553)

36 P. Jambe de Fer: *Epitome musical* (Lyons, 1556)

## 7. The structural development of the Italian viol in the 16th century

1 I. Harwood: 'An Introduction to Renaissance Viols', *EM*, vol. 2, no. 4 (1974) 235–246; I. Harwood and M. Edmunds: 'Reconstructing 16th-century Venetian Viols', *EM*, vol. 6, no. 4 (1978) 519–525; M. Edmunds: 'Venetian Viols of the Sixteenth Century', *GSJ*, vol. 33 (1980) 74–91. See also R. Hadaway: 'Another Look at the Viol', *EM*, vol. 6, no. 4 (1978) 530–539.

2 Another early 16th-century example is the viol depicted by Timoteo Viti in Urbino (*c*1505). The impact of the Spanish ancestor is there in the overall shape of the instrument, especially the length of the neck, but the method of stringing is wholly Italian (Plate 52).

3 M. Remnant: *Musical Instruments of the West* (London, 1978) Plate 42

4 J. von Schlosser: *Die Sammlung alter Musikinstrumente* (Vienna, 1920)

5 See L. C. Witten II: 'Apollo, Orpheus, and David: A study of the crucial century in the development of bowed strings in North Italy 1480–1580 as seen in graphic evidence and some surviving instruments', *JAMIS*, vol. 1 (1975) 16.

6 Edmunds (1980) 76–78

7 Edmunds (1980) 80–81

8 S. Marcuse: *A Survey of Musical Instruments* (London, 1975) 498–499

9 For Battista Ciciliano (the player) to be identified with Battista Ciciliano (the maker), it would be necessary to credit Antonio, the maker's father, with attaining a remarkable age.

If Battista was such an outstanding player by 1543 (the date of his mention in Ganassi's *Lettione Seconda*), his father could hardly have been born much after the turn of the century. According to Witten, however, he was still active in Venice in 1581. For the present, therefore, it seems safer to assume that there were two Battista Cicilianos, one a player, the other a maker.

10 Witten (1975) does not actually cite details of these Venetian documents, but he credits the information to research carried out by E. M. W. Paul.

11 Edmunds (1980) 82–83

12 The drawing is reproduced on the front cover of *EM*, vol. 6, no. 1 (1978).

13 I discussed the value of comparing surviving renaissance viols with depictions of viols in 16th-century art in a paper given at a one-day conference organised by the Viola da Gamba Society entitled 'The Viol in the Renaissance' on 16 June 1979.

14 J. B. Shaw: *Drawings by Old Masters at Christ Church Oxford*, vol. 2, (Oxford, 1976) Plate 413

15 A. Luzio & R. Renier: 'Niccolò da Correggio', *Giornale Storico della Letteratura Italiana*, vol. 21 (1893) 263

16 The 'Vohar' viol in the Dolmetsch Collection has an arched back as does the closely related instrument in Vienna (C.72).

17 Many other viol types are encountered in 16th-century Italian art. One of the more distinctive forms – albeit not very significant – was the flamboyant scallop-shaped viol. Two instruments of this type appear in Veronese's celebrated painting *The Marriage Feast at Cana* played 'per traverso'. The outline was popular in England (and might conceivably have originated there). It became the characteristic form of the orpharion and bandora; an exceptionally ornate viol attributed to John Rose (Plate 103) uses it. The German maker Vogel also used it (Plate 87).

## 8. Italian viol tunings

1 D. Harrán: 'In Pursuit of Origins: The Earliest Writing on Text Underlay (c.1440)', *Acta*, vol. 50 (1978) 217

2 A reference to the source of this tuning is given in S. Marcuse: *A Survey of Musical Instruments* (London, 1975) 497. Ms Marcuse has most generously sent me further information. The relevant copy of Michele Savonarola's cookbook was in the possession of the rare-book dealer Lawrence Witten of New Haven, Connecticut in 1957. A single sheet of typescript describing the volume and giving in full the manuscript notes on Alfonso della Viola's tunings for viol consort was prepared by Witten, and it is a copy of this typescript that I have seen. The manuscript notes are as follows:

         il modo de sonar il violon segondo alfonso
         de la viola sia lo sotto scritto et primo
         quanto all chiave di gsolreut nel soprano
la chiave de gsolreut al 3. tasto la mezzana ♭b.♮
la medesima chiave ℘ bmol, la mezzan♃ina vuoda
onde viene la chiave de csolfaut ℘ b.♮. a esser nel tenor
[There appears to be a line missing here.]
2° tasto questa sia la regola d‡ soprano
il tenor et contralto s'accordano unissonus et hanno una
medesima chiave et ℘ b.♮ et ℘ b. mol cio°, la chiave
de csolfaut ℘ b.♮ sia. la mezzana al primo tasto
et ℘ b. mol sia la mezzana al terzo tasto questa
sia la regola d‡ tenor et d‡ alto
il basso ha la chiave d'effaut nel tenore al 2° [3?] tasto
per b.♮. / et per b. mol sia la mezzan♃ina. al.

pmo tasto
    il modo d'accordar li violoni
      secondo il detto authore 3–3. $\frac{1}{4}$ : $\frac{1}{2}$
p° bisogna accordar bene quel violone col quale s'ha a son
nare il basso et poi accordare il basso dł tenor col
bordone di detto violon et il bordone dł tenor col tenor
di detto violone et il tenor dł tenore con la mezzana
dł dł basso al p° tasto la mezzana dł tenore cō
la mezzanina dł basso vuoda la mezzanina dł
tenor col canto dł basso vuodo / il tenor et alto
s'accordano unisonus / il soprano s'accorda col tenor
in questa for$^{\text{a}}$. cioe il basso dł soprano col bordon
dł tenor et cosi consequenter come hai fatto dł
basso col tenore

3  G. M. Lanfranco: *Scintille di musica* (Brescia, 1533). For an English translation see B. Lee: 'Giovanni Maria Lanfranco's 'Scintille di musica' and its Relation to 16th-Century Music Theory' (diss., Cornell University, 1961)

4  W. F. Prizer: 'Lutenists at the Court of Mantua in the Late Fifteenth and Early Sixteenth Centuries', *JLSA*, vol. 13 (1980) 15–16

5  H. M. Brown: 'Notes (and Transposing Notes) on the Viol in the Early Sixteenth Century' in I. Fenlon, ed.: *Music in medieval and early modern Europe: patronage, sources and texts* (Cambridge, 1981)

6  In *Lettione Seconda* (Chapter 22) Ganassi confirms that the fourth rule of tuning is specifically suited to five-string viols.

7  This interpretation of the fourth rule of tuning was suggested by H. M. Brown in *Sixteenth-Century Instrumentation*: *The Music for the Florentine Intermedii* (AIM, 1973) 52–53.

8  Brown (1973), Example 22, gives a series of fingering charts for 'viole' scribbled at the end of a bassus part book of about 1520 (Biblioteca Nazionale Centrale, Florence, Magl. XIX, 164–167, fols. 116$^{\text{v}}$–117). Two of these charts could be interpreted as illustrating the effect of Ganassi's fourth rule of tuning. The first chart, labelled 'Alla Bassa', gives an ascending scale of $c$, and from the tablature equivalents given below it appears that the viol is nominally tuned $a'$ $e'$ $b$ $g$ $d$ $A$. In the second chart, labelled 'All'Alta', the pitch levels are realigned by a fourth so that the nominal tuning is now $e'$ $b$ $f\sharp$ $d$ $A$. The note $a'$, for example, is now the fifth fret of the top string rather than the open top string. A part played in this tuning would thus be a fourth higher on the instrument – hence the phrase 'All'Alta'. In Ganassi's terminology, the first chart is for an $a$-tuned tenor in the 'regola seconda, ordine primo' – here it should be noted that except for the fact that the Florentine chart begins on a $c$, the two are identical – while the second chart is the 'regola quarta', applied not as in Ganassi to the $g$-tuned tenor of the 'prima regola', but to the $a$-tuned tenor of the 'seconda regola'. Though Ganassi does not say so, the application of the 'quarta regola' to an $a$-tuned tenor is a perfectly logical extension of his system.

9  Bessaraboff, for example, in *Ancient European Musical Instruments* (Boston, 1941) 357–373, attempts to reconcile the fact that some late 16th-century authorities tune the viol consort a fifth lower than others. However, as Marcuse (1975) points out, 'this seemingly irreconcilable discrepancy can be resolved very simply once we accept that these pitches were exactly what their authors said they were and that only the nomenclature differed'.

10  Marcuse (1975) 505

11  Perhaps the earliest extant treble viol is the beautiful guitar-shaped instrument by Gioan Maria, a Brescian maker resident in Venice from $c$1560 to $c$1591 in the Ashmolean Museum (Plate 85).

12  *Lettione Seconda*, Chapters 1, 2 & 3

13 These are illustrated by a woodcut of a viol with a single string showing the divisions marked off with a pair of dividers.

14 Further details about 16th-century temperaments are given in M. Lindley's article 'Temperaments' in *The New Grove* (London, 1980).

### 9. Viol-playing techniques in 16th-century Italy

1 The text of the letter is given by W. F. Prizer: 'Lutenists at the Court of Mantua in the Late Fifteenth and Early Sixteenth Centuries', *JLSA*, vol. 13 (1980) 33.

2 A. Doni: *Dialogo della musica* (Venice, 1544)

3 H. Anglés: *La Música en la Corte de Carlos V* (Barcelona, 1944) 91-92

4 An earlier portrait of a string player by Sebastiano del Piombo (*c*1515) is in the Rothschild Collection, Paris. It shows a musician holding a bow, but no instrument is visible.

5 L. Venturi: *Pitture Italiane in America* (Milan, 1931) Plate 351

6 S. Marcuse: *A Survey of Musical Instruments* (London, 1975) 498

7 For a picture of a lady playing a viol resting on a box, see I. D. Woodfield: 'Posture in Viol Playing', *EM*, vol. 6, no. 1 (1978) 38.

8 Two other paintings show a single tenor-sized viol played horizontally: the aforementioned portrait of a viol player attributed to Parmigianino (*d*1540); and a mid 16th-century depiction of domestic music-making by Calisto Piazza. For this latter example see B. Berenson: *Italian Pictures of the Renaissance*: *Central Italian and North Italian Schools* (London, 1968) Plate 1675, in which a woman is shown playing a viol 'per traverso'. It may be that women sometimes adopted this posture for social reasons, the physical position of the viol between the legs being considered unseemly.

9 R. T. Dart: 'The Viols' in A. Baines, ed.: *Musical Instruments Through the Ages* (London, 1961) 184-190

10 The title-page woodcut of Judenkünig's *Utilis et compendaria introductio* (Vienna, *c*1518) shows a standing viol player (see Plate 62).

11 The use of fingers to put pressure on the hairs of the bow by a *rabāb* player is depicted with great clarity on a late 14th-century reliquary chest from Perpignan (Plate 4).

12 R. Markowitz: 'An Iconographic Study of Viola da Gamba Bow Grips', *RIdIM Newsletter*, vol. 4, no. 2 (1979) 8

13 This contradicts Gerle (1532) and a later Italian theorist, Cerreto (1601), who both advocate placing the first finger on the first fret. The half position works well enough for simple part music but is of little use in advanced solo divisions, in which (to avoid unnecessary string crossings) the fourth finger is often required on the fifth fret. Jambe de Fer (1556) recognises that the fifth fret is valuable in playing diminutions (see Chapter 13) and thus appears to support Ganassi's fingering system.

14 I. D. Woodfield: 'Viol Playing Techniques in the Mid-16th Century: a Survey of Ganassi's Fingering Instructions', *EM*, vol. 6, no. 4 (1978) 544-549

15 For further details of Maffei's letter see M. Uberti: 'Vocal Techniques in Italy in the Second Half of the 16th Century', *EM*, vol. 9, no. 4 (1981) 486-495.

16 Translation in J. Haar: 'Notes on the *Dialogo della musica* of Antonfrancesco Doni', *ML*, vol. 47 (1966) 220

### 10. Music for solo viol in 16th-century Italy

1 H. M. Brown: *Embellishing Sixteenth-Century Music* (London, 1976) 33

2 H. M. Brown: *Sixteenth-Century Instrumentation*: *The Music for the Florentine Intermedii* (AIM, 1973) 98

3 Brown (1976) 59

4 The best study of the *viola bastarda* and its music is Veronika Gutmann's 'Viola bastarda – Instrument oder Diminutionspraxis?', *AMw*, vol. 35 (1978) 178–209.

5 Brown (1973) 56

6 Bassano does not mention the *viola bastarda* in this volume. Some of his embellishments, however, are in the *viola bastarda* style and are labelled 'per più parti'.

7 Gutmann (1978) lists the following manuscript sources of *viola bastarda* music: *Regle di contrappunto*, Florence, Biblioteca Nazionale, cod. misc. 89; *Il Dolcimelo d'Aurelio Virgiliano*, Bologna, Civico Museo Bibliografico, C. 33; British Library, Add. ms. 30491; Wrocław (Breslau) mss. 111, 112, 114.

8 For further details about players of the *viola bastarda* see Gutmann (1978) 202 & 207. On Orazio Bassani and Vincenzo Bonizzi, see also A. Newcomb: *The Madrigal at Ferrara 1579-1597* (Princeton, 1980) 184-185, 194-196. G. P. Lomazzo in his *Trattato dell'arte de la pittura* (Milan, 1584) mentions three players of 'viole da gamba' (Oratio Romano, Mauro Sinibaldi Cremonese and Ricar[do] Rognone Milanese), all presumably *viola bastarda* virtuosi.

9 A translation appears in D. Z. Crookes: 'Michael Praetorius's *Syntagma Musicum II* (pp. i-xxvi, and pp. 1-80): A Translation, Introduction and Commentary' (diss., Queen's University of Belfast, 1981).

10 Edition in *Die Improvisation in Beispielen aus neun Jahrhunderten abendländischer Musik* (Cologne, 1956) 38-51

11 Ganassi himself describes the practice of declaiming basses to the *lira da braccio* ('prattica del dire i bassi accompagnado con il suon della Lyra') in *Lettione Seconda*, Chapter 16.

12 Brown (1973) 91

13 Brown (1973) 46-47

14 Brown (1973) 98-100

## 11. The viol consort and its music in 16th-century Italy

1 G. Reese: *Music in the Renaissance* (London, 1954) 323. The implied participation of a woman in a viol consort is interesting. In the 16th century the viol remained a predominantly masculine preserve, a fact epitomized succinctly by the Frenchman Jambe de Fer in his oft-reported statement that the viol was played by 'gentlemen, merchants and other men of virtue'. For further comment on the restrictions imposed by dress on viol-playing women, see I. Woodfield: 'Posture in Viol Playing', *EM*, vol. 6, no. 1 (1978).

2 L. Frati: *La Vita Privata di Bologna* (Bologna, 1900) 121

3 G. Turrini: *L'Accademia Filarmonica di Verona dalla Fondazione (Maggio 1543) al 1600 e il suo Patrimonio Musicale Antico* (Verona, 1941). See also G. Turrini: 'Il maestro fiammingo Giovanni Nasco a Verona (1547-1551)', *Note*, vols. 4-6 (1937) 180–225.

4 Turrini (1941) 25

5 Turrini (1941) 31

6 Turrini (1941) 179

7 Turrini (1937) 193

8 A. Einstein: *The Italian Madrigal* (Princeton, 1949) 471

9 Turrini (1941) 25

10 Turrini (1941) 40

11 Turrini (1941) 34

12 Turrini (1941) 87

13 Turrini (1941) 179

14 Turrini (1941) 87

15 W. F. Prizer: *Courtly Pastimes: The Frottole of Marchetto Cara* (UMI Research Press, Ann Arbor, Michigan, 1980) 309-310

16  W. F. Prizer: 'Lutenists at the Court of Mantua in the Late Fifteenth and Early Sixteenth Centuries', *JLSA*, vol. 13 (1980) 33

17  Reese (1954) 370

18  Prizer (1980) 34

19  H. M. Brown: 'A Cook's Tour of Ferrara in 1529', *RIM*, vol. 10 (1975) 216-241

20  Brown (1975) suggests that, at least in Ferrara, there was a generally agreed method of orchestrating the madrigals and other pieces performed on these occasions. Provided that there was always one viol to a part, singers or other instrumentalists could be added at will to reinforce important lines.

21  Frati (1900) 121. Carriages transporting mixed groups of musicians outdoors were depicted in *The Triumph of Maximilian I* in 1518 (see Plate 61).

22  A. Luzio & R. Renier: 'Niccolò da Correggio', *Giornale Storico della Letteratura Italiana*, vol. 21 (1893) 263

23  D. Nutter: 'Intermedio', *The New Grove* (London, 1980)

24  E. Winternitz: *Musical Instruments and their Symbolism in Western Art* (London, 1967) 220. The favoured Florentine scoring of viols with flutes is recorded elsewhere. According to Einstein (1949) 475, a Paduan performance of the comedy *Occulta fiamma amorosa* in 1566 included an *intermedio* with 'a consort of flutes and one of viols' ('un concerto di flauti, et uno di viuole da gamba').

25  This was so throughout Europe. Payments are recorded in Lucca in 1549 to four 'viuole' and in 1570 to four 'violoni'. See E. Elsner: *Untersuchung der instrumentalen Besetzungspraxis der weltlichen Musik im 16. Jahrhundert in Italien* (Berlin, 1935) 86. Another reference dates from 1534, when the Weimar Hofkapelle paid four 'Geiger', Hans, Simon, Andreas and Walter. See A. Aber: *Die Pflege der Musik* (Leipzig, 1921) 179.

26  The changing internal balance of the viol consort in the early 17th century is illustrated by extracts from an inventory of instruments belonging to the Kassel Hofkapelle in 1613 (see Chapter 12).

27  *I Diarii di Marino Sanuto* (58 vols., Venice, 1879–1903) vol. 6, col. 175

28  H. T. David: *Eustachio Romano Musica Duorum*, ed. H. M. Brown & E. E. Lowinsky, *MRM*, vol. 6 (Chicago, 1975)

29  *Musica Nova*, ed. H. C. Slim, *MRM*, vol. 1 (Chicago, 1964)

30  Elsner (1935) 19

31  Turrini (1941) 25. About four years earlier Gombert had published a volume of four-part motets suitable for 'lyris maioribus ac tibiis imparibus'.

32  Turrini (1937) 206

33  Turrini (1937) 210

34  The passage reads: 'sonandosi questi Madrigali li mesi adrieto con le viuole da gamba'.

35  R. Donington: *The Rise of Opera* (London, 1981) 86

36  A. Segre: 'Un Registro di lettere del Cardinale Ercole Gonzaga', *Miscellanea di storia italiana*, 3rd series, vol. 16 (1913) 411

37  H. M. Brown: *Embellishing Sixteenth-Century Music* (London, 1976)

38  L. Zacconi: *Prattica di musica* (Venice, 1592); S. Cerreto: *Della prattica musica* (Naples, 1601); A. Banchieri: *Conclusioni del suono dell'organo* (Bologna, 1609)

39  M. Castellari: 'A 1593 Veronese Inventory', *GSJ*, vol. 26 (1973) 15. An inventory of instruments belonging to the d'Este court at Modena in 1625 included fourteen viols ('quattordici viole da gamba'): see E. Vander Straeten: *La Musique aux Pays-Bas avant le XIX^e siècle* (8 vols., Brussels, 1867–1888) vol. 6, 117.

40  N. Fortune: 'Giustiniani on Instruments', *GSJ*, vol. 5 (1952) 48

41  English viol players travelling to Italy in the mid 17th century confirm that the viol had fallen from favour. In 1647 the English merchant Robert Bargrave wrote from Italy that his

'little Skill on the viall' appeared to advantage 'because none else could play on it'. See M. Tilmouth: 'Music on the Travels of an English Merchant: Robert Bargrave 1628–61', *ML*, vol. 53 (1972) 143–159. Thomas Hill's letter from Lucca dated 1 October 1657 also makes this point: 'The organ and violin they are masters of, but the bass-viol they have not at all in use, and to supply its place they have the bass violin with four strings, and use it as we use the bass viol.' Cited by P. Allsop in: 'The Role of the Stringed Bass as a Continuo Instrument in Italian Seventeenth Century Instrumental Music', *Ch*, vol. 8 (1978–1979) 32

### 12. The viol consort in late 16th-century Germany

1 M. Troiano: *Discorsi Delli Triomphi* (Munich, 1568); another version with some revisions and a Spanish translation was published the following year: *Dialoghi di Massimo Troiano* (Venice, 1569).

2 *Epitome musical* (Lyons, 1556)

3 On instrumental participation in the polychoral repertory, see A. F. Carver: 'The Development of Sacred Polychoral Music to 1580' (diss., University of Birmingham, 1980) 307–337.

4 D. Alton Smith: 'The Musical Instrument Inventory of Raymund Fugger', *GSJ*, vol. 33 (1980) 36-44

5 A. Baines: 'Two Cassel Inventories', *GSJ*, vol. 4 (1951) 30-38

6 H. Zirnbauer: *Der Notenbestand der Reichsstädtisch-Nürnbergischen Ratsmusik* (Nuremberg, 1959) 6

7 J. von Schlosser: *Die Sammlung alter Musikinstrumente* (Vienna, 1920) 19-20

8 C. A. Otto zur Nedden: *Quellen und Studien zur Oberrheinischen Musikgeschichte im 15. und 16. Jahrhundert* (Kassel, 1931) 28

9 C. Sachs: *Musik und Oper am Kurbrandenburgischen Hof* (Berlin, 1910) 205

10 J. Sittard: *Zur Geschichte der Musik und des Theaters am Württembergischen Hofe* (Stuttgart, 1890) 27

11 Schlosser (1920) 19-20

12 Schlosser (1920) 20

13 Baines (1951) 33

14 C. Warren: 'Music at Nonesuch', *MQ*, vol. 54 (1968) 50

15 A. Newcomb: *The Madrigal at Ferrara 1579-1597* (Princeton, 1980) 264, document 27

16 H. M. Brown: 'A Cook's Tour of Ferrara in 1529', *RIM*, vol. 10 (1975) 216-241

17 See, for example, illustrations in G. L. Kinsky: *Geschichte der Musik in Bildern* (Leipzig, 1929; Eng. trans. 1930) 81.

18 D. Z. Crookes: 'Michael Praetorius's *Syntagma Musicum* II (pp. i-xxvi and pp. 1-80): A Translation, Introduction and Commentary' (diss., Queen's University of Belfast, 1981) 60-63

19 C. Bartlett & P. Holman: 'Giovanni Gabrieli: A Guide to the Performance of his Instrumental Music', *EM*, vol. 3, no. 1 (1975) 25

### 13. The viol in France and the Low Countries

1 N. Bridgman: *La Vie Musicale au Quattrocento* (Paris, 1964) 203

2 E. Vander Straeten: *La Musique aux Pays-Bas avant le XIX<sup>e</sup> siècle* (8 vols., Brussels, 1867–1888) vol. 7, 149

3 Vander Straeten, vol. 7 (1885) 170

4 Vander Straeten, vol. 7 (1885) 202

5 Vander Straeten, vol. 4 (1878) 188

6 M. A. Baird: 'Aspects of Secular Music and Music-making in the Pays-Bas Meridionaux during the Lifetime of Charles-Quint (1500–1558)' (diss., Queen's University of Belfast, 1958) appendix II, B.2.ix

7 Vander Straeten, vol. 7 (1885) 366

8 Vander Straeten, vol. 7 (1885) 249

9 Vander Straeten, vol. 7 (1885) 439–444

10 Vander Straeten, vol. 7 (1885) 428

11 Vander Straeten, vol. 8 (1888) 312–322

12 R. D. Leppert: 'Viols in Seventeenth-Century Flemish Paintings: The Iconography of Music Indoors and Out', *JVdGSA*, vol. 15 (1978) 12–13

13 Vander Straeten, vol. 4 (1878) 189–190

14 M. Frémiot: 'Marseilles', *The New Grove* (London, 1980)

15 H. M. Brown: *Sixteenth-Century Instrumentation: The Music for the Florentine Intermedii* (*AIM*, 1973) 95

16 D. Heartz: 'Un Divertissement de Palais pour Charles Quinte à Binche', *Les Fêtes de la Renaissance II* (Paris, 1960) 330

17 *Discours du Grand et Magnifique Triumphe* (Paris, 1558)

18 H. M. Brown: *Music in the French Secular Theater, 1400–1550* (Cambridge, Mass., 1963) 69–70

19 Brown (1963) 70

20 B. Haller: *Bern in seinen Rathsmanualen* (3 vols., Berne, 1900–1902) vol. 2, 283

21 Brown (1963) 70

22 Brown (1963) 70

23 For details of Claude Gervaise's lost tutor, see D. Heartz: *Pierre Attaingnant Royal Printer of Music* (Berkeley & Los Angeles, 1969) 372. Jambe de Fer's treatise is reprinted with an introduction by F. Lesure: 'L'*Epitome musical* de Philibert Jambe de Fer (1556)', *AnnM*, vol. 6 (1958–1963) 341–386. A facsimile reprint of Mersenne's *Harmonie Universelle* edited by F. Lesure (Paris, 1963), and an English translation of the book dealing with musical instruments by R. E. Chapman (The Hague, 1957) have been published. A translation of Rousseau's *Traité de la Viole* by N. Dolmetsch has been appearing in *The Consort* from vol. 33 (1977).

24 Heartz (1969) 373

25 H. C. Slim, in his edition of *Musica Nova*, *MRM*, vol. 1 (Chicago, 1964) xxxii, argues for a date of c1547–1556 for *Musique de Joye*.

26 R. T. Dart: 'Some Sixteenth-century French Drawings', *GSJ*, vol. 10 (1957) 88–89

27 See, for example, the illustrations in M. Sicard: 'The French Viol School before 1650', *JVdGSA*, vol. 18 (1981) 76–93.

28 F. Lesure: 'La facture instrumentale à Paris au seizième siècle', *GSJ*, vol. 7 (1954) 11–52

### 14. The viol in 16th-century England

1 C. Monson: 'Consort Song and Verse Anthem: A Few Performance Problems', *JVdGSA*, vol. 13 (1976) 4

2 E. Vander Straeten: *La Musique aux Pays-Bas avant le XIXe siècle* (8 vols., Brussels, 1867–1888) vol. 7, 160

3 Vander Straeten, vol. 7 (1885) 163

4 Vander Straeten, vol. 7 (1885) 170

5 *Letters and Papers, Foreign and Domestic, of the Reign of Henry VIII*, ed. J. S. Brewer (hereafter *L&P*), vol. 1, part 3, lxv, note 1

6 British Library, Harleian ms. 1419

7 *L&P*, vol. 2, part 2, 1501

8 *Calendar of State Papers and Manuscripts, Venice*, ed. R. Brown (London, 1869), vol. 3, 23

9 *L&P*, vol. 3, part 2, 1558

10 J. Payne Collier: *Trevelyan Papers*, part 2 (The Camden Society, London, 1863) 20

11 *L&P*, vol. 5, 251

12 J. Payne Collier: *Trevelyan Papers*, part 1 (The Camden Society, London, 1857) 201

13 J. Payne Collier (1857) 200

14 *L&P*, vol. 20, 320

15 R. Prior in 'Jewish Musicians at the Tudor Court', *MQ*, vol. 69 (1983) 253–265 has advanced the intriguing hypothesis that the consort of Italian viol players employed by Henry VIII from 1540 were in fact Jews of Iberian ancestry. The evidence he cites includes the will of another royal musician, witnessed by Ambrose of Milan, the leader of the viol consort, which he signed 'Ambrosius deolmaleyex'. Prior interprets this cryptic word as de 'Almaliach' or de 'Elmaleh', the name of a Jewish family originally from Spain. He further argues that two other string players who later joined the royal band and who were usually recorded as George and Innocent Combe or Comy, but twice as de Combre, came originally from Coimbra in Portugal.

16 British Library, Harleian ms. 1419

17 *Acts of the Privy Council of England*, New Series, vol. 3, ed. J. R. Dasent (London, 1891) 160

18 E. S. J. van der Straeten: *The History of the Violin* (London, 1933) 57

19 *L&P*, vol. 20, 320

20 For example, the Household Expenses of the Princess Elizabeth during her residence at Hatfield, 1 October 1551 to 30 September 1552, include a payment to 'the violans'. See *The Camden Miscellany*, vol. 2 (The Camden Society, London, 1853) 38. As always, however, caution is necessary when dealing with terminology of string instruments. Mid 16th-century Italian viol players would probably have referred to themselves as 'violoni' in their native tongue, and English words such as 'viallons' or 'vyalons' may have been attempts at an English version of this.

21 W. Woodfill: *Musicians in English Society: from Elizabeth to Charles I* (Princeton, 1953)

22 H. C. de Lafontaine: *The King's Musick* (London, 1909) 9

23 *Accounts of the Lord High Treasurer of Scotland*, ed. J. B. Paul, vol. 6, 261-262

24 *Accounts of the Lord High Treasurer of Scotland*, vol. 7, 118 & 199

25 Ibid. 271

26 Ibid. 328

27 *Accounts of the Lord High Treasurer of Scotland*, vol. 8, 54

28 *Accounts of the Lord High Treasurer of Scotland*, vol. 10, 95

29 Ibid. 195

30 Ibid. 415

31 *Accounts of the Lord High Treasurer of Scotland*, vol. 11, 102

32 Ibid. 242

33 In 1549, for example, in Lucca, a payment was made to Christophano de Parma with his three sons for playing 'viuole'. See E. Elsner: *Untersuchung der instrumentalen Besetzungspraxis der weltlichen Musik im 16. Jahrhundert in Italien* (Berlin, 1935) 86

34 *Accounts of the Lord High Treasurer of Scotland*, vol. 12, 322

35 Ibid. 74

36 D. Calderwood: *History of the Kirk of Scotland* (Wodrow Society, 8 vols., 1842-1849) vol. 3, 458-459

37 Historical Manuscripts Commission: *Calendar of the Manuscripts of the Most Honourable the Marquess of Bath*, vol. 5: *Talbot, Dudley and Devereux Papers 1533-1659* (London, 1980) 229

38 Historical Manuscripts Commission: *The Manuscripts of th̶ ̶D̶u̶ke of Rutland, K. G. preserved at Belvoir Castle*, vol. 4 (London, 1905) 287

39 *L&P*, vol. 13, part 2, 292

40 Ibid. 294. Cited by J. Stevens: *Music and Poetry in the Early Tudor Court* (London, 1961) 277

41 D. C. Price: *Patrons and Musicians of the English Renaissance* (Cambridge, 1981) 121-122

42 *L&P*, vol. 15, 449

43 W. L. Goodman: 'Musical Instruments and their Makers in the Bristol Apprentice Register, 1536-1643', *GSJ*, vol. 27 (1974) 9-14

44  *L&P*, vol. 20, part 2, 489

45  Ibid. 497

46  Ibid. 523

47  Woodfill (1953) 252-279

48  N. Williams: *Thomas Howard Fourth Duke of Norfolk* (London, 1964) 44

49  F. G. Emmison: *Tudor Secretary: Sir William Petre at Court and Home* (London, 1961) 210 & 212

50  G. J. Piccore: *Wills and Inventories from the Ecclesiastical Court, Chester*, part 1 (Chetham Society, vol. 33, 1857) 169-171

51  Price (1981) 77

52  Canon F. W. Galpin: *Old English Instruments of Music* (London, 1910; 4th rev. edn. 1965) 114

53  Historical Manuscripts Commission: *Calendar of the Manuscripts of the Most Honourable the Marquess of Bath*, vol. 5: *Talbot, Dudley and Devereux Papers 1533-1659* (London, 1980) 229

54  F. G. Emmison: *Elizabethan Life: Home, Work & Land* (Chelmsford, 1976) 23

55  F. G. Emmison: *Elizabethan Life: Wills of Essex Gentry & Merchants* (Chelmsford, 1978) 235

56  *Elizabethan Consort Music: I*, ed. P. Doe, *MB*, vol. 44 (London, 1979)

57  J. O. Halliwell: *The Moral Play of Wit and Science* (London, 1848) 32 & 54

58  C. M. Clode: *Memorials of the Guild of Merchant Taylors* (London, 1875) 526 & 528-529

59  R. Holinshed: *Chronicles of England, Scotland and Ireland* (4 vols., London, 1808) vol. 4, 7

60  *The Diary of Henry Machyn, Citizen and Merchant-Taylor of London, from A.D. 1550 to A.D. 1563*, ed. J. G. Nichols (The Camden Society, London, 1848) 89

61  Nichols (1848) 205

62  *Peter Philips: Select Italian Madrigals*, ed. J. Steele, *MB*, vol. 29 (London, 1970) xvi

63  *Malone Society Collections*, vol. 3 (Oxford, 1954): *A Calendar of Dramatic Records in the Books of the Livery Companies of London 1484-1640*, 139

64  Nichols (1848) 260

65  Records of the Goldsmiths Company, 30 June 1561

66  Nichols (1848) 282

67  London Corporation: *Repertories of the Court of Aldermen of the City of London*: Repertory 14, fols. 509$^v$ & 514

68  Vander Straeten, vol. 8 (1888) 311

69  H. Anglés: *La Música en la Corte de Carlos V* (Barcelona, 1944) 129

70  Records of the Goldsmiths Company, 5 June 1564

71  Emmison (1961) 215 & 288

72  T. Lennam: 'The Children of Paul's, 1551–1582', *The Elizabethan Theatre*, vol. 2 (London, 1970) 21

73  A. Smith: 'The Practice of Music . . . during the Reign of Elizabeth I' (diss., University of Birmingham, 1967) vol. 1, 169

74  Steele (1970) xvi

75  Woodfill (1953) 166

76  Woodfill (1953) 144

77  Price (1981) 54

78  W. A. Edwards: 'The Performance of Ensemble Music in Elizabethan England', *PRMA*, vol. 97 (1970-1971) 113-123. There is evidence of viol playing in the choir-schools of several English cathedrals in the early 17th century. On 21 April 1614 it was ordained that 'Nicholas Byrne shall presentlie and from tyme to tyme teach the choristers and the children of the deane or chapter, which children are or shalbe resident in Peterborough, upon the vialls and uppon the songe'. On 8 May 1617 Byrne was confirmed as a teacher of the children and choristers 'upon the vialls and songe' and two years later it is recorded that he was paid 'vj s. viij d a yeare for vyall stringes'. See *The Foundation of Peterborough Cathedral* (The Publications of the Northants Record Society, vol. 13, 1939) lii and liii. At Exeter an order was made on 6 May 1637 that 'Two new shagbotts and Two new Cornetts to be provided for the

service of the Quire, together with a sett of vyols'. See M. Lefkowitz: 'Matthew Locke at Exeter', *The Consort*, vol. 22 (1965) 8.

79 *The Dramatic Works of Thomas Dekker*, ed. F. Bowers (Cambridge, 1955) vol. 2, 284–285

80 Doe (1979) xvii

81 O. Neighbour: *The Consort and Keyboard Music of William Byrd* (London, 1978) 50

82 See *The New Grove* (London, 1980) for biographical information about these composers.

83 Neighbour (1978) 27

84 *Christopher Tye: The Instrumental Music*, ed. R. W. Weidner (New Haven, Conn., 1967)

85 Doe (1979) no. 54 & no. 57

86 Edwards (1970-1971) 116

87 *The Dramatic Works of George Peele: The Araygnement of Paris,* ed. R. M. Benbow (New Haven & London, 1970) 113

88 Doe (1979) xx

89 Doe, however, considerably underestimates the importance of viol playing in mid 16th-century England, when he writes that 'the only well authenticated group of viol players [were] the eight (seven of them Italians) listed among the royal household musicians'.

90 P. Brett: 'The English Consort Song, 1570-1625', *PRMA*, vol. 88 (1961-1962) 73-88

91 *Tom Tyler and his wife*, ed. J. S. Farmer (The Tudor Facsimile Texts, London, 1912)

92 *The Bugbears: A Modernized Edition*, ed. J. D. Clark (New York & London, 1979)

93 Clark (1979) 212–217 does not supply an editorial version of the missing lower parts and the transcription is thus full of second-inversion chords.

94 *The Play of Pacient Grissell, by John Phillip*, ed. R. B. McKerrow & W.W. Gregg (Malone Society, London, 1909)

95 I am indebted to T. W. Craik for the following analysis of the rôle of the actor–musicians. See *The Tudor Interlude* (Leicester, 1958) 47–48.

96 Others were no doubt inspired by the choirboy songs of his contemporaries. For example, Byrd's famous 'Lullabye' published in 1588 in *Psalmes, Sonets, & Songs of Sadnes and Pietie* has echoes of the Nurse's song in John Phillip's *The Plaie of Pacient Grissell* (*c*1560), line 1383 (see McKerrow & Gregg, 1909):

> The Nurse singeth
>> Lulla by baby, lullay by babye
>> Thy Nurse will tend thee, as dulie as may be
> Be still by sweet sweeting, no longer do crye,
>> Sing lulla by baby, lulla by baby:
> Let dollors bee fleetting I fancie thee I,
>> To rocke and to lull thee, I will not delay mee
>> Lulla by baby etc.

97 Calderwood (1842-1849) vol. 3, 458-459

98 P. le Huray: *Music and the Reformation in England 1549-1660* (London, 1967) 217-226

99 J. Morehen: 'The English Consort and Verse Anthems', *EM*, vol. 6, no. 3 (1978) 381-385

100 *Ralph Roister Doister and The Tragedie of Gorboduc*, ed. W. D. Cooper (The Shakespeare Society, London, 1847) 96

101 *The Complete Works of George Gascoigne*, vol. 1, ed. J. W. Cunliffe (Cambridge, 1907): *The Posies*, 246

102 *Malone Society Collections*, vol. 2, part 3 (Oxford, 1931): *Legal Proceedings of Mayor and Aldermen's Court,* 290

103 *The Diary of Philip Henslow*, ed. J. Payne Collier (London, 1845) 272

104 F. E. Halliday: *A Shakespeare Companion 1550-1950* (London, 1952) 480

105 E. K. Chambers: *The Elizabethan Stage* (4 vols., Oxford, 1923) vol. 3, 361

106 Woodfill (1953) 85

107 See the article on Norwich in *The New Grove*.

108 C. C. Stopes: *William Hunnis and the Revels of the Chapel Royal* (London, 1910) 314

109 Woodfill (1953) 86

110 R. Hakluyt: *The Principal Navigations Voyages Traffiques & Discoveries of the English Nation* (12 vols., London, 1903-1905) vol. 3, 751: 'The Voyage of M. John Winter into the South Sea by the Streight of Magellan'

111 *Accounts of the Lord High Treasurer of Scotland*, vol. 6, 261

112 Most of the following information is taken from J. Pringle: 'John Rose, the Founder of English Viol-making', *EM*, vol. 6, no. 4 (1978) 501-511.

113 English viols are known to have been circulating on the Continent about this time. In 1559 Estevan de Notero was paid for transporting to Valladolid 'a chest of vihuelas [viols] that came from England' ('un cofre de vihuelas que vinjeron de Ynglaterra'). See Vander Straeten, vol. 7 (1885) 428.

114 *Malone Society Collections*, vol. 2, part 3 (1931): *Legal Proceedings of the Mayor and Aldermen's Court*, 302

115 Puppetry and viol playing sometimes went together. In 1524 'quatre Allemans jouheurs de vyoles et maryonettes' played before Margaret of Austria (see Chapter 13).

116 The development of the structure of the 'classic' English viol of the early 17th century by makers such as John Rose, Henry Jaye and Richard Meares is beyond the scope of this study. For further information, see Pringle (1978) and D. M. Kessler: 'Viol Construction in 17th-century England: An Alternative Way of Making Fronts', *EM*, vol. 10, no. 3 (1982).

117 P. Ganz: *The Paintings of Hans Holbein* (London, 1950) 282-283

118 E. Winternitz: *Musical Instruments and their Symbolism in Western Art* (London, 1967) Plate 91

119 A large viol with violin-like corners is depicted on a 16th-century wall painting from a house in Thame, Oxfordshire, on display in the Oxfordshire County Museum, Woodstock.

120 *Accounts of the Lord High Treasurer of Scotland*, vol. 6, 261-262

121 Historical Manuscripts Commission: *The Manuscripts of the Duke of Rutland, K. G. preserved at Belvoir Castle*, vol. 4 (London, 1905) 287

122 Emmison (1961) 210 & 212

123 Woodfill (1953) 256

124 London Corporation: *Repertories of the Court of Aldermen of the City of London*: Repertory 14, fols. 509$^V$ & 514

125 E. S. J. van der Straeten (1933) 57

126 Woodfill (1953) 272

127 Stopes (1910) 314

128 W. Greenwell: *Wills and Inventories from the Registry at Durham*, part 2 (The Surtees Society, vol. 38, London, 1860) 251

129 Concerning the rise of the Jacobean viol fantasy, see D. Pinto: 'William Lawes' music for viol consort', *EM*, vol. 6, no. 1 (1978) 12-24.

130 E. Welsford: *The Court Masque* (Cambridge, 1927) 161

131 Galpin (1910; rev. edn. 1965) 67

132 Woodfill (1953) 253

133 Edwards (1970-1971) 122. See also Historical Manuscripts Commission: *Report on the Manuscripts of the Most Honourable the Marquess of Bath preserved at Longleat*, vol. 4: *Seymour Papers 1532-1686* (London, 1968) 145

134 G. Dodd: 'Alfonso Ferrabosco II - The Art of the Fantasy', *Ch*, vol. 7 (1977) 48. A vivid illustration of the growing popularity of the consort of viols in early Jacobean England amongst amateurs of good breeding comes from an extract from the will of Francis Fitton of Gawsworth co. Chester (1608): 'To my cosin Edmund Fyton, sonne and heire to my late nephew William Fitton, £20, and £10 in money which I did lend to him at his going into

Spaine with Sir Richard Leveson in consideracon of a sett of violles da la gamba of his late fathers, and also a sett of Recorders and a great gyterne, a lute and a paire of virginalles which were all his said late fathers, and by him left in my keeping, which said sett of vialles I did lend to Sir John Davers, knight, deceased, and were sithence in the handes of Dame Elizabeth Davers his late widow, and since then also in the handes of Sir Charles Davers, knight, hir sonne attainted, by whoes fall the said vialles may fortune to be lost . . .' See *Lancashire and Cheshire Wills and Inventories 1572 to 1696 now preserved at Chester* (The Chetham Society, New Series, vol. 28, 1893) 172. Also indicative of the personal interest in viol playing shown increasingly by amateurs of high rank are records of single viols being purchased for individuals. The Rutland Accounts, for example, in 1600 note the purchase of a viol for Lady Frances Manners: 'Item, 30 *Junii*, for a violl di gramba, iiij *l*: for a case, xxs., then sent to her – v *l*: See Historical Manuscripts Commission: *The Manuscripts of the Duke of Rutland, K.G. preserved at Belvoir Castle*, vol. 4 (London, 1905) 432.

# Bibliography

A complete list of all books and articles which refer to the viol and its music before 1600 would be enormous. The viol was one of the most popular 16th-century instruments and there was hardly an area of renaissance musical life in which the instrument did not figure. This bibliography is therefore highly selective. It does not, for example, include works on the following topics, even though many of them are of great importance in the study of the instrument: books on artistic history – paintings, miniatures, sculptures – essential in determining the physical structure of the instrument; editions of renaissance literature, often useful in establishing contemporary attitudes to the instrument; and historical works, political and social – official calendars of state papers, municipal documents, private wills and inventories etc. – essential for ascertaining the place of the instrument in renaissance society. Where works of this nature have yielded significant information, however, they are recorded in the Notes to the text. Also omitted from this bibliography are a large number of books, articles and editions of renaissance music in which the viol is briefly mentioned. The dividing line between such works and some of the items actually included in the bibliography is, it hardly needs to be said, at times a fairly arbitrary one.

## I *Treatises* (arranged in chronological order)

J. Tinctoris: *De inventione et usu musicae* (*c*1487); edn. in K. Weinmann: *Johannes Tinctoris (1445–1511) und sein unbekannter Traktat 'De inventione et usu musicae'* (Regensburg, 1917)

S. Virdung: *Musica getutscht* (Basle, 1511)

H. Judenkünig: *Utilis et compendaria introductio* (Vienna, *c*1518)

H. Judenkünig: *Ain schone kunstliche underweisung* (Vienna, 1523)

M. Agricola: *Musica instrumentalis deudsch* (Wittenberg, 1528 & 1529)

H. Gerle: *Musica Teusch* (Nuremberg, 1532)

G. M. Lanfranco: *Scintille di musica* (Brescia, 1533)

S. di Ganassi: *Regola Rubertina* (Venice, 1542)

S. di Ganassi: *Lettione Seconda* (Venice, 1543)

A. Doni: *Dialogo della musica* (Venice, 1544)

M. Agricola: *Musica instrumentalis deudsch*, rev. edn. (Wittenberg, 1545)

H. Gerle: *Musica und Tabulatur* (rev. edn. of *Musica Teusch*, Nuremberg, 1546)

D. Ortiz: *Trattado de glosas* (Rome, 1553)

P. Jambe de Fer: *Epitome musical* (Lyons, 1556)

M. Troiano: *Discorsi Delli Triomphi* (Munich, 1568)

M. Troiano: *Dialoghi di Massimo Troiano* (Venice, 1569)

V. Galilei: *Dialogo della musica antica, et della moderna* (Florence, 1581)

G. Dalla Casa: *Il vero modo di diminuir* (Venice, 1584)

A. Marinati: *Somma di tutte le scienze* (Rome, 1587)

S. Mareschall: *Porta Musices* (Basle, 1589)

G. Bassano: *Motetti, madrigali et canzoni francese* (Venice, 1591)

L. Zacconi: *Prattica di musica* (Venice, 1592)

R. Rogniono: *Passaggi per potersi essercitare nel diminuire* (Venice, 1592)

S. Cerreto: *Della prattica musica* (Naples, 1601)

A. Banchieri: *Conclusioni del suono dell'organo* (Bologna, 1609)

D. P. Cerone: *El Melopeo y Maestro* (Naples, 1613)

M. Praetorius: *Syntagma Musicum*: vol. 2: *De Organographia* (Wolfenbüttel, 1619)

F. Rognoni: *Selva di varii passaggi* (Milan, 1620)

V. Bonizzi: *Alcune opere di diversi auttori* (Venice, 1626)

M. Mersenne: *Harmonie Universelle* (Paris, 1636)

## II *Books and Articles*

D. Abbott & E. Segerman: 'Strings in the Sixteenth and Seventeenth Centuries', *GSJ*, vol. 27 (1974)

'Gut strings', *EM*, vol. 4, no. 4 (1976)

P. Abondance: 'La vihuela du musée Jacquemart-André: restauration d'un document unique', *RdeM*, vol. 66 (1980)

E. Albini: 'La Viola da gamba in Italia', *RMI*, vol. 28 (1921)

H. Anglés: *La Música en la Corte de los Reyes Católicos* (Madrid, 1941)

*Historia de la Musica Medieval en Navarra* (Pamplona, 1970)

J. Bacher: *Die Viola da Gamba* (Kassel, 1932)

G. T. Bachmann: 'A List of Doctoral Dissertations Accepted by American Universities on the Viola da Gamba: Its Music, Composers and Performers', *JVdGSA*, vol. 4 (1967)

W. Bachmann: *Die Anfänge des Streichinstrumentenspiels* (Leipzig, 1964; Eng. trans. 1969)

A. Baines: 'Fifteenth-century Instruments in Tinctoris's *De Inventione et Usu Musicae*', *GSJ*, vol. 3 (1950)

'Two Cassel Inventories', *GSJ*, vol. 4 (1951)

*European and American Musical Instruments* (London, 1966)

*Victoria and Albert Museum*: *Catalogue of Musical Instruments*: vol. 2: *Non-Keyboard Instruments* (London, 1968)

A. Baines, ed.: *Musical Instruments Through the Ages* (London, 1961)

F. Baines: 'What exactly is a violone? A note towards a solution', *EM*, vol. 5, no. 2 (1977)

M. A. Baird: 'Aspects of Secular Music and Music-making in the Pays-Bas Meridionaux during the Lifetime of Charles-Quint (1500-1558)' (diss., Queen's University of Belfast, 1958)

D. Baker: 'The Instrumental Consort Music of Robert Parsons', *Ch*, vol. 7 (1977)

N. Bessaraboff: *Ancient European Musical Instruments* (Boston, 1941)

R. D. Bodig: 'Silvestro Ganassi's Regola Rubertina – Revelations and Questions', *JVdGSA*, vol. 14 (1977)

'Ganassi's Regola Rubertina', *JVdGSA*, vol. 18 (1981)

'Ganassi's Regola Rubertina (Conclusion)', *JVdGSA*, vol. 19 (1982)

D. D. Boyden: *The History of Violin Playing from its Origins to 1761 and its Relationship to the Violin and Violin Music* (London, 1965)

*Catalogue of the Hill Collection of Musical Instruments in the Ashmolean Museum, Oxford* (London, 1969)

P. Brett: 'The English Consort Song, 1570-1625', *PRMA*, vol. 88 (1961-1962)

'The Songs of William Byrd' (diss., University of Cambridge, 1965)

P. Brett, ed.: *Consort Songs*, *MB*, vol. 22 (London, 1967)

N. Bridgman: *La Vie Musicale au Quattrocento* (Paris, 1964)

H. M. Brown: *Music in the French Secular Theater, 1400–1550* (Cambridge, Mass., 1963)

*Instrumental Music Printed Before 1600: A Bibliography* (Cambridge, Mass., 1965)

*Sixteenth-Century Instrumentation*: *The Music for the Florentine Intermedii* (*AIM*, 1973)

*Embellishing Sixteenth-Century Music* (London, 1976)

'A Cook's Tour of Ferrara in 1529', *RIM*, vol. 10 (1975)

'Notes (and Transposing Notes) on the Viol in the Early Sixteenth Century' in I. Fenlon, ed.: *Music in medieval and early modern Europe: patronage, sources and texts* (Cambridge, 1981)

H. M. Brown & J. Lascelle: *Musical Iconography: A Manual for Cataloguing Musical Subjects in Western Art before 1800* (Cambridge, Mass., 1972)

A. Buchner: *Musical Instruments: an illustrated history* (New York, 1973)

F. Crane: *Extant Medieval Musical Instruments* (Iowa City, 1972)

R. T. Dart & R. Donington: 'The Origin of the In Nomine', *ML*, vol. 30 (1949)

H. T. David: *Eustachio Romano Musica Duorum*, ed. H. M. Brown & E. E. Lowinsky, *MRM*, vol. 6 (Chicago, 1975)

V. Denis: *De Muziekinstrumenten in de Nederlanden en in Italië naar hun Afbeelding in de 15ᵉ Eeuwsche Kunst* (Antwerp, 1944)

'Musical Instruments in Fifteenth-Century Netherlands and Italian Art', *GSJ*, vol. 2 (1949)

B. Disertori: 'Un incunabolo di assolo per il violone', *RMI*, vol. 46 (1942)

'L'unica composizione sicuramente strumentale nei Codici Tridentini', *CHM*, vol. 2 (1957)

G. Dodd: 'Alfonso Ferrabosco II – The Art of the Fantasy', *Ch*, vol. 7 (1977)

'A Summary of Music for Viols', *EM*, vol. 6, no. 2 (1978)

*Thematic Index of Music for Viols* (London, 1980)

P. Doe: 'The Emergence of the In Nomine: Some Notes and Queries on the Work of Tudor Church Musicians' in E. Olleson, ed., *Modern Musical Scholarship* (London, 1978)

P. Doe, ed.: *Elizabethan Consort Music: I*, *MB*, vol. 44 (London, 1979)

N. Dolmetsch: *The Viola da Gamba: Its Origin and History, its Technique and Musical Resources* (London, 1962)

'Antique Bowed Instruments in the Dolmetsch Collection', *JVdGSA*, vol. 15 (1978)

D. Droysen: 'Die Saiteninstrumente des frühen und hohen Mittelalters' (diss., University of Hamburg, 1961)

M. Edmunds: 'Venetian Viols of the Sixteenth Century', *GSJ*, vol. 33 (1980)

W. A. Edwards: 'The Performance of Ensemble Music in Elizabethan England', *PRMA*, vol. 97 (1970-1971)

'The Sources of Elizabethan Consort Music' (diss., University of Cambridge, 1974)

W. Eggers: *Die 'Regola Rubertina' des Silvestro Ganassi, Venedig 1542/43: Eine Gambenschule des 16. Jahrhunderts* (Kassel, 1974)

A. Einstein: *Zur deutschen Literatur der Viola da Gamba im 16. und 17. Jahrhundert* (Leipzig, 1905)

E. Elsner: *Untersuchung der instrumentalen Besetzungspraxis der weltlichen Musik im 16. Jahrhundert in Italien* (Berlin, 1935)

C. Engel: *A Descriptive Catalogue of the Musical Instruments in the South Kensington Museum* (London, 1870)

P. Farrell: 'Diego Ortiz' *Tratado de Glosas*', *JVdGSA*, vol. 4 (1967)

N. Fortune: 'Giustiniani on Instruments', *GSJ*, vol. 5 (1952)

F. K. Gable: 'Possibilities for Mean-Tone Temperament Playing on Viols', *JVdGSA*, vol. 16 (1979)

Canon F. W. Galpin: *Old English Instruments of Music* (London, 1910; 4th rev. edn. 1965)

*A Textbook of European Musical Instruments* (New York, 1937)

I. Gammie: 'Sylvestro Ganassi: *Regola Rubertina* (1542), *Lettione Seconda* (1543): A Synopsis of the Text Relating to the Viol', *Ch*, vol. 8 (1978-1979)

B. Geiser: *Studien zur Frühgeschichte der Violine*, *Publikationen der schweizerischen musikforschenden Gesellschaft*, series 2, vol. 25 (Berne & Stuttgart, 1974)

D. Gill: 'Vihuelas, Violas and the Spanish Guitar', *EM*, vol. 9, no. 4 (1981)

G. Glenn: 'An Inquiry on the Evolution of the Viol', *JVdGSA*, vol. 1 (1964)

O. Gombosi: 'Violenduette im 15. Jahrhundert', *Acta*, vol. 9 (1937)

W. L. Goodman: 'Musical Instruments and their Makers in the Bristol Apprentice Register, 1536-1643', *GSJ*, vol. 27 (1974)

C. Gottwald: *Die Musikhandschriften der Universitätsbibliothek München* (Wiesbaden, 1968)

M. Greulich: 'Beiträge zur Geschichte des Streichinstrumentenspiels im 16. Jahrhundert' (diss., University of Berlin, 1934)

J. A. Griffin: 'Diego Ortiz's Principles of Ornamentation for the Viol', *JVdGSA*, vol. 10 (1973)

L. Grillet: *Les ancêtres du violon et du violoncelle, les luthiers et les fabricants d'archets* (Paris, 1901)

F. V. Grunfeld: *The Art and Times of the Guitar* (New York, 1969)

V. Gutmann: 'Viola bastarda – Instrument oder Diminutionspraxis?', *AMw*, vol. 35 (1978)

J. Haar: 'Notes on the *Dialogo della Musica* of Antonfrancesco Doni', *ML*, vol. 47 (1966)

D. Harrán: 'In Pursuit of Origins: The Earliest Writing on Text Underlay (c.1440)', *Acta*, vol. 50 (1978)

F. Harrison & J. Rimmer: *European Musical Instruments* (London, 1966)

I. Harwood: 'An Introduction to Renaissance Viols', *EM*, vol. 2, no. 4 (1974)

'A Case of Double Standards? Instrumental Pitch in England c1600', *EM*, vol. 9, no. 4 (1981)

I. Harwood & M. Edmunds: 'Reconstructing 16th-century Venetian Viols', *EM*, vol. 6, no. 4 (1978)

G. R. Hayes: *Musical Instruments and their Music, 1500–1750* (2 vols., London, 1928 & 1930): vol. 2: *The Viols and other Bowed Instruments*

D. Heartz: *Pierre Attaingnant Royal Printer of Music: A Historical Study and Bibliographical Catalogue* (Berkeley & Los Angeles, 1969)

R. Henning: 'Hans Judenkünig c. 1455/60–1526: Commemorating the 450th Anniversary of his Death', *LSJ*, vol. 18 (1976)

I. Horsley: 'Improvised Embellishment in the Performance of Renaissance Polyphonic Music', *JAMS*, vol. 4 (1951)

D. Kämper: *Studien zur instrumentalen Ensemblemusik des 16. Jahrhunderts* (*AnM*, vol. 10, 1970)

D. M. Kessler: 'Viol Construction in 17th-century England: An Alternative Way of Making Fronts', *EM*, vol. 10, no. 3 (1982)

G. J. Kinney: 'Viols and Violins in the "Epitome musical" (Lyons, 1556) of Philibert Jambe de Fer', *JVdGSA*, vol. 4 (1967)

G. L. Kinsky: *Geschichte der Musik in Bildern* (Leipzig, 1929; Eng. trans. 1930)

J. Lamaña: 'Los instrumentos musicales en los últimos tiempos de la dinastía de la Casa de Barcelona', *AM*, vol. 24 (1969)

B. Lee: 'Giovanni Maria Lanfranco's *Scintille di Musica* and its Relationship to 16th-Century Music Theory' (diss., Cornell University, 1961)

P. le Huray: *Music and the Reformation in England 1549–1660* (London, 1967)

F. Lesure: 'La facture instrumentale à Paris au seizième siècle', *GSJ*, vol. 7 (1954)

'L'*Epitome musical* de Philibert Jambe de Fer (1556)', *AnnM*, vol. 6 (1958–1963)

L. Litterick: 'Performing Franco-Netherlandish Secular Music of the Late 15th Century', *EM*, vol. 8 (1980)

A. Livermore: 'The Spanish Dramatists and their Use of Music', *ML*, vol. 25 (1944)

W. L. von Lütgendorff: *Die Geigen- und Lautenmacher vom Mittelalter bis zur Gegenwart* (Cologne, 1913)

V. Mahillon: *Catalogue descriptif et analytique du Musée Instrumental du Conservatoire de Musique de Bruxelles*, vol. 1 (Ghent, 1893)

S. Marcuse: *Musical Instruments: A Comprehensive Dictionary* (New York, 1964)

*A Survey of Musical Instruments* (London, 1975)

M. McLeish: 'An Inventory of Musical Instruments at the Royal Palace Madrid 1602', *GSJ*, vol. 21 (1968)

E. H. Meyer: *English Chamber Music* (London, 1946)

  *Die Kammermusik Alt-Englands vom Mittelalter bis zum Tode H. Purcells* (Leipzig, 1956)

C. A. Monson: 'Voices and Viols in England, 1600-1650: the Sources and the Music' (diss., University of California, Berkeley, 1974)

  'Consort Song and Verse Anthem: A Few Performance Problems', *JVdGSA*, vol. 13 (1976)

J. Montagu: *The World of Medieval & Renaissance Musical Instruments* (Newton Abbot, 1976)

J. Morehen: 'The English Consort and Verse Anthems', *EM*, vol. 6, no. 3 (1978)

M. Morrow: '16th Century Ensemble Viol Music', *EM*, vol. 2, no. 3 (1974)

D. Munrow: *Instruments of the Middle Ages and Renaissance* (London, 1976)

O. Neighbour: *The Consort and Keyboard Music of William Byrd* (London, 1978)

K. Neumann: 'The Renaissance Sources of the Viols', *JVdGSA*, vol. 2 (1965)

J. Noble: 'Le Répertoire instrumental anglais: 1550-1585' in J. Jacquot, ed.: *La Musique instrumentale de la Renaissance* (Paris, 1955)

C. Page: 'Jerome of Moravia on the *Rubeba* and *Vielle*', *GSJ*, vol. 32 (1979)

H. Panum: *Middelalderens strengeinstrumenter* (Copenhagen, 1915–1931); Eng. trans.: *The Stringed Instruments of the Middle Ages* (London, 1939)

H. Peter: *Regola Rubertina. Lehrbuch des Spiels auf der Viola da gamba und der Laute* (Berlin & Lichterfeld, 1972)

M. Pincherle: *Histoire illustrée de la musique* (Paris, 1959; Eng. trans. 1959)

A. Pirro: *Histoire de la Musique* (Paris, 1940)

D. Poulton: 'The Lute in Christian Spain', *LSJ*, vol. 19 (1977)

D. C. Price: *Patrons and Musicians of the English Renaissance* (Cambridge, 1981)

J. Pringle: 'John Rose, the Founder of English Viol-making', *EM*, vol. 6, no. 4 (1978)

W. F. Prizer: 'Lutenists at the Court of Mantua in the Late Fifteenth and Early Sixteenth Centuries', *JLSA*, vol. 13 (1980)

  'Isabella d'Este and Lorenzo da Pavia, Master Instrument-maker', *EMH*, vol. 2 (1982)

M. Prynne: 'A Surviving Vihuela de Mano', *GSJ*, vol. 16 (1963)

V. Ravizza: *Das instrumentale Ensemble von 1400-1550: Wandel eines Klangbildes*, Publikationen der schweizerischen musikforschenden Gesellschaft (Berne & Stuttgart, 1970)

G. Reese: *Music in the Renaissance* (London, 1954)

M. Remnant: 'The Use of Frets on Rebecs and Medieval Fiddles', *GSJ*, vol. 21 (1968)

  'Rebec, Fiddle and Crowd in England', *PRMA*, vol. 95 (1968–1969)

  *Musical Instruments of the West* (London, 1978)

J. Ribera: *La Música de las Cantigas* (Madrid, 1922; Eng. trans. Stanford, 1929)

E. M. Ripin: 'A Re-evaluation of Virdung's *Musica getutscht*', *JAMS*, vol. 29 (1976)

J. Rousseau: *Traité de la viole, qui contient une dissertation curieuse sur son origine* (Paris, 1687)

J. Rutledge: 'A Viol Bibliography', *JVdGSA*, vol. 16 (1979)

C. Sachs: *Handbuch der Musikinstrumentenkunde* (Leipzig, 1930)

  *The History of Musical Instruments* (New York, 1940)

K. Schlesinger: *The Instruments of the Modern Orchestra and Early Records of the Precursors of the Violin Family*: vol. 2: *The Precursors of the Violin Family, Records, Researches and Studies* (London, 1910)

J. von Schlosser: *Die Sammlung alter Musikinstrumente* (Vienna, 1920)

W. Senn: 'Eine "Viola da gamba" von Stephanus De Fantis', *CHM*, vol. 2 (1957)

M. Sicard: 'The French Viol School before 1650', *JVdGSA*, vol. 18 (1981)

A. Silbiger: 'The First Viol Tutor: Hans Gerle's *Musica Teusch*', *JVdGSA*, vol. 6 (1969)

H. C. Slim, ed.: *Musica Nova*, *MRM*, vol. 1 (Chicago, 1964)

R. de Smet: *Published music for the viola da gamba and other viols* (Detroit, 1971)

D. Stevens, ed.: *The Mulliner Book*, *MB*, vol. 1 (London, 1951)

J. Stevens: *Music and Poetry in the Early Tudor court* (London, 1961)

E. Vander Straeten: *La Musique aux Pays-Bas avant le XIXᵉ siècle* (8 vols., Brussels, 1867–1888)

E. S. J. van der Straeten: *The History of the Violoncello, the Viol da Gamba, their Precursors and Collateral Instruments* (London, 1915)
   *The History of the Violin* (London, 1933)
P. Tourin: *Viol list: A comprehensive catalogue of historical viole da gamba* (Duxbury, Vermont, 1979)
H. Turnbull: *The Guitar from the Renaissance to the Present Day* (London, 1974)
G. Turrini: *L'Accademia Filarmonica di Verona dalla Fondazione (Maggio 1543) al 1600 e il suo Patrimonio Musicale Antico* (Verona, 1941)
J. Tyler: 'The Renaissance Guitar 1500-1650', *EM*, vol. 3, no. 4 (1975)
   *The Early Guitar: A History and Handbook* (London, 1980)
J. Ward: 'The Vihuela de Mano and its Music (1536-1576)' (diss., New York University, 1953)
S. R. Watson: 'The "Lordly Viol" in the Literature of the English Renaissance', *JVdGSA*, vol. 1 (1964)
R. W. Weidner: 'Change and Tradition in the Early *In Nomine*', *JVdGSA*, vol. 15 (1978)
R. W. Weidner, ed.: *Christopher Tye: The Instrumental Music* (New Haven, Conn., 1967)
E. Winternitz: *Musical Instruments and their Symbolism in Western Art* (London, 1967)
L. C. Witten II: 'Apollo, Orpheus, and David: A Study of the Crucial Century in the Development of Bowed Strings in North Italy 1480-1580 as Seen in Graphic Evidence and Some Surviving Instruments', *JAMIS*, vol. 1 (1975)
I. D. Woodfield: 'The Early History of the Viol', *PRMA*, vol. 103 (1976-1977)
   'The Origins of the Viol' (diss., University of London, King's College, 1977)
   'Posture in Viol Playing', *EM*, vol. 6, no. 1 (1978)
   'Viol Playing Techniques in the Mid-16th Century; a Survey of Ganassi's Fingering Instructions', *EM*, vol. 6, no. 4 (1978)
   'Iconography of the Viol as a Research Tool for the Musicologist', *RIdIM* Newsletter, vol. 4, no. 2 (1979)
   'Viol' article in *The New Grove* (London, 1980)
W. L. Woodfill: *Musicians in English Society: from Elizabeth to Charles I* (Princeton, 1953)
L. Wright: 'The Medieval Gittern and Citole: A Case of Mistaken Identity', *GSJ*, vol. 30 (1977).

# Index

Abate, Nicolò dell', 157, 185
Aberdeen, viol players in, 209
*a braccio* (see playing position)
Africa, North
   *rabāb* in, 15, 34
   string-playing techniques in, 9, 34
   violin in, 77
*a gamba* (see playing position)
Agricola, Martin, 4, 99–102, 105–107, 109–110
Alberto da Venezia (see Venezia, Alberto da)
Aldeburgh, payments to a wait, 222
Alexander VI (see Borgia, Rodrigo)
Alexander da Milano (see Milano, Alexander da)
Alfonso della Viola (see Viola, Alfonso della)
alman, 212
Altdorfer, Albrecht, 237 n. 11
Ambroso da Milano (see Milano, Ambroso da)
Amiens, viol players in, 199
Andrea di Verona (see Verona, Andrea di)
Antonio Ciciliano (see Ciciliano, Antonio)
Antwerp, viol players in, 155, 211
apprentice viol players, 211
Aragon, Kingdom of, 16–17, 94–95
   instruments from, in England, 207
   instruments from, in Italy, 82
   musicians from, in Italy, 81
   *rabāb* in, 15–37
   *vihuela de mano* in, 38–60
Arcadelt, Jacques, 174
arm (see bowing techniques)
Arundel, Earl of, 212
Attaingnant, Pierre, 200–201
Avazini, Roberto d' (see Mantoano, Rubertino)

back
   arched, 137–138
   bend in the, 70, 104, 120, 123–124, 132
Baden-Baden Hofkapelle, viols belonging to, 192
Baer, Hans, 101
bagpipes, 101, 213
Banchieri, Adriano, 145, 189
bandora, 221–223, 239 n. 17
Barcelona, Count of, 16
Bardi, Pietro de', 188
Bargrave, Robert, 243–244 n. 41
Barnaby, Thomas, 211

*barré* (see fingering techniques)
barring (see also bass-bar), 73, 118–119, 125, 127
Bartoli, Cosimo, 127
Bassani, Orazio, 178, 242 n. 8
Bassano, Giovanni, 178, 188
bass-bar, 119
*basse danse*, 174
*bastarda* (see *viola bastarda*)
Battista Ciciliano (see Ciciliano, Battista)
belly
   arched, 73, 119, 125, 127, 131
   bent, 125, 127, 131
   carved, 125, 131, 138
   with carved 'spine', 119, 138
   'digged out of a plank', 138
   flat, 73, 76, 118–119
   ornaments on, 52–53, 71, 73
   parchment (or skin), 20–21
   thick, 119, 138
Benvenuto, Giovanni di, 14
Bermudo, Juan, 53
Berne, viol players in, 199
Bevilacqua, Count Mario, 189
Bibbiena, Cardinal, 185, 199
*bicinia* (see duo)
Binche, viol players in, 199
Binchois, 16
blocks (attached to ribs), 125
Bonizzi, Vincenzo, 178–179
Borassá, Luis, 17, 19
Borgia, Alonso, 80
Borgia, Cesare, 86, 196
Borgia, Lucrezia, 87, 89
Borgia, Rodrigo, 81–82, 86–87
bow
   for chordal playing, 163
   method of removing grease from, 106
   resin (colophony) for, 106
bowing techniques (see also notation)
   arm, use of, 161
   bow-stroke, direction of, 106, 162–163
   fingers, use of, 32, 161
   overhand grip, 9, 37
   palm, position of, 75
   reverse (or back-to-front) method, 237 n. 10
   slurring, 162, 189

257